POLITICIANS, SOCIALISM AND HISTORIANS

The Italian Problem in European Diplomacy 1847–49
Germany's First Bid for Colonies, 1884–85
The Course of German History
The Habsburg Monarchy, 1809–1918
From Napoleon to Stalin
Rumours of War
The Struggle for Mastery in Europe 1848–1918
(*The Oxford History of Modern Europe*)
Bismarck : The Man and the Statesman
Englishmen and Others
The Troublemakers
The Origins of the Second World War
The First World War
Politics in Wartime
English History, 1914–1945
(*The Oxford History of England*)
From Sarajevo to Potsdam
Europe: Grandeur and Decline
(*Penguin : Selected Essays*)
War by Time-Table
Beaverbrook
The Second World War
Essays in English History
The Last of Old Europe
The War Lords
The Russian War, 1941–1945
How Wars Begin
Revolutions and Revolutionaries

POLITICIANS, SOCIALISM AND HISTORIANS

by

A. J. P. TAYLOR F.B.A.

STEIN AND DAY/*Publishers*/New York

First published in the United States of America in 1982
This collection copyright © by A.J.P. Taylor 1980
Individual essays copyright © by A.J.P. Taylor 1952, 1953, 1954, 1956, 1957,
1959, 1960, 1961, 1962, 1965, 1966, 1967, 1969, 1971, 1972, 1973, 1974, 1975,
1976, 1977, 1978, 1979, 1980. Essays 11 and 40 © Nyrev., 1974, 1979.

Printed in the United States of America

Stein and Day/ *Publishers*
Scarborough House
Briarcliff Manor, N.Y. 10510

Library of Congress Cataloging in Publication Data

Taylor, A.J.P. (Alan John Percivale), 1906-
    Politicians, socialism and historians.

    Includes index.
    1. World politics — To 1900 — Addresses, essays, lectures. 2. World
politics — 20th century — Addresses, essays, lectures. 3. Socialism —
Addresses, essays, lectures.   I. Title.
D288.T37   1982   082   80-6217
ISBN 0-8128-2796-1   AACR2

For Eva

Contents

Preface

This volume contains a selection from my occasional writings over the last twenty-five years. None of the essays has appeared in book form before except for *Confusion on the Left* which I contributed to The *Age of Baldwin*, edited by John Raymond (1960, Eyre and Spottiswoode).

I am deeply grateful to Dr Chris Wrigley of Loughborough University for drawing my attention to many pieces I might have overlooked and for providing me with Xerox copies of them. I also record my thanks for permission to publish these essays to the editors, publishers and proprietors of *The Journal of Modern History; Wiener Beiträge; Vogue; The Observer; The New Statesman; The Twentieth Century; The New York Review of Books; The Saturday Review of Literature; The Times Literary Supplement; Encounter; The Listener* and *The English Historical Review*.

A J P T

I HISTORY and HISTORIANS

1.   Accident Prone, or What Happened Next[1]

The Journal of Modern History occasionally devotes an entire
number to a non-American historian. First came the prestigious
French historian Braudel. Then the editor hit on me as a
representative English historian which I fear I am not. The
editor asked how I had become an historian, what were my aims
and standards, what difficulties I had encountered. I had never
considered these questions previously. The result came out as
an essay in intellectual autobiography.

> A Galician priest was explaining to a peasant what
> miracles were.
> 'If I fell from that church tower and landed unhurt,
> what would you call it?'
> 'An accident.'
> 'And if I fell again and was unhurt?'
> 'Another accident.'
> 'And if I did it a third time?'
> 'A habit.'
>
> [A story told me by Lewis Namier]

In my version of history, I am told, everything happens by accident.
This, though not I think true of my books, has applied in my own
life time and again. Or perhaps such a steady record of accidents
implies some kind of predestination. It never crossed my mind, when
young, that I might become a professional historian. I did not seek
my various careers – historian, journalist, television star. They sought
me. I did not even devise the subjects of my books. All, with one
exception, were suggested to me by others. Ironically the one exception, *The Origins of the Second World War*, brought more trouble

[1]Journal of Modern History, 1977.

3

on my head than all my other books put together, trouble that I did not foresee or intend to provoke. There must be a moral here.

Certainly I loved history as far back as I can remember. I cannot explain this. It seems to me natural, just like loving music or the Lake District mountains. The first book I read, at the age of four, was *Pilgrim's Progress* – in its way a great historical work. Later I read all the historical novels I could lay my hands on : Harrison Ainsworth, Kingsley, Bulwer Lytton, G A Henty, the drabber and more factual the better. I could not take historical novels with real characters in them. That, I suppose, is why I never read Scott, greatest of historical novelists, until I was adult. Later I read indiscriminately works of historical narration. It seemed obvious to me that the historian's prime duty was to answer my childish question : 'What happened next?' It seems almost as obvious to me now. The book that pleased me most was H G. Wells's *Outline of History*, read as it came out in its original fortnightly parts – not that I accepted Wells's version of events moving inevitably toward a World State. This passion for history is still with me. Every book that arrives on my desk for review excites me, and the prospect of myself writing a book on a good theme excites me still more.

I was always a 'loner,' a solitary only child, out of step in all sorts of ways, rarely influenced by others and learning by the painful process of trial and error. I was born and grew up in Lancashire, which marked me off from the predominant, nonindustrial culture of southern England. When I first went to Oxford, I was astonished to find a town not dominated by mill chimneys and with few mean streets. I came of Radical, Dissenting stock on both sides. A collateral ancestor of my father's was killed at Peterloo. My maternal great-grandfather voted for Orator Hunt at the Preston by-election in 1830 and received one of the medals struck in honour of 'the free and independent voters of Preston.' My father was a Lloyd George Radical before the First World War. After it, when most of his fellow cotton merchants went Right, he went Left. He joined the Independent Labour party. In due course he became a Labour representative on Preston town council and was a member of the local strike committee during the general strike of 1926.

I was always on good terms with my father and went along with his Socialism. I am told this is an abnormal relationship psychologically, making one uncombative and lacking in self-confidence. I cannot say that it had any such effect in my case. On the contrary it made me more confident to have a secure family background. It is a curious thing to be an hereditary dissenter. On the one hand, you reject established views – religious in earlier times, political and social in our own. On the other, you have no inner conflict in doing so. Indeed you would have a conflict only if you accepted them. On a committee I usually put forward subversive ideas and at the same time insist that the existing rules must be rigorously observed until they are changed. Something the same applies to my books. The framework is stricly conventional – old-fashioned history, as one reviewer recently called it. But the ideas stuffed in to the framework do not conform to accepted views. This is, I suppose, why my books annoy some people – I am a traitor within the gates.

My education increased my separation from the traditional stream of English culture. I went first to a Quaker preparatory school and then to Bootham, a Quaker public school at York. At both I experienced the physical hardships which were then the distinctive mark of English education. In other ways, my schools were different. The Society of Friends is certainly a community, but one resolutely out of step with the larger one. In spirit and outlook I am closer to the Friends than to any other body, except that they believe in God and I do not. Theirs is of course a special sort of God. What they really believe in is That of God in every man, a belief I share. This has given another firm point in my life, or rather two : I am no better than anyone else, and no one else is better than me. These rules of thumb have carried me a long way.

I did not acquire much understanding of history at either of my schools. At my preparatory school I learned the dates of the kings and queens of England, went on to the dates of the kings of France and the Holy Roman Emperors, and was hesitating whether to do the sultans of Turkey or the popes of Rome next when I left the school. At Bootham I read innumerable textbooks and, when my history master challenged me to read a long book, went right through Gibbon in a fortnight. But my history was still no more than an undiscriminating appetite. Understanding came in a different way. I collected Gothic churches and abbeys, spending far more time on this than on my schoolwork. This was the first field that brought the past alive to me. I carried a tape measure and a set square and produced ground plans of impeccable accuracy, with the various styles picked out in colour. But being unable to draw freehand, I could never produce elevations. There is a parallel here with my books. They provide ground plans and the reader has to put in the elevations.

I had no doubt what I wanted to do when I left school: simply to go on with what I loved, history, though with no idea of what this would lead to or how to turn it to any practical use. Oxford was my first encounter with traditional England, and very surprising it was. For instance, though I had measured and described countless churches, I had never reflected what they were for. I had never attended a service of the Church of England and was astonished when I first entered the College chapel. I soon cried off attendance as an atheist. The dean said to me: 'Do come and talk to me about your doubts.' I answered: 'I have none.' Oxford's reaction to the general strike also took me unawares. Most of the undergraduates went off as strikebreakers. I went back to Lancashire and drove a car for my father's strike committee.

Most of my time at Oxford was spent on medieval history, then a flourishing subject. The older views were being knocked about, which had a certain charm. Otherwise not much of it interested me except for the Peasant's' Revolt. As to modern history, when we reached the Glorious Revolution, my tutor said to me: 'You know all the rest from your work at school, so we do not need to do any more.' I picked up my knowledge of modern history, such as it was, mainly from the works of Sir John Marriott, an historian now no doubt forgotten. I suspect that I am the Marriott *de nos jours,* except that he was very much on the Right and I am very much on the Left. I cultivated the revolutions of 1848 after reading Marx's *Eighteenth Brumaire of Louis Napoleon,* the book of his – apart of course from the Communist Manifesto – that I most admired. I also conceived a great admiration for Sorel's *Europe and the French Revolution,* more for its style than its content, and for many years tried to emulate his epigrammatic style, as readers of *The Course of German History* can see for themselves.

I did not go to any lectures except those of Sir Charles Oman and that only because Sir Charles, being very old, was a period piece. I never saw an original document or received any guidance in historical method. I was unaware of the existence of the Stubbs Society, the select society which promising historians are invited to join, or of the Ford Lectures, the most prestigious lectures in the English-speaking world. Now that I come to think of it, I did not have as a friend a single undergraduate who was reading history. My own friends were either literary, such as Norman Cameron the poet and J I M Stewart, later famous as a detective-story writer, or merely young men who like me were enjoying themselves.

6

I called myself a Marxist from the time I became a Socialist. But, reading more history at Oxford, I began to feel that Marxism did not work. Consider the famous sentence in the Communist Manifesto: 'The history of all hitherto recorded society is the history of class struggles.' Very impressive but not true. Perhaps all history ought to have been the history of class struggles, but things did not work out that way. There have been long periods of class collaboration and many struggles that were not about class at all. I suppose my mind is too anarchic to be fitted into any system of thought. Like Johnson's friend Edwards, I, too, have tried to be a Marxist but common sense kept breaking in.

One day a friend said to me: 'Why do you not join the Communist party?' Offhand I could think of no ready answer and on these inadequate grounds became a member of the party for a couple of years. My experiences in the general strike showed me that the Communist party played no significant part in the working-class movement, and my disillusionment was complete when Trotsky was expelled from the Russian party and then from Russia. Not that I understood the rights and wrongs of the dispute if it had any. I simply thought that a party which expelled a man of such gifts, merely because he disagreed with the accepted line, was not for me. I quietly lapsed and so escaped the soul torments over Communism that racked so many British and American intellectuals during the 1930s.

In 1927 I got a First in my history finals. This surprised me. I had thought that perhaps I was clever-clever, but certainly not that I was history-clever. Perhaps clever-clever is enough in the History School at Oxford. However it did not concern me. I wanted to escape the ivory towers of Oxford and go into what I imagined was 'real life.' Six months in a law office taught me my mistake. I drifted back to Oxford, at a loss what to do. Someone, I think Davis, the Regius Professor, suggested that I should go to Vienna and work under Pribram, who was reputed to be an authority on Oliver Cromwell. This seemed as good a way as any of learning German, quite apart from the fact that Vienna was highly esteemed in Socialist circles. So off I went and lived in Vienna for two years.

I found that Pribram had lost interest in Cromwell and had now moved on to the origins of the First World War. This was no good to me who knew no history after the Congress of Berlin. Pribram charitably suggested that I should work on Anglo-Austrian relations between 1848 and 1860 and I duly settled down in the Staatsarchiv. I received no instruction how to conduct research. I was not even warned to put down the number of the document I was copying, which caused me a great deal of unnecessary work later. I knew none of the techniques of diplomatic history. I just dived in at the deep end. Imperceptibly I found a better subject: not Anglo-Austrian relations in the void, but the diplomacy of the North Italian question during the revolution of 1848. I gradually trained myself to be a diplomatic historian and was quite competent in this modest art by the time I went on to work in the British and French archives. I suppose I ought to have worked in the Italian archives as well, but of course it was out of the question for me to go to Italy in Mussolini's time.

Though I was now doing historical research, I was far from certain that I should become a professional historian. I had no patron or supervisor in England. I did not enroll as a student at Vienna university and, though I had many social meetings with Pribram, never received any guidance from him after his initial suggestion. I vaguely foresaw that, with my newly acquired command of German, I might become a foreign correspondent. Even more wildly, I took serious steps to become an inspector of ancient monuments, a post for which, apart from my knowledge of Gothic architecture, I was totally unqualified. However, events decided for me in their usual way.

In the spring of 1930 Pribram went to Oxford and delivered the Ford Lectures. One night he sat next to Ernest Jacob at dinner. Jacob had just become head of the history department at Manchester. The professor and lecturer in modern European history had both left, and Jacob was without anyone to teach the subject in the coming academic year. He asked whether Pribram knew of anyone. Pribram, perhaps grateful for the help I had given him in translating his Ford Lectures into English, mentioned me. The next morning Jacob sent me a telegram offering me the job of lecturer. And that is how I became committed to history.

I had hardly been aware until that moment that there was a university in Manchester, and my main feeling was pleasure at going home to Lancashire. In fact the Manchester History School was at that time the most distinguished in Great Britain. The department was very small: three professors, one reader, and four lecturers in all. It never occurred to us that we might have a duty to society. Our sole task, we thought, was to train historians. No professor of modern history had yet been appointed. Hence, in my first year at

Manchester I did the work of both professor and lecturer, another case of diving in at the deep end.

I had to cover all European history from 1494 to 1914 and knew none of it except for the French Revolution and patches of the nineteenth century until the Congress of Berlin. I bought a set of old-fashioned textbooks (Rivington blue) and compiled notes for ninety-six lectures. For the period before the First World War I used the 'revisionist' books that were then in favour and produced an impeccably pro-German account. After delivering my lectures once, I decided that it would be tedious to give the same lectures year after year. I threw away my notes and thereafter lectured without notes as I have done ever since. I do not know whether I taught my enormous classes anything. But I taught myself history, literally on my feet. I also taught myself to address mass audiences without a tremor. This has often worried me. Most orators are desperately nervous before they speak – Lloyd George's shirt was always wet through. I have never trembled before either an audience or the television cameras.

When I had been at Manchester a year, Namier arrived as professor of modern history. It is sometimes said that I was his pupil. This is not so. I was already an established lecturer when Namier came and, if anything, he was my pupil, not I his. At least I tried to teach him how Manchester University worked, in which I was unsuccessful. Namier was at this time wholly taken up with English politics in the early reign of George III, a subject that did not concern me. Of course I was fascinated by his stories, but I did not share his outlook and was indeed 'the friendly critic', as he called me, who accused him of taking the mind out of history. It is strange that this great man, who deplored the influence of political ideas, should have repeatedly jeopardised his career for the sake of Zionism, a political idea if ever there were one.

My views of European history were reached independently of Namier, though we broadly agreed on most things. He had not kept up with the most recent work on the subject and occasionally I was in the happy position of telling him something instead of listening. Also our methods were different. He was a painstaking and laborious scholar. I often relied on intuition. I once made some point in a review. Namier asked me: 'How did you know that? I worked on the topic for three weeks before I found it.' I said I felt it must be so. He replied: 'Ah, you have green fingers. I have not.' Some may say that I have relied on my green fingers too much. I think I have relied on them too little. For instance I felt from the first day that van der Lubbe set fire to the Reichstag all alone. But I hesitated to champion this view against the weight of received opinion until Tobias vindicated it some thirty years afterwards.

If I had a teacher at Manchester and indeed afterwards, it was A P Wadsworth, not Namier. Wadsworth was deputy editor and then editor of the *Manchester Guardian* and also an economic historian of great distinction. He set me to writing leader-page articles on anniversaries of famous men or events and later on the interwar diplomatic documents as they came out. Wadsworth was a hard taskmaster. He constantly said to me: 'An article in *The Guardian* is no good unless people read it on the way to work.' I followed his instruction. My guiding principle, in my writings as in my lectures, has always been : 'Give the customer what he wants' — which does not of course mean 'what he would like to hear.' I worried about my style as much as about my scholarship. In my opinion a work of history misfires unless readers get the same pleasure from it that they do from a novel. My models were Bunyan, Cobbett and Shaw, though I would not claim to reach their standard. I suspect that those who are shocked by my views would be less perturbed if I wrapped them up in the prolixity usual in historical writing.

I also learned a good deal at Manchester from contemporary events and my own political activities. I advocated resistance to Hitler from the moment he came to power. But I also thought that the National government were more likely to support Hitler against Russia than to go against him and therefore I opposed rearmament until we got a change of government. In 1935 I opposed support for the League of Nations by the existing government as a fraud, which it turned out to be, and remember one splendid meeting with the entire audience, composed half of Communists and half of members of the League of Nations Union, vociferously against me. With the reoccupation of the Rhineland, I decided that we must rearm even under the National government and was convinced that if we took a firm line with Hitler there would be no war. I was one of the few people outside London who addressed meetings against appeasement at the time of Munich, and very rough they were. I have not changed the views I held then.

Though I often dabbled in politics I never devoted myself to them or sought a political career. Once when I applied for an appointment at Oxford which I did not get, the president of the College concerned said to me sternly: 'I hear you have strong political views.' I said: 'Oh no, President. Extreme views weakly held.' This has remained my position. But, growing up in a political household and myself involved in politics on the fringe, I automatically assumed that politics expressed the activities of 'man in society,' as the theme of history has rightly been called. All other forms of history – economic history, social history, psychological history, above all sociology – seem to me history with the history left out. And when I am told quite erroneously that my form of history is merely a record of events, I can only reply that so are all other forms. A ship sailing from Venice to Constantinople is as much an event as a general election or an army marching to battle. It all depends on what you make of them.

Namier affected me in one practical way. He thought we ought to have a special subject on prewar diplomacy and, being too busy to do this himself, shoved it on to me. I forgot all my previous views, and started again from scratch, reading *Die grosse Politik* and then the British and French documents from cover to cover. When I had finished, I no longer thought that Germany was the innocent victim of Entente diplomacy. I was not even sure that the First World War happened by accident. My new absorption with prewar diplomacy attracted the attention of E L Woodward, who was almost alone at Oxford in promoting its study, and in 1938 he helped me to get a fellowship at Magdalen, which I have held happily ever since.

My first real books which I wrote soon after moving to Oxford again came to me by chance. Harold Macmillan wanted a short history of the Habsburg Monarchy in its later days. Namier was again too busy and again I took it on. Then during the war PWE (Political Warfare Executive) wanted a chapter on the Weimar Republic for a handbook they were preparing. I wrote it. However, PWE found my chapter not sufficiently enthusiastic about German domocracy and therefore too depressing for their handbook. Denis Brogan said: 'Why not turn it into a book?' I took his advice and wrote *The Course of German History*. Of course both books were affected by the war, but not more, I think, than it affects me still. Since the war centered on Germany, I had to explain why the Germans got where they did. With *The Habsburg Monarchy*, I learned a great deal from central European refugees: Hubert Ripka, the predestined successor of Beneš, though he never stepped into his inheritance; Michael Karolyi, who became one of my dearest friends; and the Slovenes with whom I worked toward the end of the war in an attempt to get Trieste for Yugoslavia.

I have often been called a narrative historian, a title of which I am not ashamed. After all, the distinguishing mark of history is that events happen in order of time. How else can you present them? But these two books of mine are not really narrative; they are explanation. They try to answer the question, how did it happen? How did the Habsburg Monarchy decline and go to pieces? How did Germany remain a militaristic Power, less democratic than either England or France? The customer wanted explanations; I tried to provide them. Actually I was less affected by the war than I ought to have been. I should have seen that the Habsburg Monarchy disintegrated because of defeat in war and for no other reason. However I am still reasonably content with *The Habsburg Monarchy*. I saw German history from outside – partly as an Englishman, partly as an Austrian – and I would not claim that there is anything original in *The Course of German History*. But at least I had read Eckhart Kehr, which most English historians at that time had not.

The war affected me in other ways. It gave me a warning, which I did not always heed, against trying to learn from history. In 1940 I was convinced that the Germans would not invade England. I was right but for entirely the wrong reason. I thought that, on the analogy of Bonaparte in 1798, the Germans would make ostensible preparations to invade England and in fact invade the Middle East. The analogy was false: Hitler never had any offensive plans in the Middle East and did not invade England simply because his forces were not strong enough to do so. Later during the war I gave innumerable talks on the war and current affairs which enabled me to see the war in some sort of historical perspective. Indeed looking back I remember much more of my lectures and interpretations than of what was actually happening.

The Oxford History School, however, stopped in 1939, as it still does, and there was no academic use for my knowledge of the Second World War. I went back to my study of diplomatic history before 1914 and was wondering what use to make of this when I had another stroke of luck. Deakin and Bullock launched the Oxford History of Modern Europe. There were to be volumes on the general history of the principal nation states and in addition three on diplomatic history. I gladly undertook the middle one of these, extending from the revolutions of 1848 to the coming of Lenin and Woodrow Wilson in 1918. Thus accident had intervened again. By definition I was strictly confined to diplomatic history which suited me very well.

This was the first book I thought about before I wrote it. I should have no difficulty, except hard work, over the diplomatic details. But what about *'les forces profondes,'* as Renouvin has called them? I had difficulty, as Renouvin had, in reconciling them with the play of accident that determines the day-to-day course of events. For instance a war between the two Germanic Powers and the rest was very likely in the early years of the twentieth century. But the actual war that broke out in August 1914 would not have occurred as it did if Archduke Franz Ferdinand had not gone to Sarajevo on June 28 or even if his chauffeur had not taken a wrong turning. I suppose something the same is true of all history. *Les forces profondes* are there all right if you cover a century in a single essay, as Namier did in that wonderful essay 'From Vienna to Versailles.' But when you look at details, individual men affect even the greatest events. No doubt France would have been diminished some-how in the later nineteenth century, but she would have declined differently without Napoleon III. No doubt Germany would have become greater in any case, but the way in which she became great was determined by Bismarck. The historian, I think, just has to accept life and put up with it.

I tried to strikes a balance by drawing the general outline of these seventy years in a long introduction and then putting in the details as the Pre-Raphaelites used to do with their pictures. Maybe I did not get the balance right. When I think back to *The Struggle for Mastery in Europe*, it seems to me a fascinating recital of diplomatic episodes, each chapter suited to appear as an article in a learned journal and adding up to an unreadable book. However when I open the book again I do not see how it could have been done other-wise and there is far more in it about *les forces profondes* than I had remembered. The book established my reputation as a scholar, at any rate in some circles, and is the only one of my books to be translated into Russian. Of course the Russians paid me only in blocked roubles and it exasperates me to see copies of the Russian translation on the shelves of university libraries whenever I go to eastern Europe. Incidentally the Russian translator changed my sentence 'Wilson was as much a Utopian as Lenin' to 'Wilson was a Utopian.'

The Struggle for Mastery in Europe, though I did not know it, was virtually my farewell to nineteenth-century Europe and, in a sense, to diplomatic history also. I followed it up by a biography of Bismarck, written on the initiative of an American publisher, but the interest in it for me was not the political history, which I was now writing for the third time, but Bismarck the man. For once I tried to be a psychologist. I did not get very far. I found that Bismarck, too, got on well with his father and, according to all the rules, should have been timid and unaggressive. I decided that psychology did not provide much help to historians and that men have the disposition they are born with – a conclusion reinforced later when I wrote the life of Beaverbrook. Apart from that I fell mildly in love with Bismarck. Every historian, I think, should write one biography, if only to learn how different it is from writing history. Men become more important than events, as I suppose they should be. I prefer writing history all the same.

And now an extraordinary thing happened to me, the most extraordinary indeed that happened in my life. One evening I received an invitation to deliver the Ford Lectures at Oxford. I knew great historians gave the Ford Lectures. My friend Richard Pares had given them, and so had my colleague Bruce McFarlane. But me – the industrious hack, compiling records of events? Besides, the Ford Lectures were on English history, and I still thought of myself as an historian of Europe. I wandered out into the night, encountered Alan Bullock, and told him my plight. He said: 'You have always opposed British foreign policy. Now tell us about the men who opposed it in the past.' I was intoxicated with delight: a wonderful subject that no one had thought of before. The outcome was *The Troublemakers*, by far my favourite brainchild and the one I hope to be remembered by. I suppose it should be classed as history of ideas. For me, the ideas, the men, and the excitement of presenting them were all mixed up. *The Troublemakers* was not all praise. Michael Foot called it: 'The book in which you stabbed all your friends in the back' – a complaint he repeated about my political arguments when we used to appear together on television. All the same the Troublemakers are my heroes so far as I have ever found any.

1956 was altogether a wonderful year. I delivered the Ford Lectures. I was elected to the British Academy, according to Galbraith on the strength of my bibliography in *The Struggle for Mastery in Europe*. It was the year of the Suez crisis when I thought that the Boer war had come again and that we faced a long period of unpopularity, persecution and perhaps imprisonment. This was another error in trying to learn from history : the miserable British government could not even sin properly and called off their aggression within a week. Most of all, 1956 was the year I met Beaverbrook. The occasion for this was characteristic. He had just published *Men and Power.* In it he told how Lloyd George, when imposing convoy on the reluctant admirals, descended on the Admiralty 'and seated himself in the First Lord's chair.' I was pretty sure that there had not been a meeting of the Admiralty Board that day. I wrote asking Beaverbrook for his evidence. He invited me to lunch and said : 'I'm sure it happened' and, when I pressed him again, 'I'll ask Churchill,' which of course he never did. Years later I found that he had inserted the story on the proof in order to liven things up.

However it did not matter. I was bewitched by this master of political narrative and by the historical zest that inspired a man nearly eighty. Beaverbrook, apart from delighting me, switched my attention to English history. Another pull towards it came in a more orthodox way. One afternoon I went for a walk with G N Clark, the editor of the Oxford History of England. He said casually : 'I must do something about a final volume in the Oxford History of England, to pick up in 1914 where Ensor leaves off. Ensor was planning to do it and now he is dead. Perhaps I'll have a try at it myself.' I said : 'What about me?' and with that I was in – not only my next book, but many years of my life determined. Yet it would never have happened if G N Clark and I had not gone for a walk in Wytham Woods that autumn afternoon.

I was starting this time much more from scratch. I had never taught twentieth-century English history and had not kept up with the work on it systematically. I had reviewed most of the principal memoirs and other books as they came out. But mostly my knowledge was a matter of memory – an unreliable source. However I began to read very hard. The subject had at any rate the advantage that most of the books on it were in English and the even greater advantage that they were nearly all in the London Library. No more reading German; no more going to the British Museum. These two things were almost reward enough in themselves.

I had hardly settled down when I had to break off. Distractions made a hole in my life for two years and more. It was my turn to serve as vice-president of Magdalen College just when it celebrated its quincentenary and as vice-president I had to organise it all. This was very enjoyable and, for an historian, very interesting. But it took up much of my time : arranging dinners and parties, commissioning a fireworks display, even attending a service at the tomb of our founder, William of Waynflete, in Winchester Cathedral. I left a note of my mistakes for my successor in 2058. He will learn from it how to make new ones.

A greater distraction was the call of duty when the Campaign for Nuclear Disarmament started. This was the only public cause to which I devoted myself wholeheartedy and, I think, the one worthy thing I have done in my life. I became one of the national speakers and for two years or so toured in more halls than either Bright or Gladstone did, if only because some of the halls were not built in their time. With *The Troublemakers* fresh in my mind, I tried to achieve the same effect. Where my colleagues appealed to emotion, I relied on hard argument to show the folly as well as the wickedness of nuclear weapons. My model was Cobden – 'I know the Blue Books as well as the noble Lord does.' My best evening came at Birmingham Town Hall where I spoke precisely a hundred years after Bright delivered there his great speech on British foreign policy – 'a gigantic system of out-relief for the British aristocracy.'

The campaign was very instructive for me as an historian. Mass meetings are intoxicating for both audience and speaker. You imagine you have really achieved something when you get four thousand people on their feet with enthusiasm, and I suppose much the same is true of a successful speech in the House of Commons. This was a warning to me that politicians cannot be wholly sane. Nor were we in the great days of the campaign. We genuinely believed when we started that the whole world would be impressed if Great Britain renounced nuclear weapons and would follow our moral lead. In this way CND was a last splutter of imperial pride. The Cuba missile crisis taught us better. No one cared in the slightest whether we had nuclear weapons or not, which was of course a strong argument for abandoning them. The Cuba crisis virtually killed CND, and I have never involved myself in politics since.

Though I was too busy to do much serious research during this turmoil, I needed to write something – 'always scribble, scribble, scribble! Eh! Mr Gibbon?' I had been studying the background to the Second World War ever since the material began to come out and now could go straight ahead. This is how I came to write *The Origins of the Second World War*, the only subject I thought of myself. The title was of course wrong, as I realised when I came to write the last sentence. What happened in September 1939 was a minor episode in the Second World War, not the world war itself, which began either much earlier (April 1932) or much later (December 1941). But at this time my mind was still centred on Europe. The views expressed in the book followed logically on those I had developed in *The Course of German History*. They have now become the current orthodoxy. Indeed with Fritz Fischer and his school claiming that German statesmen actually designed the First World War and were, if anything, more extreme than Hitler, I find myself trailing far behind. However I do not intend to fight again the controversies that the book provoked. I had tried to write history in detachment; my critics were concerned to express their emotions. I will only add that, when criticising an author, I have never descended to personal abuse. I cannot say the same about my critics.

When I returned to *English History, 1914–1945*, I was not a free agent. I came at the end of a long-established series and had to conform to its pattern, putting in biographical footnotes and lists of cabinet ministers. I read all the preceding fourteen volumes in the series, though, to be honest, I managed to get right through only five of them. They troubled me. Where was the story line? Most of the books seemed to me collections of independent essays. I decided to write in the form of a continuous narrative. There was some sleight of hand about this. Continuous narrative works when you are confined to a single theme, such as the origins of a war. It is harder, indeed almost impossible, when you have to handle every aspect of national life. So I used a narrative framework and slipped in what I called 'occasional pauses for refreshment.' I maintained the solemn tone of the previous writers, pontificating about writers as though I were qualified to judge them. Somehow the book did not come out all that solemn in the end.

There were other problems. For instance, what was 'England'? All the previous writers had used England, Great Britain, the United Kingdom, and even the British Empire as synonymous terms, as they were when the series had been launched thirty years before. Now with the Scotch roaring at my back, I could not do this and yet could not write the history of twentieth-century England in isolation. This is a problem not encountered by historians of other European countries except perhaps the Germans, who, I notice, often manage to write the history of Germany without mentioning Austria. I did my best with a compromise that worked out all right.

More seriously, what England was I writing about? Again my predecessors had not worried about this and had written the history of the English upper classes. I wanted to write the history of the English people. But even in the twentieth century the English people had little history except at moments of crisis, though I do not know whether this made them happy. I kept slithering into the old fashion of writing about the 'in' classes and then pulled myself up every now and then. I must have done better than I expected. At any rate Max Beloff called me a Populist historian, which was exactly what I wanted to be.

I wrote all my earlier works virtually without consulting anybody. *English History, 1914–1945* went through the mill. G N Clark was a model editor, often querying what I wrote and then accepting it when I said it was necessary. My greatest aid came from Ken Tite, my colleague who was politics tutor at Magdalen. He should have been an outstanding political historian himself, but he was a sick man who died comparatively young without writing a book. Ken read my draft and wrote some forty pages of foolscap comments on it. I absorbed his points, and he then wrote fifteen more pages. My book was certainly chewed over, and I record with a full heart my gratitude to Ken Tite. Beaverbrook provided some of the anecdotes, not all of them reliable. More than this he gave me a firm conviction that English history was an exciting subject. Indeed on one occasion he inspired me to go on when my spirits flagged and I was inclined to break off.

There is not much to add to this record. I spent five years writing a life of Beaverbrook. This was a labour of love and does not illustrate any theory of history or biography. Beaverbrook lived a long time and managed to combine six different sorts of careers, so the book came out much longer than he would have liked. He himself came out a greater man than I had expected, but that was his doing, not mine. At any rate I wrote the book with my heart as well as with my head.

I even tried my hand at cultural history. Geoffrey Barraclough conscripted me to contribute to a series on the history of civilisation he was editing. I tried to find out what 'civilisation' meant and received many dusty answers. I decided that it meant the predominating patterns of life at any given time and, as war and economic problems predominated in the first half of the twentieth century, *From Sarajevo to Potsdam* came out political after all. My short histories of the two world wars – both suggested by a publisher – gave me greater pleasure. Without design they are curiously, and I think appropriately, different in tone. *The First World War* appears as a muddle from beginning to end. Shortly after it was published, I went to Joan Littlewood's show *Oh! What a Lovely War* and found the entire cast reading my book, delighted to have their version confirmed by a serious, or fairly serious, historian. *The Second World War* has a much firmer construction. It is, I think, the first account that binds the two wars, German and Japanese, into a single coherent pattern. I regard the book as being, in relatively short compass, the best demonstration of my way of writing history. Perhaps this is only because it is the most recent book I have written.

The difficulties I have encountered in writing history have been practical and technical. The greatest difficulty is time. You have to read a great deal, chase evidence all over the place, and make copious notes many of which you cannot lay hands on when you need them. I have of course never used a research assistant. No individual history can be written with one. As a writer my first model was Albert Sorel, and *The Course of German History* is peppered with epigrams that seek to imitate his. *The Habsburg Monarchy* often echoes the style of *The Thirties* by Malcolm Muggeridge which I happened to be reading at the time. Since then my style has been my own. It has however changed with my writing instruments. With a pen you write words. With a typewriter you write sentences. With an electric typewriter, which I use now, you write paragraphs. In military terms: bow and arrow, musket, machine gun. I try to keep up a continuous fire.

No Oxford Chair of History has come my way, though there were plenty around in my time. This was no doubt accidental, with perhaps a tinge of disapproval for either me or recent history. I was glad to escape the administrative duties that fall to a professor. My only regret is that professors tend to grab most of the research students, and I could have done with more. This has been a loss for me and perhaps for some research students.

My emancipation from teaching was completed in 1963, when the History Faculty Board terminated my university lectureship for reasons that are still obscure to me. Magdalen College gave me a reasearch fellowship, and University College, London, made me a special lecturer, which gave me just enough lecturing to keep my hand in. When I had passed the retiring age for university lectures I began lecturing again at Oxford just to show what it had missed. For this the Faculty Board paid me £40 a year. For the most part I make my living from journalism and television. Even so, I do not suppose anyone would dispute my claim to be a professional historian.

The other great difficulty is material. History, unlike poetry or fiction, does not write itself. For recent times, which I have always stuck to, there seems only too much material, and yet new evidence is constantly coming out. Often I have had to change my ground while writing a book or, still worse, after it has been written. When I finished *English History, 1914-1945* in July 1964, the fifty-year rule was in force and not a single classified British paper was available. Now the British archives are open, I suspect a little selectively, until 1945. I fear that my next task is to write the whole book all over again. If I do, it will work out differently. In the early 1960s I was still writing under the impact of the Second World War which was the most inspiring time in our history. Now I regard the state and still more the future of my country more gloomily. Indeed I often wonder whether it is worthwhile writing history at all. The record, I think, is nearly over. However history is fun to write and, I hope, fun to read. That to my mind is its justification.

On a more serious level, I believe that history enables us to understand the past better, no more and no less. This is a matter of detached curiosity, and there can be no nobler exercise of the human mind. I have never supposed, as many earlier historians did, that men can learn any useful lessons from history, political or otherwise. Of course you can learn certain obvious commonplaces, such as that all men die or that one day the deterrent, whatever it may be, will fail to deter. Apart from this, history is an art just like painting or architecture and is designed like them to give intellectual and artistic pleasure.

I have never been troubled by the dogmas of others about what history should be or how it should be written. Most of this is sales talk by academics anxious to justify their existence. My view is that they should get on with writing books in their way and I will get on with writing them in mine. I have always been conscious of the artificiality of history. We sort human beings into national or class categories, when in reality each one of them is unique. Bernard Shaw was delighted to learn from an oculist that only one man in a thousand has completely 'normal' vision. Who has ever known a typical working man or even a typical university professor? When I sit on the beach at Brighton, I am surrounded by the masses, but I do not number myself among them and no doubt each one of the others would make the same exception for himself.

Some historians understand science and technology. Some understand philosophy. I know how a newspaper office works, which makes me sceptical about studies of public opinion. I know what to do in a television studio and can talk straight to camera for twenty-five minutes, twenty-seven seconds, which allows for the commercial break. Even in my more adventurous days, I kept almost entirely to Europe. I have been to almost every European country, including Soviet Russia in the happy days of NEP. Outside Europe I went once to Morocco and once to New Brunswick. On the latter occasion I looked across the bay from St Andrews to Maine, so I can say I have seen the United States or at any rate one of them. Nowadays I stick mainly to England and recently kept my sense of history alive by walking the 150 miles of Offa's Dike.

I am English by birth and preference and, I suppose, in character. This has no relevance to my work as an historian. Seeley – or was it Freeman – said: 'History is past politics.' If this means that history should be used as a political weapon, I am not of Seeley's (or Freeman's) opinion. When I write, I have no loyalty except to historical truth as I see it and care no more about British achievements or mistakes than about any others. I was deeply concerned in the general strike, the Second World War, and the campaign for nuclear disarmament. But this does not weigh with me when I treat them historically. I think that the English people of the twentieth century were a fine people and deserved better leaders than on the whole they got. This is, if anything, the moral of *English History, 1914–1945,* but I left the reader to find it out for himself. At any rate national loyalty or even disloyalty has never been among my difficulties as an historian.

Dr Johnson said, 'Great abilities are not requisite for an Historian; for in historical composition, all the greatest powers of the human mind are quiescent. He has facts ready to his hand; so there is no exercise of invention. Imagination is not required in any high degree; only about as much as is used in the lower kinds of poetry. Some penetration, accuracy, and colouring will fit a man for the task, if he can give the application which is necessary.' That is about right, though the historian needs more invention than Johnson supposed. I am short on imagination and have never managed to write a line of poetry or a paragraph of fiction. Penetration is, I hope, another name for green fingers. Every historian tries to be accurate, though none succeeds as fully as he would like to. Style is colouring and something more : it sets its stamp on the whole work. As Johnson says, application is the main thing. Writing history is like W C Fields juggling. It looks easy until you try to do it.

2. The Historian as a Biographer[1]

A contribution to a volume of essays on History and Biography,
written at the invitation of my old friend, Friedrich Engel-Janosi,
who, alas, died before he could read my completed piece.

Inside every historian there lies concealed a biographer struggling to
get out. In his own work the historian faces an endless task. He
arbitrarily abstracts some small stretch from the seamless web of
history, knowing full well that his theme existed before the moment
when his book begins and will go on after the moment when his
book finishes. The biographer is more fortunate: the limits of his
subject are defined for him in advance. His book will begin with
the subject's birth, perhaps with some prelude of family background,
and will end with the subject's death, again perhaps with an epilogue
on the subject's legacy, political, financial or personal.

The historian looks at this good fortune with envy. How happy
he would be to enjoy the same advantages. No more need to search
for a theme; no more worrying over what to put in and what to
leave out; no more hesitation over the interpretation to set on events.
Everything is clear before him. The theme is set; the sources are
available. All he has to do is to sit down and write. Surely the
historian's training in his own craft will enable him to write a
biography without difficulty. He knows how to judge evidence and
where to find it.

Biography is only a particular form of history or so the historian
thinks. Both historian and biographer rely primarily on written
records. The biographer may get more guidance from portraits and
sculpture than the historian usually does. On the other hand the
historian gets more guidance from public buildings such as cathedrals
and castles, to say nothing of houses of parliament. The biographer

[1]*Wiener Beiträge*, 1980.

even more than the historian writes a narrative where events move in order of time. If history is essentially story – indeed the two words are the same in many languages other than English – biography is certainly a story also.

On second thoughts the historian becomes less confident. Every historian treats some aspect of man in society. It may be political man, economic man, military man, aesthetic man, but always man in society. Society comes first. The historian seeks for what is common in men, not what distinguishes one man from another. The individual is a great problem for the historian. He knows from his own experience that every man is unique. No historian for instance would admit that he is exactly like any other historian in character or achievement. Every face is different; every handwriting is different; every character is different. Nevertheless the individual has to be subordinated to the grand central design. Men have to be placed in arbitrary categories – epoch, class, nation, creed. One man has to represent the mediaeval monk or the colonial explorer; another, the merchant banker or the Jacobin revolutionary.

Of course the historian knows that these types are fictions. The men of the middle ages for instance were unaware that they were living in the middle of anything. The class-conscious proletarian is a rare phenomenon, often, as in the case of Marx, drawn from another class. Revolutionary France is often held up as the outstanding example of modern nationalism. Yet an 1850 enquiry showed that the majority of the inhabitants of France did not know that they were French. However, the historian cannot get on without these fictions and indeed soon forgets that he invented them. It is not surprising that historians have often been the ringleaders of national or class movements. Nationalism did not begin in the peasant villages; it began in academic lecture rooms.

Nowadays the historian professes to be less enslaved by national or class loyalties. In other ways the problem of how to treat the individual becomes increasingly difficult. There was a time when historians wrote mainly about the few figures at the top – the Great Man theory of history as it has been called. The fate of the Roman Empire was determined by the shape of Cleopatra's nose. Kings and Queens, Popes and chief Ministers crowded the historian's pages. History was a series of biographies, loosely strung together in a framework of general events. Gibbon, perhaps the greatest of English historians, has some splendid passages on the development of the Christian religion. But most of his narrative is a succession of

Emperors and gives the impression that their individual failings did more than crushing taxation or the barbarian invasions to bring about the Empire's fall. Ranke is generally supposed to have inaugurated a more scientific and less personal version of history. Careful reading shows that his pages often contain brilliant passages of individual characterisation, especially when the individual presented happens to be a ruler of Prussia. On a humbler level, as a boy I learnt the dates of the Kings and Queens of England and thought when I had done so that I knew the whole of English history.

The historian is no longer allowed to lapse into biography in this way. Now he must present 'the profound forces' of history. Movements, not men, are his theme. He must write about public opinion or imperialism, not about an individual editor or the founder of a colony. Indeed under pressure from the dominant school of French historians he is now ashamed to write at all about events which have become as unfashionable as the individual. The biographer is no longer an ally or a writer to be envied. He has become a deplorable example any historian would do well to avoid. The conscientious historian turned biographer has to grasp that the two tasks are fundamentally different despite their apparent similarities. To write a successful biography the historian must learn a new trade.

Often the historian fails to carry through a complete transformation. Given his training and background, he is unlikely to choose an artist or a literary figure as his subject and this cuts him off from a rich field of biography. Boswell's Life of Johnson is undoubtedly the greatest biography in the English language but its greatness does not lie in the occasional light it sheds on British politics in the eighteenth century. The historian inevitably chooses some public man : a statesman, a soldier or a political writer, someone in fact who will be an example of man in society. All the same the emphasis is changed : the individual comes first and society second.

I learnt this when I wrote my life of Bismarck. He occupied the centre of the stage and seemed to create events even when he claimed only to take advantage of them. I was back with the Great Man theory of history. Bismarck created the German Reich. He set his stamp on German society and, after designing three wars, gave Europe a long period of peace. This is not how historians now see German history. Railways and the factories of the Ruhr, not Bismarck, united Germany; the strength of the Junkers, not Bismarck, shaped German society; and the unconscious workings of the Balance of Power, not Bismarck, gave Europe first wars and then peace. However I consoled myself with the thought that even historians who most pride themselves on being up-to-date lapse into the Great Man theory, as when they treat Hitler personally as the cause of the Second World War.

However, it is not enough for the historian to write history disguised as biography. If he is to be a thorough-going biographer he must forget about events and treat his subject as an individual human being. This raises the terrible shadow of psychology. Until recently this was a subject neglected by nearly all historians and indeed by many biographers. Of course the historian was aware from his experience of others if not of himself that no man was entirely sane and rational. But he assumed that men were rational when they were going about their own business, whether it were diplomacy or running a factory. Now we are told by psychologists and particularly by the followers of Freud that the important thing is the workings of our subject's unconscious mind.

This is all very well when the psychologist or perhaps even the historian has personal contacts with a living man. Even the most uninstructed of us can form some sort of impression, noting whether our subject is bad-tempered, vain or sympathetic. The psychologist goes much deeper: he conducts prolonged interviews which he calls psycho-analysis. I have my doubts about the results achieved by these interviews. In particular I doubt whether a technique perhaps applicable to the mentally unbalanced has much relevance to those who behave in a reasonably normal way. But this is a heresy I will not pursue.

But how do you interview a dead man? The answer is: you guess. The psychologist takes concepts that he has derived from living subjects and imposes them on the dead ones. The results are far from satisfactory. The psycho-analytic biography of Woodrow Wilson by Sigmund Freud and W C Bullitt was one of the most preposterous works ever written and revealed more about the psychopathology of the two authors than of the American President. Hitler has been a favourite subject for psychologists. I read one such work recently where Hitler's character was explained by the fact that at age of three he saw his father and mother having sexual intercourse. The proof of this was that, even if he did not see them, he had the psychology of one who had and therefore must have seen them. If this sounds like nonsense, I can only plead that it represents my view of psycho-analysis as a biographical weapon.

However, the biographer must employ psychology in less extreme ways. In practical terms psychology for the biographer means two things: family background and sex. Family background sounds easy. Every man, it seems, either loves his mother and is jealous of his father or loves his father and finds his mother tiresome. The first relationship is apparently the more usual and even the more natural. Its results are said to be admirable. The subject develops a strong character by fighting with his father and at the same time a tenderness by loving his mother. The second relationship is abnormal. The subject has never fought and therefore remains an immature, unassertive character who also fails to establish any stable relationship with a woman.

In the two biographies I have attempted – one on Bismarck and the other on Lord Beaverbrook – I found this did not work out. Bismarck admired his slow, heavy father and disliked his mother from whom he got his brains. He should therefore have been weak and unassertive. On the contrary he became the most powerful figure of his age. He was combative on every issue great and small, fighting with everyone from the King of Prussia to his local tax inspector. He had a happy married life and was not above sentimental love affairs, which included the daughter of an English Duke and the wife of a Russian Ambassador. All men feared him though he could be winning enough when he wished to be. Bismarck did not confirm the psychologist's rule.

With Beaverbrook I approached the problem the other way round. I described his character to a pyschologist. Beaverbrook had a zest for power. He enjoyed making money and was captivating to women. He had also an inner uncertainty and a craving for affection which he often mistakenly thought money would win him. The psychologist answered without hesitation, 'He must have been a neglected only child.' In fact he was nothing of the kind. He was the fifth child in a family of eleven. His brothers and sisters assured me that their family life was uniformly happy and that Beaverbrook was an exception only in that he preferred to be a 'loner' – in his own words, 'a cat that walked by itself'. I decided that men have the disposition they are born with, not a helpful doctrine. Henceforward I left psychology alone.

Sex cannot be put aside so lightly. For one thing readers expect it. A biography is of little interest to them unless its subject has a glamorous love life. Sex may be important with literary figures. The Dark Lady of the Sonnets apparently mattered for Shakespeare though I think his gifts as a dramatist are to be taken more seriously. The relations of Dickens with Ellen Ternan provide an interesting gloss on his later novels but these novels read just as well without any knowledge of Ellen Ternan. Perhaps it is enlightening to learn that some novelist is homosexual, as happens often enough nowadays, but this is not what makes his novels memorable.

When we come to the political or other public figures that the historian turned biographer has to handle, their sex life has little relevance except for purposes of entertainment. Was Palmerston's foreign policy determined by the fact that he had a number of children by another man's wife? The relationship may have helped him to get the post of Foreign Secretary originally. Thereafter it does not seem to have mattered any more than if he had been married in the ordinary way. Did the longstanding friendship of Franz Joseph with Frau Schratt affect the constitutional history or the foreign policy of the Habsburg Monarchy? The platonic love that Bismarck had for Kathy Orloff makes a touching story but it did not even provide him with an excuse for meeting Napoleon III at Biarritz. Gladstone said at the end of his life that he had known eleven Prime Ministers and that seven of them were adulterers. No one, I think, could distinguish the adulterers from the chaste by examining their political activities. Lloyd George had many love affairs; Churchill had none. This had no influence on their respective careers except that Churchill claimed to have had more time for public affairs because he did not run after women.

Of course even the most political biographer finds interest in the more obvious features of his subject's character. It is useful to know how the subject handled other men; whether he was hard working or lazy; what were his gifts as a public speaker and so on. One topic neglected by most biographers is what their subject ate and drank. Bismarck ate far too much for most of his life. He drank countless bottles of champagne and brandy and smoked fourteen Havana cigars a day. Churchill also drank a great deal and lit a great many cigars though he did not keep them alight for long. Were these two great men in a constant haze of alcohol and tobacco? It does not seem so from the clarity of their speeches or state papers. Stalin is said to have drunk plain water when he appeared to be drinking vodka. I doubt whether this was the secret of his power.

The historian turned biographer has no difficulty when he is

27

merely recording his subject's career. But for a biography this is not enough. The author must also depict the subject's character, writing as though he understood what was going on in his subject's mind. Novelists find this easy. They have created the character; therefore they know everything about him. The professional biographer behaves in much the same way. He claims to know what his subject was thinking as well as what his subject was doing. He writes confidently of his subject's aims even when they were not revealed at the time. He often provides us with a vivid picture of the subject's thoughts. As a result each biographer presents an entirely different version, based more on conjecture than on evidence, and there are as many Napoleons and Hitlers as there are biographers.

The conscientious historian is at first distressed by this. He is accustomed to set down only the things for which he has evidence. Now he is required to use his imagination, not a quality with which historians are well endowed. But there is no escape from it. The historian has to recognize that biography is a literary art, much nearer to fiction or poetry than it is to serious history. However much the historian is concerned to record his subject's public acts, his essential task as a biographer is to present a single human being with all the contradictions that this involves.

Inevitably the writer of a biography becomes committed to his subject for good or bad. Some biographers come to dislike their subject and write what is commonly known as a debunking book. These books are often highly entertaining and a useful contribution to knowledge, as witness for instance that once-popular book, *Eminent Victorians* by Lytton Strachey. Most biographers, including myself, go the other way. They fall mildly in love with their subject and interpret everything in a favourable way. My admiration for Bismarck already existed before I wrote my biography of him but it may well have run away with me. With Beaverbrook I already had a deep personal affection which no doubt showed in my biography, some reviewers thought too much so. The best the historian can do when he grows attached to his subject is to keep this feeling within bounds. Even the most admirable man is all the better for a few black spots.

There are more technical problems involved in writing a man's biography. The greatest is the problem of documents. Most great men left large archives and the historian is anxious to publish copious extracts from them. If he publishes too many, he runs the risk of obscuring the subject's character. Nineteenth-century writers were fond of that composite form, Life and Letters – half a biography and half a collection of documents. The result was usually almost unreadable. With Bismarck I had little difficulty. I relied entirely on the printed sources which gave his letters and state papers and could safely refer the reader to these for further details. With Beaverbrook it was the other way round. I worked mostly from the manuscript collection of his letters and often, I am afraid, printed letters because they were amusing or eccentric rather than because they added to historical knowledge.

There is a further danger. Very often the biographer has had a predecessor; the subject himself. Many great men have been prolific writers; some have been brilliant writers. The greatest contemporary example is Winston Churchill whose version of both world wars has been indelibly stamped on the minds of most English readers. At one time historians treated Churchill's books as an impeccable source. Now we are gradually coming to realise that they are one-sided and often unreliable in their reproduction of documents. I had much the same problem with both my subjects. No one who has read *Gedanken und Erinnerungen* is likely to escape its influence. Now we know that Bismarck wrote or rather dictated it in extreme old age, often without consulting the contemporary documents and that he was more concerned to depreciate Wilhelm II than to provide an impartial account for future generations. Beaverbrook was easier. He never aimed at supreme power despite what some of his critics have said. He was an observer who witnessed with interest and amusement the struggle of others for power. As a result his two books, *Politicians and the War* and *Men and Power,* are among the most entertaining and brilliant works of memoirs ever written. All the same he was not above twisting his record of events in order to come out more creditably than he deserved.

Autobiographies by the great men are often explosive tools to be used by the biographer with caution. But the lack of an autobiography is worse. It is unlikely that either Stalin or F D Roosevelt would have written autobiographies with much literary sparkle. But surely they would have told us something. As it is both men remain, what Sukhanov called Stalin in 1917, 'a grey blur'.

I have a word of counsel for any historian who is puzzled as to how to assess an autobiography : he should write one himself. He will find that however resolutely he tries to tell the truth the narrative gets out of control. Little successes are magnified and failures passed over unless of course they are blown up into monstrous grievances. Memory becomes selective. Often you remember what you ought to have done rather than what you did. Also your actions make more sense than they did at the time. In retrospect everything can be explained, usually to your own credit. Moreover when you write of friends or colleagues you see them as they are now, not as they were once. The best that can be said for an historian as auto-biographer is that he knows he is cheating whereas the great men did not.

What applies to autobiographies applies also to anecdotes. Here the biographer has to be critical in two fields. He has to be critical about the subject. He has also to be critical about the source of the anecdote. Those who have climbed to success on the backs of great men are not likely to remember with much detachment. Alternatively the anecdotist will write with resentment against the humiliations and disappointments he had to endure. Having set down these difficulties I realise that they are much like what the historian has to face when he is working in his own field. First we have to find sources; then we have to criticise them. We are equipped to do both. After all, our training makes us more critical than other people. Hence there is a good case for historians writing biographies even if they have less imagination than the professionals.

The relationship between history and biography must also be considered the other way round. Not what contribution can the historian make as a biographer, but what use can biography be for the historian? The first answer is simple: historians have to use biographies whether they would or no. Though I do not know the statistics, I surmise that more biographies are published than serious works of history. They are our essential sources from ancient times to the present day. We accumulate pictures of individuals in the hope that they will merge into a general pattern. Not long ago Sir Lewis Namier and others set out to compile brief biographies of members of parliament. This, Namier claimed, would constitute a History of Parliament. I asked him whether this history should not rather be sought in parliamentary debates and the resolutions or bills which a parliament passed. Namier brushed me aside. History, he insisted, was to be found in the biographies of innumerable ordinary men.

I was not convinced. However much we question the Great Man theory of history, the course of events is shaped by the leaders as much as by the followers. Historians treat one aspect of this process; biographies treat another. Historians are usually more cautious and hesitant in their judgements, at any rate nowadays. Biographers provide a more vivid, but not necessarily a truer version. In the last resort their ways part. The biographer builds up his individual subject until society is almost forgotten. The historian controls his interest in the individual and imposes the needs of society. The historian is perhaps too sceptical about Freud. The biographer neglects Marx who has provided essential instruments for historians. Where would historians be without the concept of class struggles and class characteristics?

Both historians and biographers use fictions, intellectual devices to produce an illusion of reality. The biographer relies on the fiction that he can recapture a man's character by literary skill and imagination. The historian welds individuals into a composite picture to which their individual existences are subordinated. The greatest achievements have been made by mixing biography and history together. This, too, is a literary art and hard to accomplish.

3. Lancashire[1]

Since this piece was written great chunks have been hacked from Lancashire to satisfy some bureaucratic whim. I am prepared to renounce Merseyside. I shall never relinquish Lancashire North of the Sands.

Most English counties nowadays are merely administrative units, with little to show that you have passed from one to another. Not Lancashire. It is a real place, its character all its own, its people different from people anywhere else. You never have to ask yourself where you are. The talk of the people in the streets will tell you. The look of the buildings will tell you. They all say: this is Lancashire and could not be anywhere else in the world. Will you like Lancashire? It depends whether you like real life or chocolate-box beauty. Anyone who knows Lancashire finds himself at the start apologising for it: apologising for its weather, for the drab houses, for the dirt, for the general lack of smartness. Then he realises that he is apologising for life. Of course Lancashire has faults as well as virtues. You have to dig beneath the surface to discover how much greater the virtues are than the faults.

Lancashire people do not believe in showing off. You have a feeling that they were too busy in the past making money to care about appearances. I used to wonder, years ago, which was uglier – the buildings or the women. Now Lancashire, though still prosperous, is no more prosperous than anywhere else. Both women and buildings are better looking than they were – perhaps as a result. All the same, cotton, though no longer king, has set a mark on Lancashire which will take a hydrogen-bomb to rub off. The mills were built for cotton, even though they have been gutted of their spindles, the sheds of their looms, and now make anything from children's

[1]*Vogue*, March 1960. © CNP Ltd.

toys to parts of motor-cars. The long rows of houses have seen generations of cotton workers, roused by the call of the knocker-up, clattering off down the cobbled streets in their clogs. Cotton made Manchester and Liverpool great cities, though they depend on cotton no longer. Still more, cotton turned south-east Lancashire into the greatest urban agglomeration in the world, which it still is. Twenty or thirty years ago it was possible, if you were sufficiently wrong-headed, to travel for forty miles without getting away from tram-lines, and Lancashire is still the ideal county for any motorist who likes being restricted to thirty miles an hour.

To get the flavour of real Lancashire, you must forget about the two cities and go to the cotton towns which push against the Pennines – Bury and Rochdale, Burnley, Nelson and Colne. Some of them have a long history. Bolton, for instance, was a Parliamentary stronghold in the Civil War, and at Middleton there is a memorial-window (probably the first of its kind) to the men of the district who fell at Flodden. But most of these were villages until the industrial revolution and the coming of the cotton mills. Each is dominated by a grandiose Town Hall, commissioned at the height of its Victorian prosperity. Down on the plain there are great Anglican churches in Victorian Gothic. The Dissenters evidently took to the hills. Each mile up the valleys the Nonconformist chapels get bigger and bigger, until at the head they are the size of cathedrals – vast, classical temples where the hymns of the dwindled congregations now echo mournfully. Up here the rich Lancashire dialect is still unspoilt – ravishingly beautiful to those who can understand it. A woman is still *oo*, not *she*. A man takes his baggin for the mid-day break, and cows go to the shippon. Are Eccles cakes still made at Eccles? I doubt it. But there are shops which serve tripe and onions at all hours of the day. And throughout the county there is one supreme delicacy: Lancashire cheese, made in the Fylde and consumed by the inhabitants in such quantities that little makes its way to the south of England. No nonsense in Lancashire about 'cheese' (meaning New Zealand cheddar). Great Lancashire cheeses stand on the shelves, and the shopper chooses his favourite by scooping out mouthfuls with a sixpence.

Some of these cotton towns are dying with the closing of the mills. Some have switched over to new industries and have saved their prosperity without losing their character. Anyone really interested in history, and not merely in the pretty side of it, should travel far to see them. A century ago they were the wonder of the world: the centre of British wealth and, supposedly, the future pattern for all mankind. When Karl Marx described capitalism and denounced it, he had Oldham and Rochdale in mind. Now history has passed them by, and they are just curious memorials of the past like the water-mills which they displaced. It would be foolish to pretend that they will ever become places of pilgrimage even for the most romantically-minded. They are gloomy, smoke-grimed, drab. But they are not ugly: their character is too strong for that, and their brick, even though stained, gives them a warmth which is lacking in the hard stone-built towns over the Pennines in Yorkshire. Lancashire certainly has its areas of unredeemed ugliness, the more obtrusive because they straddle across the main road to the North. Coal-mining can never have attractive results, and Wigan has long been a by-word. Unjustly. Wigan has a fine situation and green, spacious suburbs. You must go to the southern edge of the county to see some of the worst surroundings which civilised man has ever created for himself. St Helens produced Sir Thomas Beecham; Warrington once had a famous Nonconformist Academy. I can think of nothing to say in palliation of Widnes. But perhaps even its inhabitants think that they are citizens of no mean city.

Such are the ravages which the pursuit of wealth has made. Yet Lancashire is full of attractions also, its greatest being the people. In southern England local differences have almost vanished. In Lancashire there is still an unmistakable character. Northerners are supposed to be hard and dour. So they are in Yorkshire, or still more in Northumberland. People in Lancashire seem brisk and business-like. But they are also sentimental and romantic. They have been softened by the damp climate and only become hard when they go south. Mrs Pankhurst was hard all right when she assaulted politicians and set fire to pillar-boxes, but what could be more romantic? And what more sentimental than to go campaigning for woman's suffrage at all? I should like to claim Joan Littlewood as a typical Lancashire woman. Unfortunately she came from London, though on foot, and merely founded in Manchester the Theatre Union which she has now taken away again, and which has grown into the Theatre Workshop. Mrs Gaskell, however, was the real thing: the most modern of Victorian novelists, and the only one who was improved by being a woman, instead of being handicapped by it. Her last gesture of romantic common sense was to leave her family mansion as a maternity home for indigent members of the middle class.

Lancashire has not run much to great men. Until the eighteenth century it was a forgotten backwater, dominated by Tory squires. The Stanleys were the only great family. They have produced generations of public men, including a prime minister, and still provide the strongest element of genuine aristocracy in the county. Gladstone was born in Liverpool, but hardly belongs to Lancashire: he was Scotch by origin and spent most of his life at Hawarden. John Bright was unmistakably Lancashire: living all his life at Rochdale, where he played for the local cricket team, and preaching a creed of pacific Radicalism which he believed to be peculiarly adapted to Lancashire's needs. His creed is supposed to have been rational and hard-headed, but he advocated it in romantic terms. I put him at the head of English orators, partly – but only partly – because I prefer his views to those of Burke or Macaulay. Throwing the net wider, one might recall that Sir Winston Churchill sat first for Oldham and then for North West Manchester in the course of the long electoral wandering which terminated at Woodford. But there would be no end to a catalogue of those who have represented Lancashire constituencies at one time or another. It includes, for instance, Lord Beaverbrook, who sat for Ashton-under-Lyne before being precipitated into the House of Lords. Ranging further back, there is the once-famous Radical, Orator Hunt, who won Preston at the height of the Reform Bill agitation. My great-grandfather was thrown out of work for voting for him and inadequately compensated with a medal.

Outside the world of politics the two universities have attracted men of great distinction. Rutherford is, I suppose, the most famous, though his feat of splitting the atom has brought us doubtful benefits. The universities give an added eminence to Liverpool and Manchester, but both have long been centres of civilisation in their own right. Liverpool, which I know less, has the higher social tone; Manchester has perhaps more to be proud of in the Hallé Orchestra and *The Guardian*. The first is still the only permanent orchestra in England with a permanent conductor: the second the only national newspaper edited and produced outside London.[1] Though Manchester naturally gets the greatest benefit from them, their influence radiates throughout Lancashire. The Hallé Orchestra visits many Lancashire

[1]Alas, this no longer true.

towns. *The Guardian* produces a late edition, much superior to that sold in London, in time for most Lancashire breakfast-tables. It does not follow, of course, that Lancashire people are particularly musical, still less that they share *The Guardian's* political outlook.

They are lucky and do not always appreciate their luck. Life in Lancashire is often dirty and usually damp – though not, as it is generally supposed, excessively rainy. But there are more cultural amenities, independent of London, than in other parts of England.

Lancashire is a good place to live. It has also great attractions for the visitor, though it would be excessive to claim that a visit is compulsory for the lover of painting or architecture. The Walker Art Gallery in Liverpool is the only collection of paintings that reaches a national level – with no disrespect to the Pre-Raphaelites in Manchester. Manchester has, however, a very fine collection of drawings in the Whitworth Gallery, an incomparable collection of historic costumes, and all kinds of precious books in the John Rylands Library. The only buildings which indisputably merit three stars (*vaut le voyage*, as Michelin says of restaurants) are both in Liverpool. The Town Hall has the most palatial state-rooms in the country: roughly contemporary with the Pavilion at Brighton, but sober with civic pride where the Pavilion is frivolous and whimsical. The city fathers are less welcoming to sightseers than Dukes and Marquises, being less in need of money and it is only possible to see the Town Hall by private invitation. Most people are unaware of its existence and confuse it with St George's Hall, which is also of the highest excellence. It has been described as the finest Greco-Roman building in existence. Certainly it is as fine a Renaissance building as any in Italy and finer in its position.

A good many places deserve two stars – worth going to see once you are in Lancashire. There are no ancient Cathedrals – Manchester being a collegiate and parish church transformed into a cathedral a century ago. But there are some fine church-fittings – stalls and screens: in Manchester itself, at Lancaster, and, best of all, at Sefton near Liverpool. St Patrick's Chapel at Heysham is unique, perhaps deserving three stars: the only work of Celtic architecture in England. If you go on to the end of the peninsula, you reach Sunderland Point, the first place where cotton was landed in England and now a ghostly parable of the cotton industry itself. Grass grows on the wharves and on the walls of the eighteenth-century warehouses. Across the estuary Glasson Dock still flourishes. According to report, it has become the congregating place for the girls who work the road houses and transport cafés in big American cars. White slaves and the ghosts of slaves rub shoulders, and of course other people rub shoulders too. But this is hearsay, a legend which perhaps one should not disturb by putting it to the test.

Furness Abbey, near Barrow, is the only first-rate monastic remain; very rewarding for the historian and winning for others from its beautiful situation and its warm red sandstone. In southern Lancashire there are a number of half-timbered houses, some turned into local museums, some falling into ruin. Indeed, Lancashire has an unrivalled record, so far as England goes, for destroying its memorials of the past. Churches and great houses were pulled down ruthlessly in the nineteenth century to be replaced by something more pretentious. Now they are merely pulled down. Knowsley, of course, is a house on the grand scale, as interesting for its associations as for its architecture and Wyatt produced one of his most accomplished works at Heaton Hall, now in a public park north of Manchester. I would put in a special word of praise for Leighton Hall near Carnforth. This has a Gothic sham-façade in front of a Georgian house. It is possible to walk between the house and the front – an unusual experience.

But Lancashire's greatest attraction from a tourist point of view is provided by nature. This surprises many people who think all Lancashire urban, like the south of England. On the contrary, Lancashire has the best of nearly everything: sea, lakes, rivers, mountains. The coast from Lytham to Fleetwood has a finer stretch of sand than the Lido, with the additional advantages of a tide and real waves. Set in the centre of it lies Blackpool, greatest of all seaside resorts. A lot of people go to Blackpool, but there is room for all and plenty to spare: miles of sand, miles of promenade. You can have a gay time at Blackpool, anywhere from the Pleasure Beach to the Tower Ballroom. You can also, with a little knowledge, doze undisturbed. Blackpool is the most innocent of resorts, or at any rate the least sinister. If anyone wrote *Blackpool Rock*, it would not be a murder-story; it would be a sentimental, and inconculsive, romance. The sea is only one of many excellencies. The river valleys, running up into the Pennines, are another: Ribble, Hodder, and Lune, each with its own quality. Associated with them is that strange mountain road, the Trough of Bowland, a feature almost unknown to those outside the county. Last of all Lancashire 'north of the sands' takes in a special chunk of the Lake District: one mountain (Coniston Old Man), two lakes (Coniston and Esthwaite), and the remote valley of the Duddon. The country-side here is gentler than in the heart of the Lake District further north; it is soft, balmy, the vegetation as rich as Cornwall. Hawks-head is one of the least spoilt places in England : mediaeval church; sixteenth-century grammar school, attended by Wordsworth; eighteenth-century Town Hall, now given over to dances. The little shops and narrow streets will be recognised by every student of Beatrix Potter. I nearly left her out. She was certainly a Lancashire author of the first rank, and a characteristic one : sentimental, hard-headed at once. Most of the land round Hawkshead is now owned by the National Trust, thanks to the profits from Peter Rabbit and Jeremy Fisher. I suppose they were Lancastrians too. Who could ask for more than a county which has Manchester at one end of it and Hawkshead at the other?

4. Acton Eclipsed[1]

Observer, 1959. A review of *Judgements on History and Histor- ians* by Jacob Burckhardt, with an introduction by H R. Trevor-Roper. (Allen and Unwin)

Lord Acton must look to his laurels. He has long reigned supreme among historians by his unrivalled skill in not writing. Others have bid for reputation by producing works in crushing volume; Acton outdid them all by remaining silent, his wisdom to be deduced only from cryptic fragments and the lecture-notes of his students. Recently a formidable competitor has been creeping up the field and now takes first place as the most powerful Bore in Christendom : Jacob Burckhardt, the sad Swiss patrician. He carries a handicap in the shape of a book on 'The Civilisation of the Renaissance in Italy,' actually published nearly a century ago and always admired. It is testimony to his quality that this handicap has been overcome. Henceforth we shall be taught to admire him for what he did not put down on paper, not for what he did.

The present book is his masterstroke. It consists of the notes which he accumulated for his lectures on general history at Basel University. No doubt they were very good lectures. It is easy to understand from the notes why Burckhardt was invited to succeed Ranke at Berlin and also easy to understand why he refused. Burckhardt surveyed the human record with gloomy detachment and yet gloomier foreboding. Progress was for him a meaningless concept; the pursuit of happiness a delusion. As traditional institu- tions tumbled down, the rule of the masses would follow. Then would come militarism, war, dictatorship and an infinity of human suffering.

This outlook put him out of tune with the brash, bustling capital

[1]*Observer,* 1959

of united Germany, but it sets him in tune with academic historians in our more sceptical age. We have emptied Progress down the drain and faith in humanity with it. The last champions of civilisation sit huddled together, waiting for the barbarous masses to break in. It is infinitely consoling for them to be told how admirable they are; to be assured that they alone are the repositories of wisdom. It is particularly consoling for them to be assured by an illustrious example that true wisdom lies in not writing books that people will read. They can thumb over these notes of Burckhardt and hail a fellow-spirit across the wastes of democracy.

Any sort of posthumous fame is, no doubt, welcome. All the same, it is a bit rough on the real Burckhardt to be enlisted in the cold war between the dons and the masses. His fragmentary writings are often worth reading, apart from their political implications. Even these notes have their lively moments. His definition of history is about as good as can be done: 'What one age finds worthy of note in another.' There is, too, a fine swipe at the endless pontificating which Acton practised and which reached a deserved climax in '1066 and All That': 'The meddling of values in world history is as if in the sea of time one wave wanted to shout insults against all the other waves.'

In practice Burckhardt did not stick to his own rule. There are plenty of moral judgements here, from the emphatic estimate of Julius Caesar early on as 'the greatest of mortals' to the persistent slamming of the French revolutionaries towards the end. No one minds that Burckhardt had an axe to grind. He too, as he confesses, had shared the faith in infinite happiness before 1848 and had been disillusioned by the outcome. The tiresome thing in Burckhardt, and in his admirers, is the claim that his axe is no axe at all and that the noise of the grindstone is never heard.

But suppose we forget for a moment all the axe-grinding, his and ours, forget about democracy and the masses and the end of civilisation, and ask instead a simple, practical question: Does this collection of lecture notes help much towards the study of history? Or, in more practical terms still: Will reading this book (as distinct from referring to it) clear the way towards a university scholarship? The answer, I fear, is: No. Better stick to Acton or even to 'Notes on European History.' The lectures were once remarkable, exciting, valuable. They have vanished. What remains are the hints with which Burckhardt sparked his mind into life or set down the broad lines which he would follow when talking. He could no doubt breathe the spirit into them. The reader is left with cold fragments.

Emulating Burckhardt's honesty, I must confess that this judgement, too, is not given in detachment. I dislike prophets of woe even more than enthusiasts for Progress. Civilisation, of course, has its ups and downs, but the present talk about its decline means only that university professors used to have domestic servants and now do their own washing-up. Except for this somewhat limited class, the present is the finest age to live in.

An historian ought to love the past, as Professor Trevor-Roper says in his introduction. But he ought to love the present, too, and even the future. The past is dead and there is a sterility in loving that alone. Burckhardt's failure to write books, or publish them, was not accidental. His thought was barren, despite his wisdom and he seems to affect his admirers. At any rate, Professor Trevor-Roper has not been stimulated into his usual originality. The student will find a comparison between the introduction to this book and the essay on the Faustian Historian in the Professor's 'Historical Essays' an interesting exercise in textual variation.

5. Peter Geyl: a great Historian[1]

Written after I had delivered a memorial address on Geyl to the
Flemish Society of Antwerp. I add an anecdote relating to Geyl's
disapproval of Toynbee's views. Shortly before Geyl's death I
met him one night walking alone down Whitehall in a dinner
jacket. I said to him, 'My dear friend, what are you doing here?'
He replied, 'I have sinned greatly. I have come from a dinner in
honour of Arnold Toynbee. He is one of my oldest friends and
I felt I had to go. Sentiment has led me to betray the cause of
historical truth.' This was the last time I saw Pieter Geyl.

What makes a great historian? By no means quantity of output.
Many small men have written long books, and some great ones have
left only fragments from which later generations must judge their
quality. Not brilliance of expression. Epigrams can spell ruin for
historians and often do. What distinguishes the truly great historian
is integrity, a single-minded devotion to the past and its problems.
  Pieter Geyl was a great historian of this kind. He presented a
shining example to other historians and commanded an admiration
which was almost without reserves. His writing was direct and
effective, but without graces. Few of his sentences lend themselves
to quotation. But there was in everything he said and wrote a
finality of judgement which gave a profound intellectual satisfaction.
  Geyl was first and foremost a patriotic Dutchman. Though he
possessed a wide European culture and aspired to be a citizen of the
world, he treasured national variety and his own nation most of
all. His life-work was a history of the Dutch-speaking people from
the revolt of the Netherlands to the present day, a work which he
left incomplete. His loyalty was not given only to the present kingdom of Holland. It extended to the Dutch or Flemish speakers on
the far side of the frontier with Belgium.

[1]*Observer*, 1967.

Geyl was one of the first who sustained this oppressed nationality. When he went to Ghent in 1908, he found a French-speaking university, where the society of Flemish students was a banned organisation. Thirty years later, Ghent had become a Flemish possession, and Henri Pirenne, the champion of an exclusively French Belgium, was a barely tolerated guest. Geyl's historical work had played a great part in this transformation. Not that it was undertaken with a propagandist purpose. It was a reassertion of historical truth.

Geyl's practical contribution to history was his fundamental revision in the story of the revolt against Spain, which split the Netherlands in two – one part independent, one part still Spanish. According to the traditional view, the division had come along religious lines. The north was Calvinist, the south Roman Catholic. This was the view expressed in Motley's famous work. Later writers suggested that the split was also national or racial – between Dutch and French speakers. Geyl demonstrated the inaccuracy of both interpretations. There were Calvinists and Roman Catholics both north and south – indeed, rather more Calvinists south than north, and the Dutch extended far south of the later dividing line. Geyl showed that the frontier was determined solely by geography. The revolt was a war of sea-power against land-power. The champions of independence won where they rested on the sea and held the line of the great rivers. They lost against the land-armies of Spain. This was a mundane, workaday explanation. But its simplicity at last made sense of what had been a confused, almost incomprehensible picture. It was a triumph of common sense.

Geyl was not content to demonstrate how history should be written. He turned also to creative criticism of other historians. For the general reader his most attractive book is 'Napoleon For and Against,' a book written in strange circumstances. During the Second World War, Geyl was active in the Dutch Resistance. He was arrested and sent to a concentration camp. There, far from his library, he meditated on what French historians had made of Napoleon. He discovered a surprising distinction in their approach. The literary historians, on the whole, admired Napoleon and made excuses for him. The academic historians exposed his failings and criticised him in the name of Liberty. It is perhaps only in France that professors are radicals, and writers the friends of tyranny. Geyl had no doubt that he was on the side of the professors. Freedom of the human spirit seemed to him the greatest of causes and he served it with all his strength.

In his later years, Geyl contended strenuously against Toynbee's interpretation of history. Some people felt that he contended too much. But Geyl felt that the cause of historical truth was at stake. He distrusted generalisations and tested them against detail. Thus, Toynbee asserted that men were stimulated by adversity and instanced the response of the Dutch to the challenge of the threat from the sea. Geyl answered that Dutch civilisation started in the lush inland areas of the Netherlands and spread from there to the sea-coast. What then, he asked, remained of 'challenge and response'? To those who like sweeping generalisations, Geyl's objection seemed trivial. What did one exception matter? To others, particularly to professional historians, it seemed decisive.

Though Geyl was often a controversialist, he contended without bitterness or malice. It was impossible to be hurt by his criticisms even when they cut deep. He often shook his head at my sallies and then softened his rebuke with words of praise. When not long ago I wrote a book implying that the Nazis were little different from other Germans, Geyl said to me: 'That was a wicked book.' I said: 'But is it true?' He replied sadly: 'Yes, I'm afraid so, but you should not say it. And yet how can you help it?'

Geyl was a great Dutchman, a great European, and a great historian. It was an honour to have known him. If I were asked to name the historian whom I have most venerated in my lifetime, I should not hesitate for an answer. I should name: Pieter Geyl.

6.   Fisher's Europe[1]

A review of *A History of Europe* by H A L Fisher (Eyre and Spottiswoode).

In November, 1870, Thiers visited Vienna and urged on Beust, the Austro-Hungarian Chancellor, that Europe should mediate in the Franco-German war. Beust replied: 'I do not see Europe any more.' Such is likely to be the feeling of a reader who emerges from the twelve hundred pages of Fisher's *History of Europe*. He will have run over a vast catalogue of facts, followed the records of innumerable wars, even observed the rise and decline of religions. But Europe will have escaped him. The countries of Europe succeed each other like the painted horses in a roundabout at a fair. Italy, France, Germany, England, Spain, Turkey, Germany, England, Holland, France – these are the topics of succeeding chapters. But where is the engine which makes the horses go round? Where even the music that accompanies their circular procession? An occasional tune reaches the ear of the observer; but the mechanics are never explained to him. Yet when the book was published fifteen years ago, it received high praise. One distinguished professor, still alive, described it as 'history, intensive and memorable'; another found in it 'the great tradition of English historiography, the tradition of Gibbon, the tradition of Lord Macaulay.' Baldwin announced more directly: 'a great book.' Now it is difficult to see in it more than a useful textbook for schoolboys, the more useful on periods off their beat where they need only a smattering of the facts.

Fisher wrote with admirable clarity and occasionally with wit. Unlike most historians, he knew something of the world. He spent part of his life in the industrial north of England, and he rose higher in politics than any English historian except Bryce and Macaulay.

[1]*New Statesman*, 1952.

Yet he remained incurably donnish. Unless men painted pictures or wrote books, he had little interest in their activities. The only Europeans he recognised were 'the small band of humanists who in every country endeavour to sweeten the bitter waters of political life', and by humanists he meant classical scholars of flippant disposition. The only public figures he admired were what he called 'long-headed men' and they make a curious selection – Leopold II of Austria, Ferdinand of Bulgaria and General Weygand are among those who earn the description. He laid down in one passage : 'peace is always wiser than war', and therefore, not surprisingly, found most of European history very foolish. He wrote in his preface : 'men wiser and more learned than I have discerned in history a plot, a rhythm, a predetermined pattern. These harmonies are concealed from me. I can see only one emergency following upon another as wave follows wave.' This was well said. The true historian has little patience with the best-selling system-makers. But have Europeans always been buffeted by the waves? have they not sometimes known how to ride the storms or even to turn their violence to good use?

Other universal historians have despised the past that they were recording. Gibbon said : 'I have depicted the triumph of barbarism and religion' – two factors that were for him synonymous. But Gibbon was confident that men had reached a securer, more enlightened age. In Fisher humanism had gone sour. The best of the story was for him at the beginning. There is no escaping the glow with which he writes of the Greeks. 'Man was essentially proud and free, on happy terms with himself, with the world, and with Olympus.' Again, 'at no time were the Greeks enslaved to a book or to a church.' From the story of Socrates he drew the comforting conclusion : 'it is idle to suppose that the influence of a great liberating mind can be stayed by persecution.' These judgements were the commonplaces of English academic education in the early twentieth century. They reach absurdity when we read of Alexander the Great : 'The great landowning nobles of Persia won from him the sympathy and respect which the spectacle of a gentleman and a sportsman never fails to evoke in the hearty nature of the open-air man.' Like the Greeks, Fisher made his peace with the Romans. They provided 'amusements on a lavish scale . . . a pleasant intercommunion, unvexed by the modern fanaticisms of creed and race . . . a wide and indulgent tolerance.' Nothing here of the endless crucifixions which lined the Roman roads. The humanist need not

46

notice these, just as he could ignore the mysteries and superstitions which were the reality of Greek life.

A classical training is perhaps not the best background for the historian of Europe or even for the modern politician. Those who think that the peoples of Europe have been wasting their time had best leave the record alone and advise their contemporaries to start again. This was the view of Rousseau and of the French revolutionaries, and a very good view too. But while Fisher disliked the past, he would not believe in the future. He wanted a static society, Chinese if not Roman. He even evoked the mythical Chinaman to pass judgement on the Reformation :

A Chinaman might well have asked himself whether . . . an attitude of mind towards the ultimate mysteries less aspiring, less heroic and less confident than that which prevailed among western Christians was not in effect more conducive to human comfort.

Yet he was equally contemptuous of the Rights of Man, which he called 'this sleek and optimistic theory.' And when there appeared a man of the east, who really rejected western values, he could only sneer at him. Gandhi, he observes, was 'not averse from availing himself of the convenience of a Ford car.' How clever that must have sounded when first said in the subdued light of New College common-room! Yet his own humanism was a little tawdry. He says rightly that at the end of the nineteenth century there was a common European culture, and he summarises its components : 'the music of Brahms, the plays of Ibsen, the novels of Tolstoi and Anatole France, the light operas of Gilbert and Sullivan, the popular songs of the English music-hall.' This cultivated man found our most characteristic contribution to European civilisation in Marie Lloyd – an excellent contribution in its way.

Two things were missing in Fisher's Europe. Both now stare us in the face – the Slavs and the class-struggle. Bismarck once said : 'Whoever speaks of Europe is mistaken; it is a geographic expression.' But at least he knew that its geography did not stop at the Elbe or even the Oder. Fisher's first reference to the Slavs is revealing. He regrets that they were not exterminated in the Balkans by Teutonic invaders : 'With a population largely Teutonic the eastern question would have assumed another and perhaps easier form.' He turned a blank eye to the great record of the Byzantine empire and maintained his ignorance of eastern Europe into modern times. Thus he implies that in 1848 Bohemia (then a part of the German Confedera-

47

tion) had no Czech inhabitants, and he supposed that the Bulgarians were not Slavs ('no hate comparable to the animosity of Bulgar and Slav' – a judgement, incidentally, quite untrue). Like most English liberals, he welcomed the triumph of nationalism when it was confined to Germany and Italy; it needed all the arts of 'a Welsh Baptist' (Lloyd George) to persuade him to tolerate it elsewhere. In his heart, he would have preferred the Triple Alliance and the Franco-Russian alliance to work against each other without British intervention : 'It is possible that if the balance of power had so been left the peace of Europe might have been preserved.' But he was by no means enthusiastic when the abortive Franco-Soviet pact attempted to revive this balance in 1935. At the end he pointed to the solution which many 'humanists' were to embrace fifteen years later : Anglo-Saxon union was to save Europe from itself, or, failing that, at least to save humanism.

Most of all, science and the machine are lacking in this history of Europe. The reader learns only casually that the population of Europe has increased at an unparalleled rate in modern times; neither the causes nor the results of this are explored. Yet other civilisations have composed poetry and devised philosophies; none other has set out to master nature. This, and none other, is the meaning of modern European history, which has reshaped the world. So far as Europe is concerned, the forms of social order make the decisive theme. Fisher could handle the French Revolution : it was concerned only with the political standing of the middle class. His understanding faltered when the masses broke into politics. There is nothing weaker in his book than the account of the revolutions of 1848 when politics escaped from middle-class control and middle-class virtues. Of course he recognised a social problem, but this had to be handled in the English way by tactful concession and by 'enjoyments placed within the reach of poor working men and women by contributions from the public purse.' He looked admiringly at the Third Republic in France, where Socialism had been 'robbed of its power to hurt by manhood suffrage.' Nothing could better reveal the outlook of English social reformers, from Disraeli to the Fabians : the masses must be given some crumbs from the table, and as time goes on more crumbs will be swept off – but principally because the feast on the table will be richer.

Yet Fisher had unconsciously exposed the weakness of this outlook on an earlier page. Writing of the monks, he says : 'like the miners of modern times, they lived a life apart and were thus peculiarly

48

prone to the acceptance of contracted doctrines in an enthusiastic form.' The monks rejected the world of their time; the miners did not belong to the civilisation of theirs. They, and the industrial workers generally, were not bought off by the humanistic prospect opened by Fisher's Education Act. Even successful social reform in England has only transferred the class struggle to the international field. No reader of Fisher's book will discover that Europe in modern times has lived on the plunder of the rest of the world; at most he will notice the glorious story of the abolition of slavery. He is left at the end with the impression only of human folly and violence, European civilisation always preserved by a handful of cultivated scholars. The last words of the epilogue sound a prophetic alarm :

> Communism as a subversive and revolutionary creed, aiming at the liquidation of the middle class by violence . . . is an evil against which every state, seeking the happinesss and harmony of its citizens, will endeavour to protect itself.

Humanists of the world unite! When Communism is defeated all will be well – pictures on the wall, philosophy on the bookshelves, port and candles in the common-room. 'As the fear of revolution recedes, the risks of war will be proportionately abated.'

7.   The Thin White Line[1]

A review of *Victorian England: Portrait of an Age* by G M
Young. (Oxford University Press, paperback edition).

It would be unfair to describe the late G M Young as the man of
one book. He wrote other books of considerable distinction. But
Portrait of an Age was his most accomplished work and the one
by which he is likely to be remembered. On its first appearance it
was described as 'the greatest single study of the age in any language'
and this judgement is very nearly true. *Portrait of an Age* can be
praised on another count. It is one of the very few successful attempts
at unified history, fusing events and ideas, laws and opinions, into
a coherent pattern.

Writers of history must envy its masterly control of the subject,
seemingly so effortless, in reality based on an almost monstrous absorption in the records of the time. After twenty-four years, it still
seems a wonderful achievement and if its limitations also now stand
out more clearly, this is not to depreciate the pleasure and profit
which it will bring to new readers in its paperback form.

There is, for one thing, a defect in its form. Originally it was not
a book, but the concluding essay in a symposium on Early Victorian
England. It was then limited to the years 1831 to 1865. This was
the period which Young knew and understood best. His essay is
beyond criticism, or very nearly. He managed somehow to bring in
everything which seemed important to the men of the age (or rather,
generation), and many things which seem important to us as well.

Then he decided to turn his essay into a book by carrying his survey on to the death of Victoria in 1901. This, as he confessed in a
preface written much later (in 1952), was a mistake: he ought to

[1]*Observer*, 1960.

have treated Late Victorian and Edwardian England as a piece and gone on to 1914. It was a mistake in another way. Young was less in sympathy with the Late Victorian age and knew less about it. What had been love of the past turned into resentful nostalgia.

Going back from this melancholy conclusion, we can grasp more clearly how narrow Young's vision was, though intense within its limitations. He asks at the beginning, 'What is history about?' He answers (and it is a good definition of one good sort of history) : 'The real, central theme of history is not what happened, but what people felt about it when it was happening.' He quotes Maitland's phrase : 'men's common thought of common things' and adds his own : 'the conversation of the people who counted.'

The shift of emphasis is significant. Maitland – 'that royal intellect,' as Young rightly calls him – sought after 'that objective mind which controls the thinking and doing of an age or race'; by 'common thought,' he meant the thought of common men. Young's interest was restricted to 'the people who counted' and by this he meant those who counted for him rather than those who shaped their age.

The men who counted in the Victorian age were surely the creators – the great engineers and industrialists, the scientists and the reformers. This was an age of material achievement; its dominant symbol was steam-power. Young closed the windows of his mind to this or, at best, noticed the smoke only to deplore it. The reader will learn from Young's book that Victorian times were dirty; he will hardly discover that these grimy years began the emancipation of the masses from their age-old poverty and misery.

Young writes as though Oxford were more important than Manchester – as, of course, it was (and still is) to some people. He mentions Newman often; Matthew Arnold a good deal; Cobden hardly at all. When he turns to economics, he dwells on agriculture and the land; he keeps clear of coal mines and almost clear of cotton mills. The people who counted seem to have been mainly country clergymen, and their conversation turns out to be very like conversation after dinner at All Souls.

Of course this is a good deal more than the book of a querulous Don, lamenting everything that has happened since the first Royal Commission on Oxford and Cambridge. Young was, in his way, a man of the world, though it was the world of Government offices. What he admired in Victorian times was 'the disinterested intelligence.' His heroes were the thin white line of administrative reformers who tempered the horrors of industrial growth.

Young's book was a portent. It was one among a number of distinguished historical works coming out roughly at the same time which exalted the Civil Servant above the political leader, and the administrator above the creator. Namier did this, or something like it, for the eighteenth century. Ensor put almost as much weight on legislation and institutions in his volume on the years between 1870 and 1914 in the Oxford History of England.

The historians of medieval England had taken the same path already. 'To be or not to be' disappeared. 'To administer or to be administered' became the choice. This is why university students nowadays tumble over themselves to become servants of the impersonal State or of the equally impersonal private monopolies. They believe that, unless they are filling up forms about others, others will be filling up forms about them.

Maybe this is now the universal destiny. Maybe the Victorian age started it. Yet there was in that age an individual roughness and vulgarity which is almost missing from Young's slightly spinsterish account. Look back to a book written some twenty years before Young's, on much the same theme: G K Chesterton's 'Victorian Age in Literature'. Chesterton's book is based on less knowledge than Young's. But it has something which Young missed: the confident beat of tumultuous life. Chesterton's Victorians shout and stamp; they laugh, cry, embrace, and shake their fists. Young's Victorians converse in a well-bred undertone.

The contrast can be shown by a single example, one which illustrates what was wrong with Young's portrait of the Victorian age. Chesterton put Dickens in the centre of the picture. Young writes: 'The political satire of Dickens is tedious and ignorant.' Young often judged supremely well, but he judged by the standards of Mr Tite Barnacle and the Circumlocution Office.

8.   Moving with the Times[1]

A review of *What is History?* by E H Carr (Macmillan).

Those who can, do; those who can't, pontificate. A chef is more
interested in taste than in vitamins; a vintner more interested in
aroma than in alcoholic content. Like Goering with culture, I reach
for my revolver when offered philosophies of history. But there are
exceptions. Occasionally a practising historian turns aside from his
work in order to explain to himself and others what he is up to. Then
we listen with respect, and no one is entitled to greater respect than
E H Carr.

He is without rival among contemporary historians. His History
of Soviet Russia is a masterpiece of scholarship and narration. No
man knows better the problems which a historian encounters; no
man has a higher sense both of the historian's responsibilities and
of his limitations. He can range from meticulous detail to wide
generalisation. He sees both the furniture of his own study and
the stir of the great world. As well, he has a beautiful gift for exposition which makes his lectures a delight to read. Who can resist a
lecture which begins with the words: 'If milk is set to boil in a
saucepan, it boils over. I do not know, and have never wanted to
know, why this happens'?

There are many fine things in this set of lectures. The layman tends
to imagine that the historian first accumulates facts and then gener-
alises from them. Carr points out that the general picture comes
first and that the facts acquire significance only in relation to this
general picture. New 'facts' emerge whenever we look at history
in a different way. As Carr says, 'the relation between the historian
and his facts is one of equality, of give-and-take.' The historian

[1]*Observer*, 1962.

sometimes shifts his standpoint because he finds new facts; he is more likely to shift it because of new experiences.

Increased knowledge of the present increases our understanding of the past quite as much as the other way round. Every historian belongs to his age, and each age gets the historians it deserves. Thus Mommsen, disillusioned by the failure of the revolutions of 1848, could dissect the last sad years of the Roman republic. At this point Carr seems to push his argument too far. Mommsen, he says, stopped at the fall of the republic because 'the problem of what happened once the strong man had taken over was not yet actual.' No Hitler; hence no history of the Roman empire. I doubt whether things were quite so simple.

Even the general principle that each age gets the historians it deserves does not work out in practice or works so haphazardly as to be no principle at all. The present day in England, when the educated classes have lost faith in the future and in themselves, no doubt deserves conservative historians, as Carr suggests: historians like the great Sir Lewis Namier and his lesser followers, who insist that history has no meaning and that it ought now to stop. How then does our disillusioned age come to deserve Carr or even me? Are we merely an antiquated hangover from the Victorians?

Carr would be cross at any such suggestion. He places himself in the vanguard of Progress and runs over with an optimism which might have daunted even Macaulay. Though he accuses others of confusion, he is himself not without sleight-of-hand. History, he insists, is movement. This is well said. But then he goes on to assert that the movement is all in one direction: upwards. Individuals, classes, nations may suffer; for the mass of mankind the march of events is set fair. Since things are getting better all the time, it follows that whatever produces these things should be welcomed by the historian.

Hence, for example, Stalin's extermination of the kulaks was justified because it helped to produce what has happened, that is, the present strength of the Soviet Union. (By analogy, though Carr does not say so, Hitler's extermination of the Jews was not justified because Germany now is not a world Power.) Carr's message is even more cheerful. Since things have got better in the past, it follows that they are bound to get better in the future. This, if I understand him, is what he means by learning from history. The duty of the historian is to keep up with the times – so much so that Carr makes Robinson Crusoe a citizen of New York.

I find all this bewildering. I sympathise with so much that Carr says – particularly with his criticism of those historians who spend their time extolling the plundering monarchs and nobles of the past. But I cannot understand how knowledge of the past provides us with morality, let alone with knowledge of the future. How can the fact that something happened prove it right or, for that matter, wrong? Again, why should knowledge of where I came from tell me where I am going to? Carr is not alone in holding that knowledge of the past enables us to behave more sensibly in the present and to foresee the future.

To me this is all sales talk: History makes the future brighter. It does not work when tested against the facts: historians are not wiser politicians or more sensible in their private lives than other men – often indeed the reverse. Was Sir Charles Oman, for instance, a particularly enlightened MP? Yet he was quite a good historian. At the present time, it is possible to guess with Carr that, by the end of the century, countless millions will be living in unparalleled happiness all over the world. It is also possible to guess, as I am inclined to do, that by the end of the century a few thousand maimed human beings will be living, near to starvation, in caves.

All history tells us is that something will happen, though probably what we do not expect. My view of history is more modest than Carr's. The task of the historian is to explain the past; neither to justify nor to condemn it. Study of history enables us to understand the past; no more and no less. Perhaps even this is too high a claim. In most European languages 'history' and 'story' are the same word. So history deserves Carr's condemnation as 'literature' after all: 'a collection of stories and legends about the past without meaning or significance.'

II POLITICS and POLITICIANS

9. The Thing[1]

A contribution to a symposium, Is there a Power Elite? I wish
I had thought of the opening by Philip Toynbee, the following
contributor; 'Who governs Britain? The governing *class*, surely'.

Lord Attlee, on some wartime journey, was reading a life of Sir
Robert Walpole. He looked across at his companion, a high civil
servant, and reflected: 'I wonder who really ran the country in those
days?' An apocryphal story no doubt like most stories about Lord
Attlee, but a reasonable speculation. In every society Lenin's rule
applies: 'Who whom?' Some men give orders; the rest obey them.
In a truly democratic society the rulers would be chosen by lot for
short stretches. Failing that we should at least postulate that every
citizen have an equal chance of reaching the top if he wants to
get there. This does not apply in any known community, not even
in Switzerland, the country that comes nearest to democarcy. Every-
where the potential ruler has to pass some test other than ambition
and ability. It may be birth, money, class, colour, religion, even (as
in old China) capacity to pass examinations. But some test there
will be. The minority that emerges will constitute the power élite
from whom the actual rulers are chosen. What we call democracy
is merely a system by which the members of this power élite receive
an occasional popular endorsement.

The requirements for entering the British power élite are fairly
well known. You must be white in colour; male; wear collar and
tie and a dark suit; and able to spend most of your life indoors sitting
down. You must also be able to dictate reasonably grammatical
English. Oratory – once highly regarded – is no longer required.
Anyone capable of reading from typescript can go to the highest
place. These are the bare essentials. The right parents are a

[1]*The Twentieth Century*, 1957.

considerable asset. It is still best to come from 'the nobility and gentry', though it is probably a mistake to be the eldest son of a peer. Parents from the professional class are good, particularly if they pay surtax. Rich business men, oddly, not at all good. If you are so foolish as to be born into the industrial working class, then you must get out of it by winning a scholarship to a grammar school or, failing this, by becoming either a trade union official or a WEA tutor. If you are born of an agricultural labourer, you should give up at the start. The right education helps. It is of little moment what you learn, though Latin is still probably the most useful subject and any form of science a handicap; the important thing is where you learn. Eton remains by far the best bet; Winchester runs it close in the Labour Party. Otherwise prefer a first-rate grammar school to a minor public school and run away to sea rather than go to a secondary modern. Oxford and Cambridge are so obvious a requirement as hardly to need mention. Any other university can be valued only for the instruction it provides. As to accomplishments, it is no longer necessary to ride a horse, shoot, fish, or even play bridge. In fact, the less accomplished you are outside your work the better. And even at work it is wiser to seem devoted rather than clever. Otherwise you are in danger of becoming a 'character', and this is hard to live down.

The picture drawn here differs little from that of the power élite in Washington or Moscow. Religion, however, provides a distinguishing mark. I use the word to mean morality and rules of conduct, not acceptance or denial of any theological dogma. You may choose anything from Roman Catholicism in its English version to 'humanism' – that is, unassertive atheism. But it must be broadly within the tradition of liberal Christianity. Fundamentalism, aggressive atheism and of course adherence to any non-Christian religion other than Judaism, exclude. In other words, the members of the British power élite observe the standards created by the nineteenth-century public schools. Once upon a time you could have found the mainspring of British public life by assembling the leading headmasters, some bishops (themselves former headmasters) and the Master of Balliol. Now the position is more complicated. By no means all our rulers have been to public schools, and even public schoolboys take much of their instruction from without the school walls. Our guardians of tradition are self-appointed; our high priests for the most part unfrocked. Nevertheless they exist and they give English life its unique flavour.

It has lately become the fashion to call them 'the Establishment'. Henry Fairlie is said to have started this, though I have also seen it attributed to myself. I regret the idea, whoever had it. The very word, so plummy, so ponderous, so respectable, tempts us to acknowledge the moral superiority of 'the Establishment'. It conjures up benign, upholstered figures, calm, steady, reliable. They would never pass a dud cheque or cheat at cards. Not intellectually dazzling perhaps, but patient, understanding, and tolerant – above all tolerant. Anyone who challenges them is disarmed by the quizzical, superior smile and the enquiry: 'Well, my little man, what is it now?' It was a great blunder to take the Establishment at its own valuation. We ought to have revived Cobbett's name: THE THING. That suggests much better the complacency, the incompetence and the selfishness which lie behind the façade. THE THING exists for the sake of its members, not for ours. They look comfortable because they are comfortable. They are upholstered because they are well fed. Their air of moral superiority is really an assumption that someone else will always cook their dinner – and a good dinner at that.

Yet in one way the word 'Establishment' has its uses. It emphasises the historical foundation of THE THING, a foundation still essential despite being obscured by later buildings. The basis of the Establishment is quite simply the Church of England as by law established. I doubt whether anyone with an Anglican background can become a true Radical. George Lansbury came nearest to it. Yet there was always a subtle dividing line between him and the rebels round him. Gladstone tried hard, but he could never rid himself of the belief that a duke or a bishop had more political sense than Cobden or John Stuart Mill. The rule still applies in the Labour Party. Its leaders with an Anglican education seek radical ideas, but they lack radical instincts. Time and again they end up on the Right without ever meaning to do so. Religious Dissent is the only safe background for a radical, but militant Dissent has long been on the decline until now the remnants of the Free Churches regard themselves as a junior branch of the Establishment. THE THING is more secure than it was fifty years ago. It runs into difficulties from its own mistakes, not from any aggressive and conscious challenge.

On paper things have changed since the classical constitution of the eighteenth century. In reality they are much the same. THE THING still assumes that it should receive all the plums and it gets them. For instance, every college at Oxford and Cambridge still has an Anglican chapel maintained from college endowments, though they claim to be members of a national university. Bishops still pontificate on every conceivable subject from nuclear fission to the private lives of unbelievers. The Test Act, though repealed, is still wondrously effective. We note with surprise when a judge is a Roman Catholic or a Cabinet Minister has been divorced. Why should it not be surprising the other way round?

THE THING has always boasted that it is not exclusive. This is true. Accept its standards, conform to its pattern, and you reap a rich reward. Incompetent in everything else, THE THING has a wonderful aptitude for seeing that there are enough plums to go round. Just as the British Empire was wasting away, the nationalised industries came along to restore the balance. There has been no such manna of jobbery since the palmy days of Sir Robert Walpole. You need not even conform to the rules so long as you pay lip-service to them. A nineteenth-century Duke of Devonshire, who lived openly with a woman not his wife, enjoyed the unique distinction of having been offered the Premiership by each political party in turn. And Stanley Baldwin did not jib at the idea that a King of England should keep a mistress.

But try to disregard THE THING. Tolerance and good behaviour vanish at once. Lloyd George is the supreme illustration. He was beyond question the greatest political genius of his time, incomparable alike in peace and in war. He had every quality except conformity. THE THING turned to him in the desperate circumstances of 1916. Once the crisis was past, it hunted him from power. Between the wars all the energies of THE THING were devoted to keeping Lloyd George out. No wonder there was nothing left over to deal with such problems as unemployment or Hitler.

Is THE THING any use? None at all except for its members. Most people lead industrious decent lives without the moral guidance of the Archbishop of Canterbury. Those who wish to read books or listen to music do so without seeking the blessing of Sir Ian Jacob. It would be a great improvement in every way if we got rid of THE THING. The country would be more alert, more receptive to new ideas, more capable of holding its own in the world. THE THING is on the surface a system of holding its own in the world. THE THING is on the surface a system of public morals. Underneath it is a system of public plunder. Its true purpose was revealed by a poster which the Chamberlain Government rashly displayed early in the war :

Your COURAGE, *Your* CHEERFULNESS, *Your* RESOLUTION WILL BRING US VICTORY

There was once, I suppose, some sense in THE THING. In former times the mass of people had to live in hardship and want. There was luxury enough only for a few; and THE THING was a reasonable device for ladling the luxury around. Now life is improving for everybody. Why should the members of THE THING get more of the proceeds than others? Already in the United States a university professor is paid less than a skilled worker in an automobile works. Economics will succeed where Dissent failed. The time is coming when the average reader of *The Daily Mirror* will get more than the average reader of *The Times*. Who will care then if the readers of *The Times* go on imagining that they are the Top People?

10.   Roasting a Parson[1]

A review of *The Trial of Dr Sacheverell* by Geoffrey Holmes. (Eyre Methuen). My favourite trial perhaps made even more attractive by the warning implied in the last sentence.

There is nothing more dramatic than a good trial. After reading Geoffrey Holmes's magnificent book I am convinced that the trial of Henry Sacheverell was the best in English history. It was an extraordinary affair: an Anglican parson solemnly impeached in Westminster Hall simply because of a sermon he had preached at St Paul's Cathedral. It is as though Malcolm Muggeridge were impeached for speaking slightingly of *The Guardian* on television. One hundred thousand copies of the sermon were sold. Mob violence on Sacheverell's behalf was unsurpassed until the Gordon Riots 70 years later. The result of the impeachment carried the Tories to victory in the General Election of 1710, and that victory in its turn almost overthrew the British Constitution. Thanks to Sacheverell, the restoration of the Old Pretender was, for a time, touch and go.

Henry Sacheverell was a dissolute Fellow of an Oxford college who specialised in violent Tory sermons. As early as 1702 he called on the Tories to 'hang out the bloody flag and banner of defiance.' Thereafter Defoe called him 'the bloody flag officer.' In 1709 his great chance came. The Lord Mayor, who happened to be a Tory, invited him to preach at St Paul's on 5 November. This was an occasion sacred to Whiggism: the day when William of Orange, the Deliverer, had landed at Torbay. Sacheverell took the opportunity to denigrate the Glorious Revolution and all its works. He argued subtly that there had been no Revolution; non-resistance was still a sacred duty; the Dissenters were conspiring against the Church of England. He had the right manner for the task. One

[1]*Observer*, 1975.

64

observer was astonished 'at the fiery red that overspread his face . . . and the goggling wildness of his eyes.' Another commented : 'I fancy he has bankrupt all the oyster-women, porters, watermen, coach-men and carmen in Town to make up his collection.'

The Whig majority in the House of Commons was in an uproar. To challenge the Glorious Revolution was sedition. It resolved 'to roast a parson.' A mere rebuke at the bar of the House would not be enough. Sacheverell must be impeached and sternly punished. Only thus could the Protestant Succession be secured. The impeach-ment was a great event: no mere impeachment at the bar of the House of Lords, but a great dramatic performance in Westminster Hall. Sir Christopher Wren was employed to set the stage and transformed Westminster Hall into an amphitheatre at the cost of £3,000. High society flocked to the trial. Queen Anne attended almost every day and listened from a private box.

There has never been a greater display of legal and political talent. Among the managers for the House of Commons were two future Lord Chancellors, five future judges, Robert Walpole, and General Stanhope. Sacheverell also had a future Lord Chancellor among his advocates. Sacheverell's stately procession to Westminster so aroused the London mob that on the evening of 1 March they burnt down six Dissenting chapels before the troops dispersed them.

The arguments were of a brilliance that defies summary. Sacheverell was no fool. He had not actually repudiated the Glorious Revolution. He had merely argued that it was open to a Tory inter-pretation. His Whig prosecutors had to show that the logic of his statements led inevitably to sedition. His Tory defenders answered that he had not uttered a single openly seditious sentence.

The Whigs had the better of the argument. No doubt their ingenuities were beyond most members of the House of Lords who had to judge. The Whigs started with a safe majority among the Lords. Gradually the softer Whigs and the Court Tories who sup-ported the Whig Government sensed that the climate was changing. The majority crumbled. In the end, though Sacheverell was found guilty, he was merely forbidden to preach for three years – no fine, no imprisonment, no standing in the pillory. A Whig MP commen-ted: 'Tis the Lords' doings, but not marvellous in our eyes.'

For Sacheverell there followed glory and a triumphal tour – 10 civic receptions, 50 public dinners, 22 private dinners, and accom-modation at many great Tory houses. In November there was the most fiercely contested except one of all eighteenth-century elections.

332 English Tory members were returned against 181 Whigs. The Tory victory turned to dust and ashes. The Dissenters were not effectively harried. In 1714 George of Hanover, not the Old Pretender, succeeded Queen Anne. The Whig Constitution was secure. But the Whigs had learnt their lesson. Never again did they attempt to roast a parson. Geoffrey Holmes concludes: 'That they also stultified church reform, and encouraged spiritual inertia, did not greatly disturb them.'

Things went well with Henry Sacheverell, if not for the Tories. He acquired the rich living of St Andrew's, Holborn, inherited an estate from a rich cousin, and married the cousin's rich widow. He lived elegantly in South Grove, Highgate. There in 1723 he slipped on the doorstep and broke two ribs. A year later he died of 'a complication of disorders.' He was buried in a vault under the communion table at St Andrew's. Twenty years later the vault was opened, and it was found that he had been buried next to a notorious prostitute. A Whig wit wrote: —

A fit companion for a high-churchman priest;
He non-resistance taught, and she professed.

I am sorry to add that Henry Sacheverell was a Fellow of Magdalen College, Oxford, indeed the most famous Fellow that college can boast of and the only one who appears in the history books. His career is a dreadful warning to any Fellow of Magdalen who neglects academic pursuits for the bright lights of publicity.

11. Talleyrand's Cut[1]

A review of *Talleyrand: The Art of Survival* by Jean Orieux, translated by Patricia Wolf. (Knopf, New York).

Talleyrand once asked a lady friend: 'What do you think posterity's opinion of me will be?' She replied: 'That you set out to stir up controversy about yourself.' Staring at her in amazement, he said: 'You are right, you are absolutely right. I want people to go on for centuries debating what I was like, what I believed, what I stood for.' This only shows that a man will go to any lengths in order to impress the woman he happens to be pursuing. For there is no mystery about Talleyrand except that created by writers who wish to turn an honest penny. He liked women; he liked money; he liked an easy comfortable life. To his misfortune he was caught in the storm of the French Revolution. He waited for it to blow over and sometimes tried to help on the process. He said many things that were esteemed witty at the time. His career was unusual even in a revolutionary epoch. But a great man? A statesman? It is hard to believe it.

M Orieux, however, has no doubts. His book is in the worst style of French writing – rhapsodical, disorderly, overblown, more a cheap romantic novel than a work of history. Perhaps it is tolerable in French; it is unreadable in English. M Orieux is given to addressing his characters. Here is an early example. Talleyrand's foot was injured at birth. His mother thought this disqualified him from becoming head of the family and turned him into a priest, remarking, 'My son is well adjusted to his new profession.' On which M Orieux breaks out:

[1]*New York Review of Books,* 1974. Copyright © 1974 Nyorev, Inc. Reprinted with permission.

What profession? Buttoning a cassock over one's ordinary dress and playing choirboy is not a profession, Madam, it is a travesty. . . . You did an astonishing thing, Madam: without knowing it, you turned your rejected son into the most illustrious member of your race. . . . Measured against a mother's initial betrayal, all subsequent betrayals were insignificant.

At any rate Talleyrand became a bishop, duly collecting the rewards in money and women which this brought. In 1789 he went with the Revolution, perhaps from conviction. When his acts provoked the disapproval of the Pope, he wrote to a friend: 'You know about my excommunication. Come cheer me up and dine with me. As no one will offer me fire or water, we will have to make do tonight with cold meat and iced wine.' Comment by M Orieux: 'O flippant statement if there ever was one.' M Orieux also remarks:

> His critics never mention that one major failing of his, far more serious than his love of gambling, women and money: a flabby will that brought his worst instincts into play. Napoleon forgave all his faults except his alarming pliability – and he knew the man he was dealing with.

If Talleyrand had not been pliable, he would have been guillotined during the French Revolution and no one would have heard of him. As it was, he celebrated an open-air mass on the anniversary of the taking of the Bastille and whispered, as he clambered on to the platform: 'Don't make me laugh.' He left France before the Terror, first for England and then for the United States, where he ran some successful land speculation. His favourite American word, he said, was 'sweetener,' and when later he squeezed £50,000 out of American negotiators, remarked that since the Americans had invented such an appropriate word they must know how to use it.

Talleyrand returned to France under the Directory when the worst days of the Revolution were over. He made love to Mme de Staël, and she thrust him on the Directors. When asked who she was, he replied: 'An intriguer, to such a degree that I am here in the foreign ministry because of her.' And in answer to a further question whether she was a good friend: 'Friend? She would toss her friends in the river in order to fish them out.' Being without a carriage, he drove to meet the Directors in Mme de Staël's and, as he did so, muttered under his breath that he would make '*une fortune immense, une immense fortune.*'

So he did. Probably no foreign minister has ever made so much money while in office or continued his activities over so long a time. He was paid by everybody – by Napoleon, by German princes, by Tsar Alexander I, by the British government. His foreign policy, so far as he had one, was often directed to the best interests of France, but he saw no reason why he should not be paid for promoting them. With this fortune he acquired a great landed estate and the vast château of Valençay. He was also a compulsive gambler, running through millions of francs.

Napoleon Bonaparte was the decisive figure in Talleyrand's life. Talleyrand helped Bonaparte up the ladder, served him as emperor, and then engineered his overthrow. Even after this he wrote: 'I loved Napoleon. I became personally attached to him despite his faults; at the start of his career I felt drawn to him by the irresistible magnetism exerted by all great geniuses.' It was Talleyrand who encouraged Bonaparte's expedition to Egypt. M Orieux accepts Talleyrand's explanation that the expedition was intended to 'turn official thoughts and acts away from revolutionary Europe' – an unlikely proposition. The Egyptian expedition was a quick alternative to the invasion of England which had proved impossible.

A transaction just before Bonaparte left was characteristic of both men. Bonaparte was short of money, and Talleyrand lent him 100,000 francs. On his return Bonaparte repaid the money and asked: 'Why did you lend it to me? I have often wondered about it and could never understand your motive.' Talleyrand replied: 'I had no motive; you were young and made such a vital, intense impression on me that I wanted to help you without any ulterior purpose.' To which Bonaparte remarked: 'In that case you acted deceitfully.'

Talleyrand's great days came when he was Napoleon's foreign minister – great at any rate from the point of view of making money. He began well. When Napoleon asked him how he had made so much money, he replied: 'Oh, that's simple. I bought bonds on the 17th Brumaire and sold them three days later.' 17th Brumaire was the day before Bonaparte seized power. Thereafter Napoleon used to say: 'His great ancestry makes up for everything.' There was little skill or originality in Talleyrand's policy: he did what he was told and pocketed his percentage. Napoleon summed up his qualifications: 'Sophistication, first-hand knowledge of the courts of Europe, a shrewd tongue that says just enough and no more, an inscrutable countenance that never changes, and finally a great name.' In later years Talleyrand made out that he had always opposed Napoleon's pursuit of conquest. He did so only when it began to go wrong.

Even then his opposition was confined to private mutterings. The idea that he contributed to Napoleon's overthrow is pure myth, partly manufactured by himself and partly by Metternich, who was another character of the same kind. In 1809 Metternich reported from Paris that Talleyrand and Fouché were preparing to resist Napoleon. They 'are firmly resolved to seize the opportunity if the opportunity arises, lacking courage to provoke it.' The opportunity never arose. Talleyrand and Fouché contributed to Napoleon's overthrow only in the sense that the so-called German Resistance contributed to Hitler's. Napoleon ruined himself by his limitless ambitions; his overthrow stemmed from the Russian army. When all was over Talleyrand stepped on to the scene and headed the French Provisional Government. He said with some excusable exaggeration: 'The only conspiring I have ever done was when I had the majority of France as an accomplice and was seeking hand in hand with her the salvation of my country.'

Talleyrand did not long remain in power. The restored King Louis XVIII no doubt disliked him. M Orieux remarks that he was not Cardinal Richelieu or even Mazarin. He lacked strength of character and needed a master. Also he was lazy: alert in a crisis and off on pleasure the next day. Talleyrand made some stir at the Congress of Vienna, though circumstances made this easy, when all the victorious powers except Prussia wanted to keep France active in the balance of power. After this he departed to a profitable retirement until the French Revolution of 1830 when he became French ambassador in London and secured the independence of Belgium. His last negotiation was a prolonged bargaining whereby he made his peace with the Church a few hours before he died. When he received extreme unction he held out his clenched fists instead of his palms and said: 'Do not forget that I am a bishop.' He had received episcopal unction on January 16, 1789. Much had happened since then including the secularisation of church lands on

Talleyrand's initiative and his own marriage. However the Church was ready to welcome the belatedly repentant sinner.

Considerable ingenuity is needed to deduce any significant principles of foreign policy from Talleyrand's career. He was an adroit and unscrupulous negotiator. He never conducted a negotiation without financial profit for himself. He distrusted the arrogance of power and did not regret the loss of Napoleon's conquests. If pressed to define what he believed in he would have answered with his favourite refrain: '*Une fortune immense, une immense fortune.*'

Talleyrand had unparalleled success with women despite his lameness and clumsy figure. He shared Madame de Flahaut with Gouverneur Morris, the American minister in Paris, and of course with her husband. Their son, the comte de Flahaut, following his father's fashion, had a son by Queen Hortense, Napoleon's stepdaughter, and their offspring, the duc de Morny, was able to boast: 'I am the great-grandson of a king, grandson of a bishop, son of a queen, and half-brother of an emperor.' Morny's daughter married a marquis of Lansdowne, and their son became the British foreign secretary who created the *Entente Cordiale* – altogether a distinguished record for Talleyrand's descendants. When Talleyrand became foreign minister he ousted his predecessor from the marriage bed as well as from office. The outcome of this was Eugène Delacroix, the great Romantic painter, whose career Talleyrand followed with paternal solicitude.

Talleyrand's last mistress was his niece by marriage, Dorothy, whose mother the duchess of Courland was also his mistress whenever she could afford the time to come to France. Yet even his lovemaking was pursued with indifference. He was a voluptuary, not a seducer, and Madame de Flahaut complained that, though *suaviter in modo*, he lacked *fortiter in re*. Talleyrand would probably have accepted this as a flattering verdict. He never did anything with energy or conviction except of course when he laid his hands on money. If indifference, lack of principle, and self-interest are the essential qualities for diplomacy, Talleyrand was perhaps a model diplomat after all.

12.   The Steam Intellect Man[1]

A review of *The Life of Henry Brougham to 1830* by Chester W New. (Oxford University Press.) Brougham deserves a further tribute for the Continental church-furnishings which he added to St Wilfred's Chapel at Brougham. Of course it cannot rival the parish church of St Ninian, a mile or so away.

Lord Grey said in 1809: 'The first man this country has seen since Burke's time is *Brougham*.' The tribute was already deserved, although Brougham was then only on the theshold of his career. When he died half a century later, the *Daily Telegraph* called him: 'The old *drum-major* of the army of *liberty*.'

No man did so much for so many great causes. Emancipation of the slaves; popular education; university education; religious freedom; freedom of the Press; parliamentary reform; reform of the law. The list of Brougham's acts is a catalogue of Great Britain in the age of Reform. He was the greatest parliamentary speaker of his day, the only man who could rival Canning.

Politics did not use up his energies. He was an outstanding member of the Bar, and defender of Queen Caroline. He filled the pages of the *Edinburgh Review* with his essays, much to the annoyance of the young Macaulay, who wanted to fill them himself. He had opinions about everything and did not keep them to himself. The remark of Rogers after a week-end with Brougham is well known: 'This morning, Solon, Lycurgus, Demosthenes, Archimedes, Sir Isaac Newton, Lord Chesterfield and a great many more went away from Panshanger in one post-chaise.'

It is hardly surprising that a man of such universal accomplishments has had to wait more than a century for a biographer. Apart from other difficulties, the task demanded knowledge of every

[1]*Observer*, 1961.

aspect of early nineteenth-century life. Professor New laboured for thirty years. When his work was nearing completion, the Brougham manuscripts were bought by University College, London – some 50,000 items; and Professor New had to begin all over again. He finished this first volume; passed the proofs; and died. The second half of Brougham's life, more obscure but equally fecund, remains to be treated by another. Perhaps a further thirty years will pass before this is done, though no biographical task is more urgent or more rewarding.

It is sad indeed that the present work breaks off halfway, and sad too that Professor New cannot read the tributes to his work. This is the most important political biography which we have had for a long time. It is not a work of dazzling literary character. The writing is pedestrian, the arrangement sometimes casual and episodic. But there is a powerful grasp of the sources and a guiding clarity which picks out the essential features. Brougham emerges as a man and also as a political figure of the first importance. He had every great quality except discretion. Bagehot said, wickedly but not without reason : 'If he were a horse, nobody would buy him; with that eye no one could answer for his temper.' Brougham quarrelled with many people in the course of his long life, but he invariably forgave those whom he had injured. His charity was not always reciprocated.

Like Burke, Brougham made himself by his genius. Unlike Burke, he never found a patron or needed one. His pen and his tongue carried him to triumph. He had energy without parallel. One episode, told in this book, illustrates his quality. In 1828 when he was also busy founding London University and launching Mechanics' Institutes throughout the land, he took up the cause of law reform. He was coached by Bentham, who wrote to him with a characteristic mixture of efficiency and imbecility : 'It shall have, aye that it shall, the dear little fellow, some nice sweet pap of my own making, three sorts of it. (1) Evidence (2) Judicial Establishment (3) Codification Proposal. ... all sent this very blessed day.' On 7 February, 1828, Brougham addressed the House of Commons for six hours and three minutes; in print his speech took up 168 pages. During his speech, he sucked oranges, cursing in a low voice whenever he sucked a bad one. His speech outlined virtually every law reform which was carried in the next 100 years.

Brougham is perhaps the supreme example of the reformer who won the day by argument and rhetoric. Of course he used agitation also. During the election of 1830, though in full practice on the Northern Circuit, he rode out from York to the various towns, and addressed meetings of 15,000 to 20,000 people. (Or so he said. My experience is that speakers add a nought to their audiences.) But his great reliance was on the strength of his case, repeated time and again. His time, not the eighteenth century, was the great age of reason, in political matters at any rate. Historians may talk of the Nonconformist conscience, of growing pressure by the rising middle class, or of working-class discontent. The truth is that the Bad Old Cause was argued out of existence, and Brougham was the greatest arguer. The privileged classes are often said to have yielded from fear. Perhaps they did; they were always a timid lot. But they yielded far more because they had grown ashamed. Reason brought them down.

Peacock laughed at Brougham and his Steam Intellect Society. Brougham was indeed the Great Eastern of politics, a man too big for his age. In later life, his outsize engine ran him on to a sandbank. He became a figure of fun, remembered only for the Promenade des Anglais at Nice. Yet his great powers were always used for good, and no man has a higher claim to be numbered among the makers of the modern age.

13. Orange Peel: The Cotton Spinner's Son.

Reviews of *Mr Secretary Peel: The Life of Sir Robert Peel to 1830*[1] and *Sir Robert Peel: The Life of Sir Robert Peel after 1830* by Norman Gash.[2] (Longman's.)

I.

Between the wars streamlined biographies were in fashion. Eminent statesmen were dug up from the ponderous Lives which enshrined them; their personalities were displayed, and their public labours passed over briefly. The fashion has changed. Historians have become the new resurrection men, providing revised versions of the standard Lives rather than cutting them down to the size of a novel. Dr Plumb is doing this for Walpole. There is a new life of Disraeli, and a new Asquith. Now Norman Gash presents two substantial volumes on Sir Robert Peel.

There is good excuse for this. Peel was in the first rank of nineteenth-century statesmen. He carried Catholic Emancipation; he repealed the Corn Laws; he created the modern Conservative Party on the ruins of old Toryism. Yet, strangely enough, his Life has never been written. The three volumes by C S Parker, though a valuable source, are simply a collection of letters, with little attempt at narration, and Parker's editing leaves much to be desired. Peel's papers have long been in the British Museum, waiting for a biographer, and Gash has used them thoroughly. His book, in the conventional phrase, fills a long-felt gap. It takes its place at once as a standard work on nineteenth-century British history.

Gash writes competently. His scholarship is careful and exhaustive. His clear narrative rests firmly on the sources and is sound in its

[1]*Observer*, 1961.

interpretation. Nevertheless his book is somewhat dull. Peel himself is partly to blame. Though a sensitive and perhaps an interesting nature lay behind his cold exterior, he took care not to reveal it. He wrote few letters of a personal kind and destroyed those which he did. He was content to survive only as a 'public man' and there is not much fun in that. Moreover, history is one thing, and biography another. Most historians are not greatly interested in human nature or, if they are, do not know how to reveal it. Gash is no exception. None of his figures comes alive. He has a historian's zest for detail and spares the reader nothing.

The first volume deals with Peel's life only to 1830. During this time he was chief secretary for Ireland and Home Secretary. The book tells us a great deal about Irish conditions and about Peel's reform of the criminal law. It dissects the personal intrigues and manoeuvres within the Tory Party. It displays the relations between Crown and Cabinet in the last years before the great Reform Bill. These things are interesting; some of them are important. But it is really excessive that we should have to read nearly 700 pages in order to learn about them. Every historian is reluctant to throw away even the tiniest scrap of information about the past. But even historians should bear in mind the great principle of economy of effort, both for themselves and, still more, for the reader. Gash has disregarded it.

It is not as though there were any great mystery about Peel or his policy. By inclination he was simply a first-rate administrator with a tidy mind, the sort of man who in a slightly later period would have gone into the Civil Service. He had no desire to change things nor any belief that change would do good. He said: 'We are told that we cannot stop where we are; I answer that we are more likely to stop where we are, than we shall if we advance to the point to which we are invited.' When he became Member for Oxford, he accepted the principle that his views would never change. One of his supporters wrote to him: 'It is change and versatility in any way which will at any time injure the reputation of the Member for the University in the University itself.' Hence Peel never met trouble half-way. He waited until the trouble came and then succumbed to it.

Catholic Emancipation was the great example. Peel was for many years the outstanding spokesman of the 'Protestant' cause, always ready to jump into the breach. Emancipation, he argued, would destroy the historic constitution; it would threaten the security of

76

the Established Church; it would not satisfy the Irish. Faced with rebellion in Ireland, he turned round, jettisoned his previous arguments, and announced that Emancipation was the only way to keep Ireland quiet. Both sets of arguments made sense but not in the mouth of the same person. Yet Peel was impatient, too, with those who changed their minds before he did.

Peel had almost every gift of statesmanship except foresight, and here he set the pattern for Conservatism to the present day. When our rulers announce that they will never do this or that and then do it, we recognise that the spirit of Peel is still with us. Daniel O'Connell was the first to benefit from Peel's policy or lack of it; Jomo Kenyatta, at present, the last and there are sure to be others. Peel charted the course for British Conservatism: 'no concessions – except to threats.' Even concessions thus extracted are better than none at all. But it is strange that Peel and his followers never appreciated that telling men they will get concessions only if they make trouble is hardly the best recipe for a quiet life.

2.

'I will not be the Peel of my party.' Thus Balfour, leader of the Unionist party, in 1910. At first sight a curious remark. Balfour had been a singularly ineffective leader and was destined to be unshipped by his own followers the year after he made the remark. His record as prime minister was distinguished only by an Education Act that was in a minor way a betrayal of what his followers believed in. Against this, Peel's record as leader and prime minister was perhaps the greatest that any modern British statesman has to show. He gave England an unarmed police force under civilian control; a fiscal and financial system that lasted for nearly a hundred years; a political system freed from religious monopoly; and above all Free Trade. In 1848, thanks to Peel, England experienced only the Chartist picnic on Kennington Common when nearly every European country was gripped by revolution. Yet it was all in vain. On two occasions – Catholic Emancipation and the repeal of the Corn Laws – he put nation before party. His name became a byword among politicians and has remained so to the present day.

Of course most leaders have trouble with their party, particularly when they are in office. Every leader has then to water down the

²*New Statesman,* 1972.

principles that he previously professed. Conservative prime ministers are harassed from the right, Liberal and Labour prime ministers from the left. Again, nearly every leader practises the doctrine that David Low attributed to Baldwin: 'If I hadn't told you I wouldn't bring you here, you wouldn't have come.' Disraeli led the aristocratic Conservatives to household suffrage. Asquith led the pacific Liberals into the Great War. Macmillan led the Imperialist Conservatives into discarding the British Empire. Even splitting the party, as Peel did in 1846, has been repeated. Gladstone split the Liberals over Home Rule; MacDonald split Labour by forming the National Government in 1931. In both these cases the impact was less. Gladstone retained the allegiance of the majority of Liberals. MacDonald took so few followers with him that the unity of the Labour Party was not affected. Peel held a third of his followers, including all the able administrators – enough to cripple the Conservative Party and not enough to start a party of their own. This was not the worst. Peel's real offence was to disregard almost without warning principles which his supporters cherished and to which he himself had professed unquestioning devotion.

It was not that Peel was a casual or incompetent party leader. His construction of a modern Conservative Party from the Tory fragments shattered by the passing of the great Reform Bill was an incomparable achievement which brought its reward. The general election of 1841 was the first occasion in British history when a party, as distinct from a conglomeration of groups, won a clear majority, and the feat was not repeated until after the second Reform Act of 1867. As prime minister, Peel dominated his cabinet and seemed to dominate his party. In those great days he was the only British statesman, apart from the aged Duke of Wellington, of clear national stature. Whence then the catastrophe? Was it all an accident or were there in Peel hidden weaknesses?

These are topics which those interested in political history, from Bagehot to Crossman, have often debated. Norman Gash makes a contribution of unique importance in this, the first serious biography of Peel. The first volume which brought Peel to 1830, though eminently sound, was, I thought, on the dull side. The second volume however is a wonderful book, as good a political biography as has appeared for many years past. It contains no surprises. As Gash remarks, the Memoirs which Peel wrote after leaving office 'still stand as an authentic record of the events with which they are concerned'. Gash has added a great deal more from the various sources which he uses with unobtrusive skill. His presentation never allows the ample details to obscure the march of events. Gash has matured into a beautiful biographer. Occasionally, being a Conservative himself, he takes the rhetoric of the time a little too seriously, and this may make the less engaged reader giggle. Thus he writes of the attempt to reform the Irish corporations:

> The reform in the abstract was unexceptionable. The practical effect, however, would be to install Catholics in power in nearly every Irish borough. It raised therefore the constant dilemma which dogged all Irish politics: how to apply rational and acceptable reforms to Irish institutions without destroying the Protestant ascendancy.

How indeed?

Gash's book is strictly political biography, just as the biography of a general should be about war. Some prime ministers, perhaps most great ones, have been interesting in themselves. They were eccentrics in either character or behaviour. Gladstone appeared extraordinary, for good or ill, to everyone who met him. Disraeli was odd in the highest degree. Palmerston was a law unto himself. Lloyd George was like no one who had ever been. Even Baldwin was decidedly rum. But unless Peel had been prime minister, and a great one, there would have been little to say about him. He was a faithful husband. Gladstone said that he had known eleven prime ministers and that seven of them were adulterers. Peel was certainly one of the virtuous four. He was very rich – Gash computes his income at £40,000 a year or more. He was also very generous, giving inconspicuous assistance to writers and artists. He collected pictures, sticking to the Dutch, Flemish and English schools then in vogue. When tempted towards the Italian primitives by Prince Albert, he replied: 'I think we should not collect curiosities.' Gash gives some examples of his lighter remarks. They are all right, acceptable enough at the dinner table. But any man with a turn for conversation could have done as well.

The effect is very different as soon as politics enter in. Peel had a mastery of performance that has rarely been equalled. Disraeli described him as the greatest parliamentarian that ever lived, though the remark was not meant as a compliment. Peel was conscious of his gifts. Shortly after becoming prime minister for the first time (in 1834), he wrote:

I do not hesitate to say that I feel that I can do more than any other man can who means his reforms to work practically, and who respects, and wishes to preserve, the British Constitution.

The Bank Charter Act of 1844 is a good example of Peel's art. Without any specialist knowledge of banking, he picked up from bankers a grasp so clear that the system he devised lasted for nearly a century. Bagehot's famous diagnosis of ordinary ideas and extraordinary abilities was unfair. It was rather that Peel carried practical ideas to an extraordinary level.

Peel grew up in politics as the servant of the Crown and, though he used party as an instrument for gaining power, never reconciled himself to the fact that as the party leader he must be to some extent its servant. After his fall in 1846 he rejoiced at his 'freedom from the base servitude to which a minister must submit who is content to sacrifice the interests of a great empire to those of a party'. Gash is content to make the contrast between national statesman and party leader without going further. Peel is presented as a great administrator impatient with party considerations much as present-day civil servants are impatient with their political masters. In this view Peel was a forerunner of Hankey or Warren Fisher.

There was surely a more positive reason for the cleavage between Peel and his party. He was consciously leading his followers where they did not want to go, pushing them into the nineteenth century and industrial England. Gash points out that in the general election of 1841, though the Conservatives were still 'primarily the party of England and above all of the English counties', there could have been no Conservative victory without the 44 Conservative MPs returned for the larger boroughs. Peel's aim was to create an alliance between landowners and capitalists, to make in a sense a single nation of all those with a stake in the country. Bismarck, who avowedly modelled himself on Peel, had the same aim when he pushed the Prussian Junkers into accepting national middle-class Germany. And Bismarck, like Peel, got precious little thanks from the class that he preserved.

There was a further factor that made Peel's offence the more heinous, a factor that Gash does not perhaps sufficiently develop. Bismarck caused the Junkers much trouble, but no one could deny that he himself was a Junker and stuffed with Junker prejudices. Peel was to outward appearance a Tory – upper-class education, a great landowner and much given to cracking up Tory beliefs, such as the Protestant ascendancy or the Corn Laws. But his Toryism was only skin deep. Consider for instance the Church of England, the institution that Tory squires loved above all else. Here is Peel's definition of it:

> *That* is the Established Church of England to which the King must conform – whose chief ministers have a right to seats in the House of Lords – which has an unalienable claim to ecclesiastical property.

In fact a mere property-owning organisation like any city company. Once the Catholics were emancipated, Peel hoped that their priests too would be endowed – then presumably there would be nothing to choose between the two Churches in his eyes.

Similarly over the Corn Laws he never seems to have grasped that they symbolised the traditional social superiority of the landed classes. He said in 1845:

> I am afraid of other interests getting damaged in this struggle about the Corn Laws: already the system of promotion in the Army, the Game Laws, the Church are getting attacked with the aid of the League.

A felicitous list indeed: the Game Laws and the purchase of commissions put on the same level as the Established Church – all privileges of the landed classes and all, in Peel's eyes, increasingly indefensible. Peel let slip the truth about himself in 1835 when he boasted 'that the King had sent for the son of a cotton-spinner to Rome, in order to make him Prime Minister of England'. Maybe he never realised how much his origins removed him emotionally from historic Toryism. Though he resided in a great mansion at Drayton, he still belonged spiritually to Oswaldtwistle. In his later years the cotton-spinner's son predominated more and more. When he first avowed his loss of faith in the Corn Laws, he defined his real belief:

> We must make this country a cheap country for living, and thus induce parties to remain and settle here, enable them to consume more by having more to spend.

It is not surprising that when Peel resigned he said that the main credit for the repeal of the Corn Laws should go to Cobden. Peel was not out-argued by Cobden. He was not even converted by Cobden. He discovered to his surprise that he had really agreed with Cobden all along. The cotton-spinner's son returned to his true allegiance.

14. Hero or Humbug?[1]

A review of *John Bright* by Keith Robbins. (Routledge.)

John Bright has been with me for a long time. When I was a boy at Bootham just a hundred years after he had been, I was offered him as a hero and thought him an old humbug. Later, after studying his speeches on the Crimean war I decided that he was a hero. Now the excellent biography of him by Keith Robbins, flatteringly dedicated to me, convinces me that I was right both times: Bright was a hero and there was something of the humbug in him as well. Henry James characterised him well : —

> He gives an impression of sturdy, honest, vigorous, English middle-class liberalism, accompanied by a certain infusion of genius, which helps one to understand how his name has become the great rallying-point of that sentiment.

It gives added piquancy to this impression that it was recorded when Bright and Henry James were guests of the Earl of Rosebery at Mentmore – surely an odd place to meet the great denouncer of 'our effete aristocracy.' Not at all: Bright was equally at home with the Duke of Argyll at Inverary, with the Earl of Aberdeen at Haddo and with the Duke of Devonshire at Chatsworth.

Bright's great strength was as a speaker at mass meetings, though also in the House of Commons. His speeches are incomparable, greater than Gladstone's, greater than Lloyd George's. They rank with Burke's as the only speeches in English which can still be read as literature. I rate highest Bright's speech at Birmingham on 29 October 1858, if only because it contains the best survey ever given of British foreign policy from the Glorious Revolution to the

[1]*Observer*, 1979.

middle of the nineteenth century. All Bright's speeches combine wisdom, advocacy and humour. His oratory was purely English: he never studied the Greek and Latin classics and was soaked in the English classics instead.

Bright was carried to the public platform by the campaign against the Corn Laws and was rightly a little jealous when Cobden claimed to have imposed their repeal all on his own. Thereafter Bright outstripped Cobden as a popular leader. His sustained criticism of the diplomacy that preceded the Crimean war, though unsuccessful at the time, triumphed eventually in the long period of Splendid Isolation.

Bright did not carry his Quakerism into public life. He was an isolationist, not a pacifist. He agreed reluctantly with the military suppression of the Indian Mutiny; he applauded the victory of the North in the American civil war. But he was steadfastly against any entanglement in European affairs, even if it was disguised as a crusade for national liberation: 'It is not my duty to make my country the knight-errant of the human race.' He resigned from Gladstone's Government in 1882 in protest against the bombardment of Alexandria and the conquest of Egypt – acts as foolish and wicked in their way as the later incursion at Suez. All the same he had some odd ideas about Europe, as when he wrote in 1870: –

> France is deposed and Germany is exalted, a great gain I think for liberty and for peace. It will be a great gain too for Protestants and the imposture which is still throned on the seven hills will be less able to claim military support.

Bright had one great practical achievement: he did more than anyone else to promote the second Reform Act which established household suffrage, though it is characteristic that he stayed away from the great demonstration in Hyde Park which ended in rioting. His political radicalism had strict limits. He opposed universal suffrage and was even firmer against votes for women: 'men-women are not a pleasant addition to our social arrangements.' He opposed the factory acts or any other interference with 'the natural laws,' of which trades unionism was the worst. Thus he wrote of a strike at Preston in 1853: –

> The battle must be fought out, when combinations are entered

into. When once the natural adjustment of wages is departed from, then there remains only to learn who is the strongest.

Twenty years later, during a period of trade depression, he was still saying the same: without trade unions 'the labour markets would have been more steady and the enormous loss caused by strikes would have been avoided.' He also opposed any interference with the sale of alcohol and said of the temperance reformers, 'It is always so when great questions get into the hands of weak people – weak heads are liable to be run away with.'

Bright began well over Ireland. He was among the first to advocate a system of land purchase which would transform Ireland into a community of peasant proprietors and he pushed this cause hard throughout the 1870s. The Home Rule Party, as led by Parnell, forfeited his sympathy by their aggressiveness. Perhaps he resented their interruptions of his speeches. The Parnellites became for him 'rioters' and 'rebels,' unfit to rule their own country. Belatedly he discovered, too, the Protestant cause in Ulster. Bright contributed as much as Joseph Chamberlain to the defeat of Gladstone's Home Rule Bill in 1886, a sadly conservative end to a radical's career.

Beneath an appearance of charm and benignity there was a complex character. He had two serious breakdowns which took him out of public life for years at a time. He was also very selfish. He led an active social life in London at the tables of the great. His wife was left in Rochdale for months on end to care for their considerable family. Nor did she accompany him on his excursions to Scotland or abroad. He sometimes gave the impression that he was prouder of his 'magnificent barouche' than of his political achievements. Perhaps he secretly reproached himself. He wrote in 1876, when invited to accept some office in the Society of Friends : –

The labours of life have taken me out of the way of service for our little Church. I feel that there is nothing above the humblest office – shall I say that of doorkeeper? which I could properly undertake.

Yes, he certainly was an old humbug. Or so I think until I read again one of his speeches. Then I must acknowledge that he really was a great and noble man.

15. The Oath Man[1]

A review of *The Bradlaugh Case* by Walter Arnstein (Oxford).

Constitutional law, though no doubt important for the student of English history, is not a gay subject. There are many ingenious arguments, some odd tangles and occasionally a decision of real significance. There is also a great deal of drab, legal prose. Two men have enlivened this unromantic field. In the eighteenth century John Wilkes provided both fun and drama, while striking more than one blow for liberty. In the nineteenth century Charles Bradlaugh also struck his blow for liberty and even provided fun in a rather solemn way. Bradlaugh's name still rings a bell in any well-informed mind. He was the most famous of English atheists; he produced with Annie Besant the first book which popularised contraception; and he did something or other about the oath taken by members of parliament.

What exactly did he do? Here even the well-informed are less confident. Many, including knowledgeable historians such as Philip Guedalla, assert that Bradlaugh refused to take the oath. On the contrary, there was never a more assiduous oath-taker. He demanded to take the oath again and again. When this was refused him, he administered the oath to himself more than once. I knew that bit, but I got others things wrong. I assumed that Bradlaugh was excluded altogether from parliament between 1880 and 1886. Not at all. He was merely excluded from the debating chamber. He spent much of his time in the House of Commons library, preparing for his next legal engagement, and often attended debates, just outside the bar. For some months, from July 1880 to March 1881, he actually sat in the chamber after having affirmed and, on two occasions, voted against motions for his own expulsion. Professor Arnstein

[1]*New Statesman*, 1965.

is the first to clear up every aspect of this complicated case. His book is a model of precise history. It is beautifully written and unfailingly accurate. It brings Bradlaugh to life. It illuminates Gladstone's intellectual complications. It further discredits that overrated figure, Lord Randolph Churchill.

Bradlaugh was a thoroughly Victorian character. No one could have been more earnest, more worthy, more sincere. Even his atheism showed this. His views were little different from those of the agnostics. But he claimed that, being 'without god', it was more honest to say so, instead of covering himself with a respectable phrase. He was not concerned to promote atheism when he became a parliamentary candidate. He had more usual Radical aims in view – land reform, proportional representation, repudiation of Beaconsfield's foreign policy, and almost apologised to the electors 'because in my speculative opinions I differ from many of you'. In 1880 Bradlaugh was elected for Northampton along with Labouchere, who liked to call himself 'the Christian member for Northampton'. In fact Labouchere's 'speculative opinions' were much the same as Bradlaugh's, and he once told the House of Commons that the words of the oath were 'just the same superstitious incantation as the trash of any Mumbo-Jumbo among African savages.' Bradlaugh, however, took the oath more seriously. He paid Christians the compliment of assuming that they meant what they said or swore, an attitude which greatly exasperated most of them. Bradlaugh therefore decided to affirm.

Here the legal tangle began. An act of 1866 allowed Quakers, Moravians and Separatists to affirm instead of taking the parliamentary oath. (Query – has any Moravian ever taken advantage of this?) Acts of 1869 and 1870, which Bradlaugh had helped to promote, allowed atheists to affirm in the law courts. Bradlaugh therefore claimed that he had the same right in parliament, and the law officers agreed with him. To make matters certain, he formally asked permission from the Speaker, Brand. There was thus no fumbling by Brand, as Ensor for instance alleges. Bradlaugh himself raised the question. Brand referred the question to a select committee, which decided against Bradlaugh by the chairman's casting vote. It was assumed that Bradlaugh would now take the oath. He resolved to do so. But he was also resolved to make his own beliefs clear. He wrote a letter to *The Times*, explaining that he would take the oath, 'although to me including words of idle and meaningless character', in order to perform his duties to his

87

constituents. This was an open challenge. The Conservatives took advantage of this. The Speaker, having once consulted the House, had to do so again. Bradlaugh was not allowed to take the oath.

Gladstone, although prime minister at the head of a great majority, failed to give a lead. On one occasion he formally indicated this by appearing 'in his grey-cream summer coat with gloves and walking-stick rather than in his customary black frock-coat.' In Gladstone's view, Bradlaugh's rights ought to be determined in the law courts, not in parliament, a characteristic evasion. In any case, this method turned sour. The House of Commons tried to escape its troubles by allowing Bradlaugh to affirm after all. He did so and duly took his seat. All seemed over. A common informer, Henry Clarke, claimed the penalties which an MP incurred by voting in parliament without having taken the oath. Clarke won. Bradlaugh was again excluded from the House. The victory incidentally rebounded on Clarke. Bradlaugh was later able to show that Clarke was being 'maintained' by Newdegate, a fanatical Protestant MP, and recovered damages in his turn.

Each year, at the opening of the session, Bradlaugh presented himself and demanded to take the oath. Each year he was refused. In 1882, having been again refused, he ingeniously administered the oath to himself and then voted against the resolution which again expelled him. Bradlaugh tried the courts, as Gladstone had urged him to do, only to be told that they could provide no remedy. He tried demonstrations of violence and vainly sued the officers of the House. Gladstone belatedly acknowledged his own responsibilities. In 1883 he reluctantly promoted a bill which would allow atheists to affirm instead of taking the parliamentary oath, and delivered what was perhaps his greatest speech when introducing it. Asquith, for instance, devoted almost an entire chapter of his autobiography to it 40 years afterwards. However, it failed at the time. The bill was defeated by 292 votes to 289, largely on the strength of quotations from Gladstone's own writings.

In 1881 the House declared Bradlaugh's seat vacant; in 1882 Bradlaugh was expelled from the House; in 1884 he himself vacated his seat by taking the Chiltern Hundreds. On each occasion he was returned at a by-election. In 1884 he again administered the oath to himself, actually at the Speaker's Table, and this time voted twice before being turned out. In 1885 he was again prevented from taking the oath. It seemed to have become a habit for all concerned. In 1886 there was a new parliament, and the affair was expected to begin over again. Peel, who was now Speaker, ruled that the resolutions of the previous house had lapsed and that there could be no 'inquisition as to what may be the opinions of a Member when he comes to the Table to take the Oath.' Bradlaugh was sworn along with a mob of other members. The affair was over. In 1888 he promoted an act allowing anyone to affirm who wished to do so. In 1891 the House unanimously expunged Bradlaugh's original exclusion from parliament. Bradlaugh was on his deathbed and too ill to understand. He died two days later and was buried without ceremony of any kind.

The appearance in parliament of an avowed atheist certainly raised an awkward problem for Christians who tried to combine tolerance and intense religious conviction. Much of the outcry against Bradlaugh, however muddled, was sincere. Much was not. Randolph Churchill used the affair solely to harass both Gladstone and Sir Stafford Northcote, his own nominal leader. Bradlaugh, in an open letter to Churchill, referred to 'old English gentlemen' as 'a class to which I, as well as yourself, am a stranger – I from birth, and you from habit.' The conduct of the Irish Home Rulers was equally discreditable. Bradlaugh had been a good friend to Ireland, and most of the Irish were in the House only because of an Emancipating Act in 1829. But Parnell, apart from wanting to please the priests, was playing for Conservative support and, besides, always enjoyed tormenting Gladstone. The Home Rulers voted almost solidly against Bradlaugh, a prelude to their wrecking tactics in the general election of 1885. Cardinal Manning took a similar line, in a bid to make himself recognised leader of Christian England. Newman for once successfully pulled the rug from under Manning's feet. He issued a statement about the Affirmation Bill :

It little concerns Religion whether Mr Bradlaugh swears by no God with the Government, or swears by an Impersonal, or Material, or Abstract and Ideal Something or other, which is all that is secured to us by the Opposition . . . Looking at the Bill on its merits, I think nothing is lost to Religion by its passing, and nothing gained by its being rejected.

Manning retreated into silence. The Archbishop of York, not to be outdone, summarised Bradlaugh's beliefs as 'No God, No King, and at least for the present – as few people as possible.' A Northampton clergyman reported a poor woman as saying: 'When Bradlaugh gets in the Queen'll have to do her own washing.' No such luck. The Thing, having made a fool of itself, then gave Bradlaugh concessions to keep him quiet. In the long run the adherents of Mumbo-Jumbo triumphed over Bradlaugh's earnest sincerity. Anyone who doubts it should turn up the record of the Privy Council when the members of the present Labour Cabinet were admitted. A small honourable minority affirmed. Most of those who took the oath had not previously been distinguished for religious belief. Perhaps, following Labouchere, they may be called 'the Christian members of the Cabinet'.

16. The Uncrowned King.[1]

A review of *Charles Stewart Parnell* by F S L Lyons (Collins)
and *The English Face of Irish Nationalism: Parnellite Involve-
ment in British Politics, 1880–86* by Alan O'Day (Dublin:
Gill and Macmillan).

Charles Stewart Parnell is one of the most interesting characters in
modern history. He is interesting politically. More than any other
man he gave Ireland the sense of being an independent nation. As
Gladstone said, he did for Home Rule what Cobden had done for
Free Trade: 'he set the argument on its feet.' Parnell is also interesting personally: a Protestant landowner who became the most
powerful leader Ireland has known and a successful statesman who
threw everything away for the love of a woman. There can never
be too many books about him.

Leland Lyons, now Provost of Trinity College, Dublin, tells
Parnell's story with incomparable scholarship and literary grace.
This is a classic biography which will be read as long as anyone
cares about Irish history or for that matter about history at all. It
is a biography in the strict sense. Parnell always occupies the centre
of the stage and even the greatest figures such as Gladstone never
steal the limelight from him. The decisive events are treated only
in so far as they concern Parnell. Thus in 1886, when he had almost
carried Home Rule to victory, his hopes were ruined by Chamberlain's revolt and the defeat of the Home Rule Bill in the House of
Commons. Lyons passes over the debates with hardly any mention.
Again the Special Commission of 1889 which restored Parnell's fame
yields little drama. Of course we get Pigott and his 'hesitency' –
'with a small h, Mr Pigott, a small h'. But essentially all that
matters to Lyons is that Parnell won.

[1]*New Statesman*, 1977

More remarkable still, though Lyons shows how Parnell built up his mastery over the Irish Nationalist party, he does not discuss the character of that party in any detail. This is where O'Day comes in. Lyons's book is about Parnell without the Parnellites; O'Day's is about the Parnellites without Parnell. O'Day is analytical where Lyons is biographical, and by this approach he lays his finger on one decisive weakness in Parnell's position. Parnell wanted the Irish party to be strictly independent, manoeuvring between the British parties without committing itself to either of them. But most of the Parnellites had little to distinguish them from British Liberals. They had the same Liberal outlook. The most prominent of them lived in England and followed careers there in journalism or at the bar. Even in the days of their parliamentary obstruction they served loyally on parliamentary committees. They were members of London clubs, one of them even a member of the Savile, which was alleged to be almost as good as being a member of the Athenaeum. How could such men wage a political war for Irish independence? As O'Day rightly remarks, the Home Rule Bill would merely have transferred some power from the British ruling class to the moderate representatives of the Catholic Irish nation. The son of a once-famous Home Ruler said to me: 'We would have run Ireland for you if you had let us.'

The truth is that the Irish MPs were always threatening to bolt, and the O'Shea divorce case gave them their opportunity. Until then they were whipped into line by Parnell's will. All of them trembled before him. Parnell could be a delightful dinner companion, gentle, amusing and sympathetic. But at the first hint of opposition his 'Red Indian' eyes flashed fire. Parnell had virtually no experience of politics before he began his abrupt rise to the top. He was unshakably convinced that he was a man born to rule. He had one particular asset which is often unnoticed. He was an Englishman in background and upbringing with all the arrogance of an imperial race. All Irishmen are in the last resort soft. Parnell's will made them seem hard. He took his ascendancy for granted. He kept aloof from his followers and in his later years hardly attended the House of Commons. Lyons thinks he had lost interest. Surely it was rather that, like Napoleon, he had become too confident of his despotic power, particularly of course when he took up with Katharine O'Shea.

Parnell had other gifts beyond mere will-power. Though not a great orator in the nineteenth-century style, he captivated mass audiences by his uncompromising determination and the impression he gave of extremism. Behind the scenes he was a negotiator of the first rank who knew how to take every advantage. He was a match even for Gladstone, the most ingenious negotiator of the age. He was more than a match for the Irish Nationalists who turned against him. No man ever 'bested' Parnell. It was circumstances that brought him down.

Conor Cruise O'Brien argued some 20 years ago that Parnell's aims were essentially constitutional and the argument has been generally accepted. Ireland should receive Dominion status and would then cooperate with Great Britain as an equal. Certainly Parnell tamed the men of violence as firmly as he dominated the parliamentarians. Certainly he rejected the idea of a revolutionary war on the practical grounds that Ireland was not big enough to run away in – an argument where Sinn Fein was to prove him wrong. But his rejection of extremism and violence was one of expediency. His aim was an uncompromising independence, not a legislative adjustment of Irish administration. 'No man can set bounds to the march of a nation.' This was Parnell's basic principle.

Parnell was ingenious but in some ways he was outwitted by British politicians, especially by Gladstone. Parnell rose high with the backing of Irish agrarian discontent. Gladstone quieted the discontent by his Land Act of 1881. Again Parnell secured a commanding position in Parliament by bargaining with both Liberals and Conservatives over Home Rule. Gladstone took the Home Rulers prisoner when he produced his own Home Rule Bill. Parnell still tried to keep free and maybe even welcomed the O'Shea divorce case for this reason. The other Home Rulers never escaped. They were shackled to the Liberal Party for the rest of their existence.

Parnell's relations with Katharine O'Shea were to cause his downfall. The story is still full of mysteries and always will be. We know why Parnell allowed the affair to drift on unacknowledged; he and Katharine O'Shea were waiting for the money she would inherit when her rich aunt died. For the same reason O'Shea made no fuss. But there is much more that needs explanation. Why did Parnell remain friendly with O'Shea when he was already Katharine O'Shea's lover? Even stranger, why did O'Shea remain friendly with him? The friendship was not merely personal. O'Shea was Parnell's political adviser and his intermediary with Gladstone and Chamberlain. Parnell must surely have known that O'Shea was an unreliable negotiator, evading the decisive issues and promising more than he could perform. Why did Parnell use him in this way? And why did Gladstone and Chamberlain, shrewd men and experienced politicians, accept O'Shea at his face value? Surely they could see that he was a light-hearted, garrulous rogue. Perhaps there was more to O'Shea than comes out in the accounts. O'Shea himself aspired to become Irish Secretary. Was this pure fantasy? Or did others take him seriously? The answers are beyond conjecture.

Lyons makes somewhat heavy weather over Parnell's love affair, producing psychological explanations that Parnell wanted a home and domesticity. In fact when a man is in love, he is in love and that is all there is to it. Parnell, in his usual arrogant way, was careless over the practical side of the affair. He seems to have thought that he could justify his position, if challenged, by proving that O'Shea had condoned the affair. Apparently it never crossed his mind until too late that such proof, though certainly forthcoming, would bar the way to a divorce and to what he wanted: Katharine O'Shea as his legitimate wife and their children acknowledged as his. His last stroke of ingenuity was to assert that Gladstone was seeking to dictate who should lead the Irish party. Even Parnell's most devoted followers could hardly have believed this but it inspired his last and most romantic fight. Though Parnell did not achieve Home Rule he made Ireland a nation. He was the uncrowned king of Ireland. He was also Katharine O'Shea's King and she was his Queenie. He did not found a dynasty. His only grandson became an officer in the British army and died in India of enteric fever in 1934. As Leland Lyons concludes: 'The line of direct descent from Parnell therefore ends in a cemetery at Lahore.'

17. Imperial Miscalculations.[1]

A review of *Joseph Chamberlain and the Tariff Reform Campaign: The Life of Joseph Chamberlain.* Volume 5: 1901–1903. Volume 6: 1903–1968. By Julian Amery (Macmillan). Though I have written about Joseph Chamberlain before, the topic of these two volumes seemed different enough from its predecessors as to justify inclusion.

Joseph Chamberlain was the greatest force in British politics between the decline of Gladstone and the rise of Lloyd George. He was a pioneer in social reform and municipal enterprise. He defeated Irish Home Rule. He inspired a new era in British Imperialism and directed its triumph in the Boer War. When old age was already upon him, he challenged the accepted dogmas of Free Trade and launched the movement for Tariff Reform, which was to transform British economic life a generation after his death.

Despite these achievements, nothing went right with him. He stands pre-eminent as a Splendid Failure. Only the six counties of Northern Ireland remain in the United Kingdom, and even they have Home Rule. South Africa is a republic, dominated by the Boers. The British Empire is little more than a memory, and the last fragments of Imperial Preference survive only as an embarrassment for those who are clamouring to make Great Britain part of Europe. Chamberlain, it seems, was successful only in destruction, bringing ruin first to the Liberal, and then to the Unionist, party. Was he too impatient, too self-centred? Did he misjudge the climate of the times? These are riddles perhaps without an answer.

He has triumphed belatedly in one field. No man not a Prime Minister has had a biographical monument of such grandeur raised

[1]*Observer,* 1969.

to his memory. J L Garvin, the famous editor of *The Observer*, produced three volumes of Chamberlain's Life more than 30 years ago. Julian Amery, taking over the unfinished task, added a further volume and was then distracted by political activities. Electoral defeat has at last freed him to finish the work and with a grandiose conclusion. The two volumes now presented run to more than a thousand pages, though they cover only three years of Chamberlain's fully active life. The first hundred pages, it is true, are taken over from Volume IV, in order to make the story of Tariff Reform complete, and the last 70 pages continue this story from Chamberlain's death to the present day. Still, there is a formidable amount of reading.

The enthusiast for political biography would not have the book a page shorter. The details have the fascination provided by the analysis of a game of chess. Each pawn has its significance. Each move helps to determine the future. Chamberlain does not stand alone. All the great names in British politics pass before us. The Duke of Devonshire confesses : 'My knowledge of political economy is small, and I should find it very difficult to argue with either an expert Free Trader or Protectionist, and I am too old to begin.' Balfour of course is the key figure, perhaps concerned, as Mr Amery suggests, to hold the Unionist Party together, perhaps, however, even more concerned to defeat Chamberlain without caring much about either Free Trade or Protection.

Chamberlain set out to undo the work of Richard Cobden 70 years before. The Anti-Corn Law League was much better run, with better organisation and more skilful speakers. Cobden gave the impression that he was really conducting a crusade. Chamberlain presented Tariff Reform as the offshoot of a Cabinet squabble, which indeed it was. The campaign was started without adequate preparation. Chamberlain and his followers were not clear what British industries would benefit from Colonial Preference. They could not determine how much British food prices would rise – if at all. There were few reliable statistics and little practical information. The current talk was of 'a scientific tariff,' but the only science involved was guesswork such as is shown at the gaming tables. In all the arguments, summarised by Mr Amery, the critics not surprisingly came off best. Chamberlain scored off Balfour; Asquith scored off Chamberlain; the sophisticated ingenuities went round and round.

Chamberlain had a vision of a united Empire. Reading his speeches one after another, it is hard to feel that he ever translated this vision into practical terms. He initiated his campaign for Colonial Preference as a matter of Imperial sentiment. This led him to advocate taxes on imported foodstuffs as the only counterpart which Great Britain could offer to the colonies. But the colonial advocates of Preference were industrialists. The colonial farmers were Free Traders, who in any case were already exporting all their wheat. In exchange they wanted cheap industrial goods and did not care whether these goods were British or American. Next, talk of food taxes raised the claims of British agriculture, a deserving cause which had little to do with Imperial sentiment – and where Chamberlain was ignorant. Then, if British agriculture needed protection, why not British industry also? Yet Chamberlain asserted: 'I am not a Protectionist.' He favoured tariffs only against dumping or, as Balfour did, for purposes of retaliation – putting them on in order to compel other countries to take them off.

The bewilderment of the voters was not surprising. This was an argument where the protagonists knew only that they disagreed with one another and hardly knew why. The practical decision sprang from 'stomach taxes.' It was the feeling against these which defeated Tariff Reform. Balfour recognised this, as Bonar Law and Baldwin did after him. The latter-day outcome has been paradoxical. Though we are still without food taxes, British agriculture now flourishes as never before, and such Imperial Preference as remains provides us with cheap food. Once the British people were asked to accept dear food for the sake of the Empire. Now they are asked to accept it for the sake of Europe. Maybe the fear of stomach taxes will work its old magic and keep us out of the Common Market. All this is far from Chamberlain. His campaign, despite Mr Amery's epilogue, has become an historical curiosity.

Chamberlain's personality remains a puzzle even after six volumes of biography. He commanded great devotion, inspired great enthusiasm. He also provoked great hostility, perhaps more than any other British political figure in modern times. Even Lloyd George got off more easily. Mr Amery suggests correctly that he was never accepted by the political Establishment, and this was particularly tough in the Tory Party. He had also an arrogance which provoked and almost justified dislike. He had virtually no friends in politics – certainly not Balfour, despite their exchange of polite phrases, maybe only John Morley, and that friendship was little more than a reminiscence.

Fate worked against all the Chamberlains. Joseph, Austen and Neville in their different ways deserved better of their times than they achieved. Evidently bad luck becomes a habit, much like anything else. Now, however, the run is broken. Joseph Chamberlain has at least been lucky in his biographer.

18. Rational Martyr.[1]

A review of *The Riddle of Erskine Childers: a biography by Andrew Boyle* (Hutchinson).

Who was Erskine Childers? One Erskine Childers was a patriotic upper-class Englishman who served in the Boer war and the Great War and wrote a famous book, *The Riddle of the Sands,* which was both a sensational thriller and a powerful piece of anti-German propaganda. The other Erskine Childers was an uncompromising Irish Republican who was condemned to death by the Free State government as a member of the illegal IRA. It seems impossible that they should both be the same man. But they were. Here is a riddle to delight that accomplished biographer, Andrew Boyle. His last book was on Brendan Bracken, a Catholic Irish Nationalist by birth who turned himself into an English Protestant Tory. His present book is something of the same story, only the other way round. Of course there are differences. Bracken, that man of mystery and invention, destroyed all his records. Childers left a plentitude of evidence both in print and in manuscript. Despite this he remains at the end the more mysterious of the two.

There was nothing in Childers's background to suggest anything unusual. His father was of Yorkshire gentry stock, his mother was Anglo-Irish; his uncle was Chancellor of the Exchequer in Gladstone's government. Losing both parents early in life, Childers found a home with his Anglo-Irish cousins at Glendalough in Wicklow. But there was nothing Irish about his upbringing. This was impeccably English: Haileybury and Trinity College Cambridge. His friends were cool, enlightened Liberals like himself: Walter Runciman. G M Trevelyan, Eddie Marsh. Tennyson was his literary idol:

[1]*New Statesman,* 1977.

There is hardly a good aspiration or a good motion in me which has not either been heightened or originated by him . . . Such a life, such a life's work, and such a death are a treasure of unimaginable value to all English-speaking people.

Childers adopted the most conventional of careers and became a clerk in the House of Commons, a post that suited perfectly his orderly, disciplined mind.

There was also an adventurous side to him. He was an accomplished yachtsman – hence *The Riddle of the Sands*, which derived from his exploration of the islands off the Dutch coast. He volunteered for the Boer War and had a gallant career. His experiences there made him critical of British generals and sympathetic towards the Boers. After it he aspired to enter politics as a staid Liberal. In this he was unsuccessful. His first interest in Irish affairs came in as a side wind from his sympathy with the Boers. This interest remained remote until the revived controversy over Home Rule. Ulster gun-running seemed to him unfair. He decided to run guns for the Irish Nationalists and did so successfully. Significantly all his crew, male and female, had an Anglo-Irish background except for his American wife, who in time became as passionately Irish as he was.

The Great War brought Childers back on a patriotic course. His expert knowledge made him invaluable over the somewhat fanciful plan of a British expedition to seize and hold the island of Borkum. Later he went to the Dardanelles and then to the western front. He was a skilled map reader, first with motor boats and then with aircraft. His deeds of gallantry were rewarded by the DSC. At the end of the war he was the close adviser of Trenchard, another of Boyle's heroes, in planning the bombing of Germany. His reputation as an outstanding fighting man was secure. This was not all Childers did during the war. He served on the abortive Plunket commission which sought an agreed solution of the Irish question. By now he himself favoured Dominion Home Rule for Ireland, a respectable enough programme.

After the war Childers sought a new Byronic adventure. He and his wife moved to Dublin and took up the cause of Sinn Fein. He became the political adviser and publicist of Sinn Fein. De Valera regarded him as 'the model of all I'd wish to have been myself'. In 1919 Childers voiced the claims of Ireland at the Paris peace conference. In 1921 he rose higher. He went to London as secretary of the Irish delegation that negotiated the Irish settlement with Lloyd George. Here his training as clerk in the House of Commons asserted itself. The Irish delegates thought in terms of high principle and political realities. Childers looked after the commas. His own position was simple : Sinn Fein stood for an Irish Republic embracing all 32 counties, hence anything that derogated from this was unacceptable. For him, as for De Valera, the treaty which instituted a Free State for 26 counties only was a betrayal and must be rejected.

This was the decisive moment of his life. Where once he had been a patriotic Englishman he now became an Irish rebel, rebelling not only against the British government but against the established Irish government as well. The opposition of this 'damned Englishman', as Arthur Griffith called him, exasperated the Irish supporters of the treaty. Though Childers took no active part in the republican insurrection, he came to symbolise all the extremism and irrationality of the IRA. Andrew Boyle writes :

Childers's very Englishness, the air of indefinable superiority which, according to critics, he exuded like a smell that stank in good Irish nostrils, had not been the least of his handicaps, the greatest being his temerity.

A Dublin friend remarked, 'It was his sniff of disdain which got him killed.'

When arrested, Childers was holding a little souvenir revolver Michael Collins had given him. This was enough. Childers was shot on the order of the Free State government in November 1922. Andrew Boyle puzzles why this happened. He writes: 'Childers's potential greatness was marred by an ungovernable tendency to stand in his own light and confound even those who knew and loved him best.' Sean O'Faolain said that 'he was what the Russians call a "fatal" character and the shadow of his doom was over him from the first'. I find this somewhat mystical and perhaps characteristically Irish.

The true explanation is perhaps more straightforward. Childers regarded the treaty as untidy and that was enough for him. He gave his life as a protest against slovenly drafting. He was not a martyr to romance; he was a martyr to rationalism, a grave fault indeed in the world of politics. Childers's last request to his son, who subsequently became President of the Republic of Ireland, was : 'If ever you go into Irish politics, you must not speak of my execution in public.' The son never did. Andrew Boyle has at last done justice to Erskine Childers even if he has not wholly solved the riddle. Perhaps Childers himself could not have done that.

19.   The Gowk.[1]

A review of *C P Trevelyan 1870–1958: Portrait of a Radical*.
By A J A Morris (Blackstaff Press).

In the eighteenth century there was a politician known as Single-Speech Hamilton, who achieved fame by his first speech in Parliament and never made another. It would be unfair to credit Charles Trevelyan with only a single decisive act. For one thing he was a highly progressive president of the Board of Education in the two interwar Labour governments. Nevertheless, his importance stems from what he did in August 1914. Though not the only Liberal minister to resign in protest against the British declaration of war on Germany, he was the only one to state publicly the reasons for his resignation, when both Burns and Morley remained silent. He went on to rally the few dissenters and with them founded the Union of Democratic Control, perhaps the most formidable radical body ever to influence British foreign policy.

Trevelyan's dissent and his leadership thereafter were unexpected and seemingly out of character. He came of impeccable Whig stock, Macaulay was his great-uncle. Sir George Otto Trevelyan, his father, was a middle-of-the-road Liberal who dithered towards Unionism before returning to the Gladstonian fold. His two brothers had considerable literary gifts: Robert as a poet, George as the last great exponent of Whig history. Charles had no such gifts. He took a second at Cambridge and could not aspire to the fellowship at Trinity College which was almost an hereditary Trevelyan perquisite. In 1899, when he first became a Liberal MP, he regarded himself as a Liberal Imperialist, supported the Boer War and looked to Asquith and Haldane as his leaders. He took a modest view of his abilities and wrote to his future wife:

[1] *New Statesman*, 1977.

So little do I think there is any good chance of rising to very high position with my mediocre store of knowledge and ability, that I shall tend less and less to try for position and more and more to take a line I think right.

No wonder Trevelyan's father-in-law called him a 'damned serious gowk'.

Trevelyan's judgement of himself helps to explain his political development. Not caring for advancement he could stick to his principles and develop them; unconsciously he perhaps believed that being a Trevelyan was advancement enough. He became a typical radical in the days of Asquith's government: an advocate of taxation of land values, ready for Lib-Lab cooperation in social reform, and eager for a conflict with the House of Lords. He shared, too, the radical outlook over foreign affairs. He was against excessive naval expenditure in 1909 and again in 1914. Like other radicals he began with great faith in Grey, writing in 1909, 'There was never a saner man at the head of foreign affairs than Sir Edward Grey.' In 1912 he was disillusioned: 'I am afraid I am becoming more and more definitely opposed to Grey and his whole outlook and policy, his reticence and his sympathies.'

The difference between Trevelyan and other radicals was that they were carried away by Grey's speech of 3 August 1914, when he justified war against Germany by talk of the British obligation of honour towards France. Trevelyan was outraged. Grey and Asquith had repeatedly denied that there was any British commitment to France. Now Grey was invoking it. 'I never was clearer in all my life . . . We have gone to war from a sentimental attachment to the French and hatred of Germany.'

A few other radicals shared Trevelyan's outlook; hardly any were prepared to act. C P Scott wrote, 'I agree with your objects, but I should be apt to part company with you as to methods. So I am better out of it.' Trevelyan and Morel launched the Union of Democratic Control. Morel provided the ideas. Trevelyan provided much of the money and become the principal UDC spokesman in Parliament throughout the war. Bernard Shaw thought that Trevelyan should be prime minister: 'You can very soon become the visible alternative nucleus to the George gang and the Asquith ruin' – a characteristically Shavian exaggeration.

Trevelyan lost his seat in 1918. When he returned to Parliament in 1922 it was as a left-wing socialist. As usual he began with great faith in MacDonald and even in Baldwin, 'the two finest men heading the two main political parties that there have been in my time'. As usual he was disillusioned. When MacDonald failed to back his admirable Education Bill during the second Labour government, he resigned, thus escaping the agonised disputes over the financial crisis. There can, however, be no doubt that he would have gone along with the cabinet minority who rejected the cuts in unemployment relief. Trevelyan again lost his seat and never returned to Parliament. He had a last moment of triumph at the annual Labour Party conference in 1933 when he moved a resolution committing the Labour Party to a general strike in case of any threat of war. He wrote: 'It is a quite immensely important decision. It puts the organic Labour movement against *all* war under any circumstances.' Events did not work out like that, as Trevelyan recognised when he supported wholeheartedly the British war against Hitler.

Trevelyan had a happy old age. He became Lord Lieutenant of Northumberland. This alarmed some of the neighbouring gentry who might have swallowed his eccentric politics but were shocked at his stripping to the waist when out rabbit-shooting on a hot day. He inherited the Wallington estate on his father's death in 1928 and devoted himself to restoring it. Wallington became a centre for left-wing politics and culture, housing the People's Theatre of Newcastle and providing youth hostels. In 1941 he handed over Wallington with a large endowment to the National Trust. Charles Trevelyan died in 1958 in his 88th year, still young at heart. I wish Mr Morris had given us more passages from Trevelyan's correspondence in his later years when he was still vocal over political matters. Michael Karolyi told me that Charles Trevelyan was the British politician whom he most esteemed. This was no mean tribute.

20.   The Black Book.[1]

A review of *Salome's Last Veil: The Libel Case of the Century*
by Michael Kettle (Granada). Another of my favourite trials,
made even more delightful by the additional fantasies that the
author contributes.

The suit for criminal libel by Maud Allan, stage dancer, against
Noel Pemberton Billing, Independent MP, in 1918 undoubtedly
provided the finest legal entertainment of the twentieth century,
transcending even that of the Rev Harold Davidson, Rector of
Stiffkey. Billing was a wild patriot, convinced that the Germans
were aided by perverts in high places. When Wilde's play *Salome*
was given a private performance – and when it was proposed to
trundle the play round Europe as an example of British culture –
Billing saw that his chance had come: here was sexual corruption
at work.

Billing was aided by Captain Spencer, former British intelligence
officer, who had been discharged from the army after being certified
insane. Spencer revealed to Billing that there was a German Black
Book containing the names of 47,000 British perverts in the political
and social worlds. Spencer also wrote the attack on Maud Allan who
had played Salome. Unable to accuse her of being a sodomite, the
usual term of abuse, he consulted a local doctor who provided a
sensational title, The Cult of the Clitoris. Such was the innocence
of those days that both Mr Justice Darling, who presided at the
trial, and the prosecuting counsel had to be enlightened as to the
meaning of the word. They were also in the dark about 'orgasm'
and 'sadism'.

Further reinforcement came from Mrs Villiers-Stuart, another

[1]*New Statesman,* 1977.

intelligence agent, who was instructed to discredit Billing by luring him into a homosexual brothel. Instead, she informed him that she had actually seen the Black Book. She had been shown it by Neil Primrose, her alleged lover. Subsequently, the British authorities had arranged Primrose's death in Palestine. In fact he died fighting gallantly, though this did not come out at the trial.

Mrs Villiers-Stuart was Billing's star witness. Although she had only turned over the pages of the Black Book, she was able to recall the name of almost any prominent figure mentioned. Mr and Mrs Asquith were in the Book. So was Mr Justice Darling, who expressed no surprise at his inclusion. Captain Spencer discoursed on the sexual frenzy provoked by the cult of the clitoris. A doctor held forth at length on sadism, a theme he had learnt from the works of Krafft-Ebing, Lord Alfred Douglas, once Wilde's catamite, who had translated *Salome* into English, now appeared as a reformed character, testifying that Wilde had written *Salome* with the deliberate purpose of sexual corruption.

The case was accompanied by constant uproar. Billing, who conducted his own defence, disregarded all the rules of evidence and denounced Darling's attempts to check him as giving deliberate assistance to the German enemy. Loud applause from the public galleries followed each of Billing's outbursts. Towards the end, Billing, who had pleaded justification, withdrew his charge that Maud Allan was a lesbian. His plea of justification therefore failed. Darling, however, did not remark on this and the jury acquitted Billing.

Such was the case of the Black Book. Billing, though crazy, was a formidable litigant. Darling prided himself on his wit and was delighted to be told that George Robey was the darling of the music hall. This time Darling's wit miscarried. It is said that the case showed the hysteria of the British people in the last year of the first world war. In all probability a firmer judge would have blown Billing's case to pieces in no time.

Mr Kettle gives a fuller account of the case than has ever been given before, and every word is a delight. Clearly he does not think that there was anything in Billing's case. There was no German Black Book; there were no sexual perverts in high places, or not more than the usual number; there was no plot. However, Mr Kettle has discovered two plots of his own in which Billing played a subordinate part. The first was the Generals' plot which was designed to supersede civilian authority by a military triumvirate —

Sir William Robertson, formerely CIGS; Colonel Repington, military correspondent of *The Times*; and General Maurice, formerly DMO. Maurice had fired the first shot by his letter to *The Times* which accused Lloyd George of lying about the strength of the British army in France. Mr Kettle thinks the accusations well-founded. However that may be, Lloyd George triumphed in the House of Commons by revealing that the figures he gave had been supplied by Maurice's own department.

Billing was then pushed into action by the conspirators to undo the effects of Maurice's failure. It is difficult to understand how civilian authority could be discredited by accusations of sexual perversity against Asquith, leader of the Opposition and the generals' friend, while no such accusations were made against Lloyd George, the Prime Minister. But let that pass. All plots have loose ends.

There was also a plot by the politicians. Lloyd George and Bonar Law were designing to make a compromise peace with the Germans, disguised as negotiations in Holland over the exchange of prisoners of war. They trembled at the patriotic protests that Billing would make and therefore pushed Maud Allan into taking action in the belief that Billing would be discredited. They even, it seems, rigged the case beforehand. In Mr Kettle's words, 'The Pemberton Billing case . . . was basically a struggle between Billing and Bonar Law.' The politicians' plot also miscarried. There was no compromise peace. Billing emerged more formidable than ever and plagued the government throughout the remainder of the war by a campaign demanding the internment of all aliens.

In a sense, however, Pemberton Billing should be acclaimed as the man who won the war. The reports of the case aroused such hilarity in the trenches that the soldiers were inspired to withstand the great German onslaught of April to July 1918 and then to launch their own offensive, which carried the Allied armies to final victory.

21. Fascism.[1]

A contribution to a series of articles on The Isms in 1957.

The oddest thing about Fascism nowadays is that even its advocates have to pretend to be ashamed of it. Fascism has become a dirty word, and a speech in its favour can be identified at once by the unfailing phrase: 'Of course I have no sympathy with Fascism but . . .' We have to make do with less branded words like totalitarianism, authoritarianism, demagogy, and so on. It will save a lot of trouble when Fascism gets back into currency.

Fascism is a disease of democracy or at any rate of the mass-age. Dictatorship alone is not Fascism if it relies simply on force and has no popular backing. Fascism demands a mass-party where a few self-chosen leaders control a body of disciplined followers drawn from the disgruntled elements of society. Here is the starting-point of Fascism: a sense of grievance, social, political, national, even personal, it really does not matter what. But the psychology of resentment must be there, and if the resentment is unfounded so much the better. A Fascist party exists to express emotions, not to achieve results. Its programme is a mere rigmarole of high-sounding phrases, and if any of its aims are in fact achieved then others equally irrelevant have to be hastily botched up. Hence the futility of concession or appeasement to a Fascist party or country. Indeed, concession aggravates the resentment by exposing its irrational basis. Fascism has to be kept on the boil by parades and uniforms. Its demonstrations release pent-up emotions and at the same time generate fresh ones rather as an atomic reactor turns out more power than it consumes. The demonstrations must threaten violence. Later they must apply violence against some element felt to be outside the Fascist community – Jews, Slavs, coloured peoples. The actual choice of the

[1]*Saturday Review*, 1957.

victim has no practical sense. Hatred and persecution are practised for their own sake.

Fascist leaders are concerned only with power. Usually indeed they claim to be serving some national cause and boast of their patriotism. But this nationalism is not essential and the few avowed survivors of Fascism now present themselves as having been 'good Europeans' before NATO and the rest of it were ever thought of. Fascists will use any ideological cover so long as it brings them nearer to dominance over others. What do Fascist leaders do with their power when they get it? Mainly they destroy the obstacles to its unrestricted exercise. Fascists hate the Christian churches, the law courts, the trade unions, not as rivals but simply as brakes. They have nothing to put in the place of these institutions. Fascist law is merely the rule of the stronger. Fascist creeds are a jumble of dark emotions, incoherently expressed. Fascist morals, too, simply provide unlimited sexual gratification for males whose appetites are usually greater than their powers.

Is Fascism necessarily anti-Socialist or even anti-Communist? In the days when Hitler was coming to power much play was made with the idea that Fascism was the last defence of a declining capitalism. As a matter of fact, capitalism seems to get along much better in a sensible democratic community. It is true that the rich retain their riches in a Fascist state and even add to them. Probably the capitalist classes in Germany and Italy are still proportionately better off than their counterparts elsewhere as the result of Fascist rule. But though the capitalists keep their wealth, they lose their power just like everyone else and as individuals they are equally exposed to the irrational tyranny of the Fascist bosses. Many German magnates had time to decide in a concentration camp that they had been ill-advised to finance Hitler.

Other writers turn the analysis upside down and make out that Fascism and Communism are indistinguishable. This is an unnecessary confusion. Fascism sometimes parodies Communism just as it parodies almost everything else, but it lacks the practical economic aims which make Communism a rational, though materialistic, creed. What Fascists like in socialist measures is the power they offer, not the results they produce. Where socialists, let us say, might advocate rationing in order to secure fair shares, Fascists rejoice in the regimentation involved.

A final point is often ignored. Even Fascist leaders cannot be irrational all the time. If they were, they would be certified and locked up before they had started on their political career. Since, by definition, they have no rational principles, they are wholly selfish in their sane moments. There is no example on record of an honest Fascist leader. All of them – Hitler, Mussolini, their followers and imitators without exception – grabbed at wealth as well as power. When you find a political community in which all the leaders are corrupt, you may guess that it is on the way to Fascism. Indeed, Fascists in power (or out of it) plunder on such a gigantic scale that one is tempted to believe that they are rational after all – cheats and swindlers, not psychopaths. But this is wrong. Fascism is the irrational made vocal, and therefore any attempt to reduce it to rational terms defeats itself.

22. Sly, Sir; devilish sly![1]

A review of *Baldwin: the unexpected Prime Minister* by H Montgomery Hyde (Hart-Davis, MacGibbon).

In December 1935 Baldwin, then Prime Minister, was gravely menaced by the storm of indignation that blew against the Hoare–Laval plan. Sir Austen Chamberlain, who shared this indignation, held the life of the Government in his hands. Baldwin sent for him and said: 'Austen, when Sam [Hoare] has gone, I shall want to talk to you about the Foreign Office.' Chamberlain thought he was being offered his old office and defended the Government in the debate. After it Baldwin saw Chamberlain again. This time he said: 'If you had been 10 years younger, there would be no doubt in my mind that you should have it. As it is . . . I have decided to offer it to Anthony [Eden].' Or, as Chamberlain put it, more crudely: 'He told me I was ga-ga.' Chamberlain penned this bitter verdict:

> The public think him a simple, hardworking, unambitious man . . . a man too of wide and liberal mind who has educated his party.
> And we know him as self-centred, selfish and idle, yet one of the shrewdest politicians, but without a constructive idea in his head . . . 'Sly, Sir; devilish sly!' would be my chapter heading and egotism and idleness the principal characteristics that I should assign to him.

Curzon saw in Baldwin 'a mixture of innocence, ignorance, honesty and stupidity – fatal gifts in a statesman when wholly dissociated from imagination or vision or *savoir faire*,' Lloyd George called him 'the most formidable antagonist whom I ever encountered.'

[1]*Observer*, 1973

112

Baldwin's record was certainly formidable. Almost single-handed he overthrew Lloyd George, the greatest statesman of the age. He routed the TUC. He defeated Beaverbrook, a far cleverer man. He drove Churchill into isolation, casually and without effort. He dethroned a king. His career was littered with the corpses of friends and foes whom he had politically massacred. Yet he remained Honest Stan the country-lover, asking plaintively, 'Cannot you trust me?' and always, or nearly always, receiving an affirmative answer. Here is a subject of endless fascination.

Baldwin has had bad luck with his biographers. G M Young 'fell out of love with his subject – even began to dislike him.' Middlemas and Barnes were more interested in the history of the times than in the man and produced an unreadable volume of over 1,000 pages. Historians, it seems, do not make good biographers. At last a true biographer has appeared. Montgomery Hyde has behind him a life-time of writing biographies and never loses sight of his subject in the turmoil of events. This is Baldwin as he really was : idle, subtle, even on occasion treacherous, but as one of his juniors put it : 'Fundamentally a nice man,' Or in G M Trevelyan's words : 'In a world of voluble hates, he plotted to make men like, or at least tolerate, one another.'

Baldwin did not like clever men – Lloyd George, Birkenhead, Churchill. At the end of his life he said : 'The only man he could never forgive was Beaverbrook' – perhaps because Beaverbrook beat him in the competition for the affection of Bonar Law. He told a Glasgow audience that he 'had never known a good workman who could talk nor a good talker who was a good workman.' Yet Baldwin was himself one of the greatest talkers of the age – unrivalled at the microphone, master of the House of Commons, and for ever delivering speeches on literature, if the works of Mary Webb can be dignified with that name. When he spoke at an Athenaeum dinner after his retirement, Lord Macmillan, the chairman, declared : 'As Ben Jonson said of Bacon, "the fear of every man that heard him was lest he should make an end".' Conventionally middle class himself, he was the idol of the staid and respectable men full of good will so long as it did not affect their pockets or their social standing.

There was in Baldwin a personal magic that bewitched men and sometimes lured them to destruction. Despite the interminable speeches and the Cabinet discussions, the impression remains that Baldwin had not an idea in his head: lovable maybe, human cer-tainly, but totally unconstructive. All he wanted was a quiet life for himself and others. On holiday after settling a strike in the coal fields, he wrote of 'those wretched miners whom I hoped never to see again.' At the end of his life he told R A Butler: 'One of the things that comforted me when I gave up office was that I should not have to meet French statesmen any more.' No public man has groaned more over his official work and none has done less, sniffing at his papers instead of reading them, just as the crossword was the only part of a newspaper that interested him. Why did he not give up and embrace the country life for which he was always hankering? To judge by his own professions, Baldwin should be called the reluctant rather than the unexpected Prime Minister. But, of course, it was play-acting, the role for which Baldwin had cast himself and of which the public never tired.

On the positive side there is not much to record: a lessening perhaps of class conflicts that was coming in any case for more fundamental reasons. And, of course, the dethroning of a king. This is the one subject on which Montgomery Hyde writes too much. It is all known, except for some titbits of legal curiosity. The king's affair, as it was known, is now almost incomprehensible. No one from start to finish ever inquired about Mrs Simpson as a human being. Could she make Edward VIII happy as she so triumphantly did? Had she the qualities to rise to the challenge of becoming queen? No, she had been the innocent party in two divorce cases and was thus civilly dead. No one, including Montgomery Hyde, has ever pointed out that the easy ending of the affair owed more to Mrs Simpson than to anyone else. I wonder what would happen in a similar situation nowadays.

Montgomery Hyde's book is readable, historically impeccable, and does not push Baldwin's virtues too hard. Montgomery Hyde misses one good story and, I think, spoils another. We do not hear Mrs Baldwin's answer when asked how she endured the conceiving of her children: 'I closed my eyes and thought of England.' And surely what Churchill said of Baldwin before their reconciliation was: 'What, is the candle still guttering in that old turnip?'

23. Baldwin's Fall Guy.[1]

A review of *Sir Samuel Hoare: A political Biography* by J A Cross (Cape).

Sir Samuel Hoare, later Lord Templewood, had many great achievements to show. Early in his career he helped to organise the overthrow of Lloyd George. Towards its end he was instrumental in keeping Spain neutral during the Second World War. As Secretary for Air he secured the independence of the RAF. As Secretary for India he was the principal architect of the Government of India Act which, if it had been carried out, might have given India a more peaceful path to independence.

All those who worked with him acknowledged his intelligence and administrative skill. Many saw in him a future Prime Minister. But something went wrong. In his few months as Foreign Secretary his very intelligence caused him to stray beyond redemption. His name was for ever associated with the Hoare–Laval plan and he joined that great class of future prime ministers who never made it.

Hoare has had to wait long for a biographer. He has not waited in vain. Professor Cross's book is a model of careful scholarship: fully based on all the available sources; favourable towards Hoare but frank about his shortcomings; and with a firm grasp of political events. There is not much to say about Hoare's personality. He made a loveless marriage. He had high ambitions but was content to wait. He had few strong convictions and described himself as 'a Liberal among Conservatives and a Conservative among Liberals.' He was also somewhat sanctimonious, perhaps a legacy from his Quaker forebears. In 1912 a London paper said he had 'a simpering voice that suggests a newly ordained and nervous curate,' and a

[1]*Observer*, 1977

Labour member reduced the House to laughter by interjecting in a weak, piping voice, 'Dearly beloved brethren.'

For a long time everything went well with Hoare. As a British intelligence officer in Italy he subsidised Mussolini's pro-war Socialist paper, though the two men never met. He was a stalwart figure in Baldwin's government of 1924–29. His conduct of the Government of India Bill through the House of Commons was a masterly performance. Hoare challenged Churchill and defeated him. The conflict left a lasting mark on both men. Hoare wrote:

> I shall never forgive Winston. He and his friends are completely unscrupulous. They stick at nothing. They misrepresent everything that is said and spread about all kinds of groundless charges and baseless rumours.

Churchill, too, did not forget. As Prime Minister he refused to appoint Hoare Viceroy of India despite the enthusiastic and repeated recommendations of the responsible Minister. As Cross says, 'the widely held view of Churchill as a man without rancour seems in need of some revision.'

Though there have been many accounts of the Hoare–Laval plan, Cross's is the best up to now. He overlooks one point. While Hoare was thinking solely in terms of foreign policy, the Cabinet and especially Baldwin had other preoccupations. They had the shadow of the Peace Ballot behind them. In the middle of the Abyssinian crisis they fought and won a general election on the ticket of loyalty to the League. Like Hoare, his colleagues wanted to do a deal with Mussolini but it had to be wrapped up in League principles – an impossible combination. Hoare contributed to the confusion by promising full British support for the League on condition all the other members were as wholehearted. Hoare attached most importance to the condition; the British public heard only the promise.

The documentation, particularly from the Cabinet records, is, however, clear. In the view of the British Government the League existed to preserve peace and, once Italy had invaded Abyssinia, the League had failed. There was no thought of punishing Mussolini or of enforcing international justice by war or even by effective sanctions. The only concern of British policy was to discover a price at which Mussolini would stop the war. The Cabinet agreed on this again and again. Even the election slogan, 'all sanctions short of war,' really meant 'no sanctions that implied any risk of war.'

Hoare's job as Foreign Secretary was to devise a price that would satisfy everybody, ending the war without totally discrediting the League. When Hoare went to Paris and reached agreement with Laval, this was not the aberation of a sick and tired man. It was the logical consequence of British policy and what Hoare had been told to do. Moreover the Cabinet endorsed the Hoare–Laval plan. The public outcry frightened Baldwin out of his wits. He repudiated Hoare and the Cabinet followed his lead. Though Hoare was compelled to resign, he refused to recant. He still insisted that he had been right, and so he had been within his terms of reference.

This was a discreditable episode for everyone except Hoare. Even Vansittart, who largely devised the plan, made out in his memoirs that he was in Paris only by accident when it was concluded.

For good or ill Hoare was ruined. In November 1939 a member of the Foreign Office recorded a remarkable conversation with Herbert Morrison:

If this country were heavily attacked, or if the Prime Minister's health prove unequal to the strain upon it, he said ... that he supposed the Lord Privy Seal [Hoare] would succeed him, a decision which he thought would be unwelcome to all Opposition parties. The Opposition disliked the idea of the Lord Privy Seal, feared [Churchill] succeeding as Prime Minister, and would welcome the Foreign Secretary [Halifax] in that capacity, though he feared it was constitutionally impracticable.

Hoare had indeed fallen low when even Lord Halifax was preferred unto him.

24. The Chinese Cracker of Cliveden.[1]

A review of *Nancy* by Christopher Sykes (Collins).

The first woman to sit in the British House of Commons was an American who got there only because her husband had been unwillingly elevated to the House of Lords. That was an odd twist, but with Nancy, Lady Astor, odd things were happening all the time. It is as an oddity – a 'caution' in the North-country phrase – that a biography of her is justified. On a serious political level there is little to report about Lady Astor except that she was a Member of Parliament for twenty-six years. She did something to promote nursery schools. She retarded a relaxation of the divorce laws – a perverse achievement considering that her own first marriage had been dissolved. She raised the age at which young people could be served with alcohol in a public house from sixteen to eighteen. Having been a fervent supporter of Chamberlain she was one of the honourable forty who wrought his downfall in May, 1940. During the Blitz she was courageous and indefatigable in Plymouth, the city which she represented and of which her husband was Lord Mayor throughout the Second World War. That is about the lot – hardly enough to cover a memorial tablet, let alone to fill a book.

The most important event in Nancy Astor's life was her marriage to Waldorf Astor and not her election to Parliament, which was indeed a consequence of the marriage. Before then Nancy Langhorne was a somewhat wild Virginian girl, much given to rushing her fences, a character all right but with no public significance. She made an unfortunate first marriage, got out of it, and came to Europe to recover. She certainly knew how to follow the dictum, 'Do not marry money, but go where money is.' On her first visit she captured the affections of Lord Revelstoke, the banker, and

[1]*Times Literary Supplement,* 1972.

imagined that she was in love with him. She soon wearied of his overriding concern with business affairs. On her second visit to Europe she won the more welcome attentions of Waldorf Astor and married him in 1906. Waldorf's father, William Waldorf Astor, was a fantastically rich American expatriate who gave Cliveden to Waldorf and Nancy as a wedding present. A little later he aquired *The Observer*, also an attractive inheritance. Waldorf was less pleased when his father alleviated the boredom of the First World War by buying a title. It was this which consigned Waldorf to the House of Lords in 1919, when the first Viscount died, and so propelled Nancy into the House of Commons.

The Astors lived on a grand scale. They had Cliveden for the weekends, a big house in London, another at Sandwich for the golf, and yet another in Scotland. They often gave dinner parties in London for fifty or sixty guests and at Cliveden had fifty gardeners, to say nothing of a chef with five assistants. Waldorf and Nancy were for many years a happy couple – she impulsive and unpredictable, he cautious, restrained and yet devoted. Nancy liked other men to be in love with her, though at a respectful distance. No guest at Cliveden went padding back from his hostess's bedroom in the early morning, as they did at other Edwardian houses. Some of these lovers had, however, a profound effect on Nancy, more indeed than Waldorf had. Philip Kerr, later Lord Lothian, converted himself from Roman Catholicism to Christian Science and then converted Nancy also. From Kerr Nancy learnt, too, her passionate and unreasoning hostility towards 'RCs' – an obsession enshrined for many years in *The Observer*'s trust deed.

Christopher Sykes suggests another paradoxical source for this obsession. Hilaire Belloc was a friend of Nancy's, as many unbalanced letters in this book show. His obsessions were against the rich and the Jews, obsessions that Nancy did not share. But she picked up the trick of obsessions from Belloc and switched it against Belloc's own religion. This was a characteristically wrong-headed performance. Later Bernard Shaw replaced Belloc as the chief literary lion of Cliveden. He and the Astors visited the Soviet Union in 1931, one of the great comic episodes of our time. Shaw claimed to have been a Marxist socialist for sixty years, though it is clear that he did not have much idea what this meant. Having praised Stalin, he went on to praise Mussolini and Hitler, in the latter of whom he discovered 'the greatest living Tory' with *Mein Kampf* as 'really one of the world's bibles'. Though Shaw was a vegetarian and a teetotaller, he liked the good things of life. No doubt Nancy's principal attraction for him was that she was a very rich woman.

Wealth was not of course Nancy's only asset, though it enabled her to use her other gifts. Shaw said after a visit to Cliveden that he had spent Sunday with a volcano. Nancy Astor was not big enough to be a volcano. She was a Chinese cracker, discharging sparks in all directions. Some of them were dazzling, some merely painful. When she proposed to write her autobiography, one of her sons suggested that it should be called *Guilty but Insane*. The remark was not spoken altogether in jest. In public, rudeness was Nancy's principal stock-in-trade. At election meetings she could shout down and silence the most persistent heckler. In Parliament she maintained a stream of interruptions, some of them relevant. Mr Sykes prints from Hansard Nancy's silly interruptions which almost wrecked the great speech that Churchill delivered after the Munich conference. Her own speeches were, for the most part, rambling and ineffective and became worse as she grew older.

When Nancy first ran for Parliament she declared: 'I am not standing before you as a sex candidate.' But she knew how to play on her sex once she arrived. Her first prank was to steal the seat traditionally reserved for Sir William Joynson-Hicks, and there is nothing funnier in the book than the bumbling old gentleman solemnly drawing the attention of the House to this outrage. During the 1920s she carried the concerns of women and children almost alone. In 1929 the women MPs rose to fourteen. Nancy invited the nine Labour women to lunch and proposed that they should drop their Labour allegiance in favour of a Women's Party under her leadership. One of them remarked: 'If only she did not have to boss us!' Thereafter Nancy ran down. She was never happy except in opposition, and yet had to support the National government. She became a nuisance, a figure of fun.

Though her husband owned *The Observer* and her brother-in-law owned *The Times*, Nancy often had a bad press. In her early days, Horatio Bottomley discovered that she was described in *Who's Who* as 'the widow of Robert Gould Shaw', though Shaw was in fact still alive. This was meat for Bottomley, who ran a campaign headed: 'A Hypocrite of the First Water – The Poor and the Rich'. Later Bobby Shaw, the only son of her first marriage, caused her further trouble. He was convicted of a homosexual offence. Beaverbrook, though not acquainted with the family, ensured that the story was not mentioned in any newspaper. For this act of disinterested charity he earned no thanks but instead persistent abuse in *The Observer* for his manipulations of the press. Mr Sykes passes over this episode in a single embarrassed sentence.

The worst trouble came in the later 1930s, when Claud Cockburn, editor of *The Week*, discovered a nest of appeasers in 'The Clive-den Set'. Mr Sykes shows painstakingly that there was not much in the story. There were appeasers at Cliveden such as Tom Jones or for that matter Lothian. There were many guests of an entirely opposite conviction. Nancy had not the persistence to be a con-spirator. But she was often rash. She gave a lunch for Neville Chamberlain to meet overseas correspondents, and he revealed his plans for betraying Czechoslovakia. When the news leaked out, Nancy denied that the lunch had ever taken place. The next day she retreated and explained that she had only meant to say that Chamber-lain had not given any official interview.

Her last years were sad. Though she did much to inspire the citizens of Plymouth, she also sought advantages for herself. When a consignment of chocolates arrived from America for the Plymouth women and children, she wanted some. Waldorf refused and, when she flew into a temper, withdrew into another room where he had a heart attack. After the war their relations grew worse. Nancy wished to run again for Plymouth; Waldorf prevented her doing so, and she never forgave him. The final blow came when Waldorf allowed *The Observer* to go left. He and Nancy became virtual strangers, meeting only for occasional weekends. As compensation for abandoning Plymouth, Nancy wished to be made a peeress in her own right. James Stuart, the Tory Chief Whip, put the idea to Churchill; there was no answer. Mr Sykes later protested to Stuart that there must have been an answer of some sort. Stuart replied : 'Oh, well, if you call an embarrassingly long silence fol-lowed by an angry grunt an answer, there was.' The mutual dislike between Nancy and Churchill was always intense. She once said to him : 'If I were your wife, I'd put poison in your coffee.' Churchill replied : 'And if you were my wife, I'd drink it.'

In her last years she still fired off sparks, but increasingly at ran-dom. There were also flashes of kindness. During the Profumo case some of the dirt washed on to her son Bill, then the third Viscount Astor. The news was kept from her. The newspapers were cut before they reached her, and some friend always rang up just before the six o'clock news. One morning she collected the papers herself and read the story. She said : 'We must go to Bill at once.'

On the way there she forgot what had happened and asked: 'Why are we going to see Bill?' Her last words were: 'Am I dying or is it my birthday?'

Mr Sykes has drawn a beautiful portrait of this strange, difficult woman. For her early years he has used the autobiography that Nancy began. He has built up a fund of reminiscences, his own and also those of others. He has skilfully worked in material from other books. This is a most winning biography, sympathetic and almost convincing. Nancy Astor was a fascinating woman. She was brave and stimulating. She certainly stirred things up. But she was also a spoiled child of fortune. She captivated men and then tormented them. Despite her kindness, she was indiscriminately cruel, a bully who knew that her great riches made it impossible for most others to hit back. Many of those who knew her, including some who suffered from her, loved her. The detached reader, however, who did not know her, is left with an enormous sense of relief that he escaped this ordeal.

25. Nobody's Uncle: The Tiger who walked Alone.[1]

Reviews of *The Life and Times of Ernest Bevin*. Volume One:
Trade Union Leader 1881–1940. Volume Two: *Minister of
Labour and National Service 1940–1945*. By Alan Bullock.
(Heinemann.) A third volume is still to come.

I.

Alan Bullock is a biographer in the Victorian manner: solid, accurate, exhaustive. There is no showing-off by the author, and no
amateur psycho-analysis. The record is left to speak for itself, and
if the result is sometimes pedestrian, that is how it was for Bevin.
Though Bullock admires Bevin as much as he detested his previous
theme, Hitler, this difference of feeling has not produced any
difference of treatment. Bevin, like Hitler, is presented from 'outside', as a public figure. '*Life*' and '*Times*' merge into each other
after the first few pages. Alan Bullock stands 'outside' Bevin in
another sense. He is not a Trade Unionist or even a member of the
Labour movement. This detachment has its advantages. No living
writer could have presented a fairer, or more informative account of
Bevin's life. But detachment has its own disadvantages. Bullock,
being on the outside, has failed to realise how much Bevin was on
the outside too. The reader is made to feel – from the sub-title on –
that Bevin was a characteristic Labour leader of the early twentieth
century. In fact he was unique for good and ill, a strange, solitary
character, self-made in career and, still more, in ideas.

Bevin was a man without roots or background. Father unknown;
left to fend for himself at the age of eight; never acquiring a craft
or skill. He remained all his life a casual labourer, ready to turn
his hand to anything and without much belief in the trained expert.
An engine-driver or a maker of precision-tools would never have

[1]*Encounter*, 1960, and *Observer*, 1967.

challenged the bankers as ruthlessly as Bevin did at the time of the Macmillan Commission. He would have been taken in by them and assumed that, as experts, they knew what they were talking about. Bevin, the casual labourer, always knew better than the experts, and often with justification. But there were many things he did not know. He knew little or nothing of industrial England. Bristol, where he grew up, was an isolated pocket of urbanism in a rural sea, and even as a town it was a backwater in Bevin's time. In a curious way, Bevin did not know anything about the Industrial Revolution. The transport and general workers whom he organised could all have existed just as well without it, except for the bus-drivers who depended on the internal-combustion engine. Bevin dealt with docks and transport undertakings, with hotels and restaurants. He never dealt with factories or engineering-shops. Alan Bullock quotes Bevin's favourite saying: 'I like to create.' This was the one thing he never did. The members of his Unions were moving things about, not creating them. Even when Bevin drew up schemes for European co-operation, they were the dreams of a trader, not of a creator. There was something lacking in a Labour leader who knew little of industry and nothing of the north of England.

It is easy to see what Bevin lacked. He lacked comradeship, the unconscious solidarity which the Labour movement represented. Of course there was plenty of spite and intrigue in the Labour movement, as I daresay there is even in the Church of Rome or the Communist Party. The pull of comradeship was strong all the same. That is why the open breach with MacDonald was such a misery and a torment in 1931. But not for Bevin. He always treated the Labour movement as his personal property. The members of his Union were for him 'my people'. He did great things for them, but in the feudal way that a duke might look after his retainers. 'Loyalty' was the great cause which Bevin preached; it is a feudal word. If anyone was disloyal – that is, went against Bevin – then no consideration of comradeship could save him. Ben Tillett was no doubt a tippling old bore when Bevin drove him out of the Presidency of the Union. All the same, no other Labour leader would have been so merciless. Lansbury and Bevin had worked together for years on the board of the *Daily Herald*. Did this deter Bevin when he marched up to denounce Lansbury for hawking his conscience round the Labour movement? It did not. The delegates to the Conference voted for Bevin and against Lansbury; but there was not one who, in his heart, would not have liked to be Lansbury and none who wanted to be Bevin.

Bevin was solitary in another, even more significant way. He played politics by ear and with total disregard of ordinary patterns. He often displayed a dislike of intellectuals. This made him popular with the English upper classes who also dislike intellectuals, and I suspect that Alan Bullock gets some pleasure from the way in which Bevin slammed the impractical theorists. Yet Bevin was not really, to borrow his own phrase, a guileless practical man. He was a rival intellectual, playing the same game but with rules of his own. His mind ran over with cock-eyed ideas; and his rambling talk, if taken down, could have gone alongside Hitler's *Table Talk* as an intellectual curiosity. Bevin could never have had a two-volume *Life* or won the admiration of the Foreign Office if he had stuck to trade-union organisation. It was his chaos of dynamic ideas which made him count in British politics. He saw things which his more humdrum colleagues missed. Often he saw aright. He appreciated earlier and more clearly than others the futility of a non-revolutionary General Strike; though it is fair to add that he saw through the General Strike more quickly because he had believed in it more passionately. This was a typical intellectual's change of front which would not have disgraced Crossman: all for the General Strike one day, dead against it the next. Bevin transformed the emphasis of Trade Union action from strikes to negotiation, and no man used the new method to better effect. It is hardly an exaggeration to say that Bevin laid the foundations of the Welfare State. But, lacking a theory or any general conception, he left the Labour movement in the bewilderment over the Welfare State which still bedevils it. He prided himself on never reading a book. Perhaps he was lucky to escape Marx; but if he had read William Morris, or even Ruskin, we should not now be in such confusion.

Bevin had also the intellectual's consuming interest in foreign affairs. He became the appointed negotiator for the Trade Unions – Labour's Foreign Secretary – as early as the Councils of Action in 1920. Again he played by ear, and he played alone. Once more it was exchange of goods, access to raw materials, which interested him. These were the obsessions of a transport-man, and they produced strange results. Intellectuals said many silly things between the wars. Did any intellectual say anything sillier than this: 'The old Austro-Hungarian Empire was economically perhaps the soundest thing that existed in Europe'? The Empire was a device by which Magyar landlords and German capitalists exploited oppressed populations, yet Bevin took it as his example in 1937. He was always dreaming of vast Free Trade areas, sometimes for the Commonwealth, sometimes for Europe, without any thought how they contradicted each other. He once wrote to Cole: 'Really, old man, look how you have boxed the compass.' In fact, Cole erred, if at all, from rigidity of principle; it was Bevin who boxed the compass at a moment's notice, and, when he changed, everyone had to follow him.

Bevin's obsession with trade also made him exaggerate the efficacy of economic sanctions, just as he treated the League of Nations as the Transport and General Workers' Union on a larger scale. His denunciation of Lansbury at the Labour Party Conference of 1935 was the highlight of Bevin's pre-war career. Lansbury's pacifism has been dismissed as impractical. Was Bevin's line any better? This sane, practical man committed himself to the extraordinary proposition that Baldwin's Government could be relied on to support the League of Nations against Mussolini. Lansbury seems a monument of common-sense in comparison to this. Bevin battered down opposition. He won; he did not persuade. Men feared him; some admired him. But few felt for him the affection that they felt for Arthur Henderson – a man of equally impeccable working-class origin, who rose as high but by less ruthless methods. Bevin had many great qualities. He had one great defect: nobody called him Uncle.

2.

Ernest Bevin was a big man with a strong personality and a mighty voice. Beaverbrook called him, rightly, 'a powerful beast'. He probably ranks first among British trade union leaders of the twentieth century. His contribution to the Second World War was magnificent and decisive. Without Bevin as Minister of Labour there would not have been a contented working class. After the war, he was a forceful Foreign Secretary, though opinions differ about his achievements.

All the same, three large volumes of biography make a heavy call on our interest or admiration, particularly when Alan Bullock, the biographer, rivals the ponderous style of his subject. The first volume, on Bevin's career as a trade union leader, was perhaps justified. Four hundred pages on Bevin the war-time Minister of Labour are not designed to stir eager curiosity.

The length could be excused if Bevin had left a large number of private papers, full of revelations. There is virtually nothing of this kind – merely notes for a few speeches and two or three cantankerous letters. Some war-time leaders, notably Churchill and Eden, were allowed to use the official records. Alan Bullock has been barred by the 50-year, soon to be the 30-year, rule. The bulk of his material comes from parliamentary debates, Bevin's speeches, newspaper articles, and the volumes in the official Civil History of the Second World War.

The analysis of Bevin's policy and achievements is, of course, competently done, but there is nothing new in it, at any rate nothing new for the student who has worked through the official histories. Occasionally Alan Bullock claims too much for Bevin. He seems to forget that the final word on manpower lay with Sir John Anderson, who conducted the manpower budget; perhaps Bevin forgot it himself.

Of course Bevin became a Minister in order to do a vital job and Alan Bullock is right to lay most emphasis on this. Though Bevin told a startled Labour conference: 'I am here as one of your nominees in the War Cabinet,' he was, in fact, Churchill's nominee and no one else's. He said to one of his friends: 'You know, Harry, I'm a turn-up in a million,' and he cared little about either the Labour Party or individual colleagues. When the Parliamentary Labour Party voted against the Government in order to demand firmer action on the Beveridge Report, Bevin not only voted with the Government, as other Labour Ministers did. He turned up at the party meeting the next day and insisted that, as he had broken standing orders, he must be expelled. Though the party did not oblige him, Bevin ignored it for the next 18 months. His idea of party democracy was that, once anything had been carried by the block-vote of his union, everyone must conform implicitly.

As man and Minister, Bevin had two sides. He was, without dispute, a marvellous boss. He knew how to get the best from those round him, and they repaid him with deep affection. He said characteristically to one subordinate: 'Anything you make a mistake about, I will get you out of, and anything you do well I will take the credit for.' Only the first part of the remark was true.

Bevin showed a different spirit towards colleagues, whether of his own party or not. He trampled on opposition and rejected proffers of reconciliation. Thus Citrine tried to remove a misunderstanding. Bevin replied: 'I respect other people's positions and opinions but I expect mine to be respected also: and that is all.' He girded constantly against Morrison and said: 'Don't you believe a word the little b—— says.' He snubbed Morrison's attempt to discuss post-war policy and answered only: 'When the Leader puts a policy before all of us we shall have to give it our serious consideration.' He was furious when Morrison released Sir Oswald Mosley from detention. This showed, Bevin declared, that Morrison was not to be trusted. He spoke openly of resigning from the Government and was only talked out of it by Brendan Bracken of all people.

Bevin's greatest dispute was with Beaverbrook, a dispute which raged for nearly two years. There was a clash of principle and method. Beaverbrook improvised; Bevin advanced by slow, methodical stages. There was still more a clash of personality. Beaverbrook despised and neglected committees. Bevin arranged that the Production Executive should meet in Beaverbrook's own room. Beaverbrook retaliated by continuing to work at his desk during the meetings.

Here again the hand of friendship was refused. Beaverbrook wrote: 'How I would like to give support in complete agreement with you and your policy.' Bevin replied: 'I have no policy or platform except that of the Government as a whole, arrived at through the War Cabinet.' In the summer of 1942, according to Bevin's own account, which no doubt grew in the telling, Beaverbrook, then out of the Government, told Bevin that Churchill was on the way out and offered to help make Bevin Prime Minister instead. Bevin indignantly went off to Churchill, who refused to believe him. Bevin complained of Churchill's relationship with Beaverbrook: 'He's like a man who's married a whore: he knows she's a whore but he loves her just the same.'

Despite his parade of loyalty, Bevin usually spoke of 'my policy' and described the working class as 'my people.' Any workers who opposed him were liable to be dismissed as Trotskyites – a charge which even Alan Bullock finds difficult to sustain. Beaverbrook once described himself as 'the cat that walks alone.' Bevin was a tiger who walked alone, and woe betide any who came near him. He was an elemental force, invaluable in wartime. But it is not surprising that other members of the Labour Party fell out with him. Bevin often bullied for a good cause: he was a bully all the same.

III WRITERS

This section is regrettably short. I originally aspired to be a literary critic and indeed the first article I published, now lost in the sands of time, was on Forster's Life of Dickens. *I have read most of the English classics, often many times over, with Boswell's Johnson of course at the head of the list. But my mind was too prosaic to cope with the higher flights of literature and I settled for history which, I suppose, is a modest form of literature itself. However by a fortunate chance this section present the contemporary writers whom I read most often and with most pleasure, perhaps even with most profit, when I was young.*

26. Shaw The Court Jester.[1]

An article written for the centenary of Shaw's birth on 26 July, 1856. Perhaps this essay is a little ungrateful in view of the pleasure and intellectual stimulus I derived from Shaw's writings. Even if he had nothing to say, he said it incomparably well.

Bernard Shaw lived to be ninety-four, and we are still dominated by personal memories on the hundredth anniversary of his birth. In time these will fade. The rich brogue and challenging beard, the homespun knickerbocker suit and the infectious laugh, the inexhaustible appetite for jest and controversy – they will become incidents in volumes of reminiscences. Sooner or later we must ask – what of Shaw as a writer? Still more, what of Shaw as he claimed to be, a sage and philosopher? Will he last as long as Shakespeare? Or will he be forgotten like his contemporary Stephen Phillips?

We ought to be able to answer these questions even now. For though Shaw the man was with us until just the other day, Shaw the writer had worn out long before. Indeed, the creative Shaw had a curiously short run. He wrote his first play when he was nearly forty. *Saint Joan*, his last serious achievement, came out in 1924 – a working span of less than thirty years and an ironic comment on his view that men would achieve more by living longer.

Shaw had one superlative quality. He was the greatest arguer there has ever been. All Irishmen have the gift of the gab. Shaw out-talked everyone for fifty years. He was greater than Burke, greater than Swift, in the art of political advocacy. Start reading a preface or play at any point, and you are swept away by the torrent of words, all criticism or doubt bludgeoned down. But scramble to

[1]*Observer*, 1956.

the bank, recover your sense, and look around. Shaw was marvellous over a short distance; he could not sustain an argument for more than a paragraph.

This is why plays suited him so well. A second character could always interrupt when the first ran dry. There is no development; only statement and counter-statement. All Shaw's plays anticipate the round-table discussions which are now a stock-in-trade of radio – discussions without shape or conclusion, designed to show off the personality of the four distinguished contributors.

The Intelligent Woman's Guide showed most clearly Shaw's lack of staying-power. Though no one else could have written such dazzling pages, any intelligent woman could have written a better guide to almost anything – as one intelligent woman, Beatrice Webb, remarked.

Shaw was an Irishman of the ascendancy, straddling between England and Ireland, and despising both. He had the arrogance which comes of belonging to a master-race – always ready to assert his own opinion and to reject authority. But he had also the sycophancy which comes of being a poor relation. Just as Burke always curried favour with his patron, the Marquis of Rockingham, so Shaw never offended his patrons, the enlightened *rentiers* of Edwardian England who filled the stalls for his plays and bought his books. He was outrageous only on things that were too silly to matter – defending the Flat Earth theory or jeering at medical science. Fine stuff to make a boy think when he is working for a scholarship, but not dangerous.

On all serious questions Shaw came down firmly on the side of the stronger, though satisfying his conscience by the use of perverse arguments, much like Sir Henry Wilson – his fellow Irishman. He supported the Boer War and welcomed the first war against Germany as 'the last spring of the old Lion'; the neutrality of Belgium was, he held, a fiction, and British policy a trap for Germany deliberately laid by Sir Edward Grey. He worshipped strong men. In his prime he chose Julius Casear and Napoleon as the heroes of his historical plays; and he outdid all contemporaries in his admiration for Mussolini and Stalin. Even when he glorified a heretic he took care to choose Joan of Arc – someone safely canonised and not associated with any really dangerous idea. William Morris dreamt of John Ball. But Morris had really burnt his boats so far as the governing classes were concerned. Shaw was a court jester who never lost his place at the high table.

He was certainly a Socialist, and a hard-working one. But his Socialism was 'off-stage,' like Rigoletto's life with his daughter. And even this Socialism sprang from intellectual arrogance, not from sympathy. To Shaw every workingman was a Caliban, to be despised or, sometimes, feared. The working-classes were brought in to his plays as comic relief – dustmen or chauffeurs, caricatured and debauched to make sport for their betters. Shaw was the most snobbish of all English writers; the more offensive when he disguised his snobbery as worship of the Superman.

Revealed religion had lost its force in the England of his day, and instead every literary man was expected to have a 'message.' Shaw did his best to oblige; he, too, would be a moral teacher. A comparison with Wells shows how tawdry Shaw's message was. Wells really understood the barrenness and frustration of contemporary society, and he had a vision of a more constructive, hopeful future. Shaw was merely impatient with human stupidity, and supposed that this would be cured if men tried to live longer. He learnt a twaddle of biology secondhand from Samuel Butler, and the only man who has ever applied this Shavian biology is Lysenko, hardly a disciple to be proud of.

Shaw despised humanity, despite his desire to prolong men's days. He was himself always rational, never knew passion either for good or ill. He was incapable of resentment, but also incapable of love. This gives his plays their peculiar character. The essence of drama is human tension : there is no tension in Shaw's plays, only debate. What playgoer has sat forward in his stall, racked with anxiety whether Ann Whitefield will marry John Tanner?

Shaw was a materialist in the strictest sense – a true representative of the Edwardian age in which he flourished best. He loved money, and the things that money would buy – tasteless comfort in *de luxe* hotels, swimming in heated baths and warm southern seas. He was a teetotaller, a vegetarian, a non-smoker, not from asceticism, but in order to savour the pleasures of life more. One has the feeling that Shaw was never unhappy, and therefore he was never happy either. He knew only pleasure, a very different thing.

At the end of his life Shaw confessed that he stood for Nothing. He, the missionary, the advocate, the Socialist, might have been expected to bequeath his hoarded wealth to some great cause. The only one he could think of was the promotion of a new alphabet –

not even words, but letters. The magic of Shaw's words may still bewitch posterity. It will applaud the last sentence of *Man and Superman* : 'Go on talking.' But it will find that he has nothing to say.

27.   The Man Who Tried to Work Miracles.[1]

An article for the centenary of H G Wells's birth on 21 September 1866. Though I owe more to Bernard Shaw than to any other single writer, I owe more to H G Wells's *Outline of History* than to any other single book.

H G Wells did not expect to last. He did not even want to last, or so he claimed: 'What I write goes now – and will presently die'. He was not interested in being a literary artist, though he had in fact great literary gifts. He was, he insisted, a journalist, someone who wrote for the day and who 'delivered the goods.' He would be disappointed if the hundredth anniversary of his birth were marked only by discussions of Wells as a novelist. He would want to know what had happened to his ideas. Had men listened to his message? Had they taken what he believed to be the only way to salvation? The answer would be at first sight even more disappointing for him. His novels and scientific romances survive as entertainment – widely read in paperbacks. Hardly anyone bothers about Wells as a thinker, perhaps no one except a devoted young American, W Warren Wager, who has written a book about *H G Wells and the World State* and has produced more recently an anthology of Wells's prophetic writings.

Still I would not dismiss Wells lightly. Going back to his books after not reading them for many years, I found all sorts of ideas which are running round the world with little appreciation that Wells started them. Not that his ideas were as original as he claimed. Wells was more a representative man than an originator. This does not make him any the less interesting. Of course his literary gifts are what really count, whatever Wells said in depreciation of them.

[1] *Listener,* 1966.

Taken simply as a writer, Wells had two qualities, and these keep him alive. The first was a gift for social comedy. His best book, *The History of Mr Polly*, is a work of irresistible fun. I would say the same, with some reservations, about *Tono-Bungay* and, with more, about *Kipps*. But even his least inspired books have occasional flashes of the same spirit. None of his characters is real – and that goes, to my mind, even for the much-vaunted *Ann Veronica*. They are caricatures or Humours in the Jonsonian sense. Mr Pooter, also a comic figure, is a hundred times more real than Mr Polly – you can still meet him in many a suburban street. Does anyone believe in Mr Polly, in Uncle Ponderevo or in Kipps? They are creatures of fantasy to whom comic things happen.

And not only comic things. Each book by Wells begins more or less realistically, usually in rather depressing surroundings, and then the principal character escapes by a miracle. I do not mean merely by an unlikely twist. I mean by something preposterously impossible. Mr Polly finds an impossible plump middle-aged woman, who owns an impossible riverside inn. Uncle Ponderevo invents an impossible patent medicine and makes an impossible fortune. Kipps comes into an impossible fortune not once but twice. None of Wells's characters gets out of his difficulties by his own strength. The escape comes from outside. It happens to him. The characters who do not escape go off at the end of the book to 'think things out', an implication that they will rescue themselves. But if they have not managed to 'think things out' during the course of a long book – and they never have – why should they succeed afterwards? Thinking things out only means waiting for a miracle instead of experiencing one.

The need for a miracle even in Wells's apparently realistic novels was of course much greater in his scientific fantasies, was indeed the essence of them. This was Wells's other great gift, one still more unusual – I would venture to say unique. He could pretend and then take the pretence seriously. He would postulate one simple impossible step – a food which produced giants, a man who slept for 200 years, a war of the worlds – and then he would work out calmly, realistically, what would follow. The overwhelming feature of his scientific fantasies is that they are not fantasies, except for the one impossible twist. They are exactly what would happen 'if only . . .'

Wells could really live in the imaginary situation which he had created and sometimes, to his dismay, his imagination took him prisoner. He always wanted a glowing future, but the future of his fantasies often turned out to be most unpleasant. At any rate, for good or ill, Wells in these fantasies was 'the man who could work miracles' – the title of one of his stories which was later made into a film.

Wells, the thinker and prophet, was the same: he could work miracles, or at any rate wanted to work them. Here again he had the right patter and often the right imagination. He made many inspired guesses about the future developments of machines. For instance he described full-scale battles in the air almost before heavier-than-air machines had got off the ground. He announced more than fifty years ago that men would get to the moon, though he did not foretell correctly what they would find when they got there – but this is hardly surprising, for it seems that they found precisely nothing. At a time when motor-cars had hardly started, Wells foresaw that the traffic in cities would grind to a halt, as we all know it is doing, and he anticipated other, more sensible forms of transport, such as moving platforms – an idea which is just being aired now. He also foresaw that, thanks to the motor-car, everyone would desert cities for the country and that, in this way, the country would disappear, another gloomy and correct prophecy. He had unbounded faith in the beneficent effects of electricity, a faith which he shared with Lenin, and expected that electrical devices would end the drudgery of housework. And so they have, though only at the price of turning the housewife into their slave. He was sure that one day we should all live on a scientific diet of pills, another prophecy which threatens to come true.

These prophecies were wrapped up in scientific jargon. Underneath they were merely inspired guesses and just as likely to be wrong as right. Wells did not really understand what he was talking about. If he wanted something, he assumed that there was a way in which it would happen. For instance, in 1903 he foresaw mechanical monsters fighting each other in a future war and was later aggrieved when the credit for inventing the tank was denied to him. But he had never faced the technical problems involved in building tanks. He merely described what he wanted and left someone else to work it out. And, though he was right about tanks, he was wrong about the answer to them. Writing in the nineteen thirties about the next war, he imagined that tanks would be stopped by vast ditches dug across Europe and filled with slime. The more prosaic, successful answer was the anti-tank gun. Wells's inventions for the future brought him much reputation, but of course they were the product of a lively imagination, not the serious work of a disciplined technician. This hardly mattered. They were fun, and the books built round them made good reading.

But the mix-up between what could be and what Wells wanted mattered a good deal more when he came to deal with man. This was Wells's serious concern as a thinker. He was amused to speculate on the ways in which machines could develop. He was passionately resolved on changing man's behaviour, and he believed that this could be done only by changing man himself – changing him in a specifically biological way. Wells claimed that the miracle could be worked by Science, very much with a capital S. Actually it was his own obstinate will: an impatient insistence that the change must happen. The word science was used simply as an incantation. Wells himself claimed to be a scientist. At any rate he had had some elementary training in biology under the great T H Huxley. He learnt the doctrine of evolution at its most confident. But he does not seem to have understood what he learnt. If evolution teaches anything, it is that the process of biological change is very slow. It took millions of years to evolve mammals; hundreds of thousands, if not millions, to evolve man. It is surely inconceivable that there should have been any biological evolution in man – any change in his natural make-up – during the few thousand years of civilisation, and still more inconceivable that man should have changed during the 150 years or so since the French revolution and the coming of modern industry.

Wells seems to have expected that men would change, you cannot call it evolve, more or less overnight, say in a couple of centuries; and of course men do change their behaviour and even, to some extent, their physical character quite quickly. For instance, the average height of Englishmen has increased markedly in the last fifty years, but such changes have nothing to do with biological evolution. They occur because of what happens to men after they are born, not because of a change in their nature. Englishmen are taller because they, and particularly the lower classes, are better fed than they used to be. Put them back on their old, inferior diet, and the next generation would be back where they started. It is the same with behaviour. Men are warlike or peaceful, brutal or tolerant, religious or atheistic, because that is what they have been taught to be, not because of something in their nature. Wells's appeal to evolution was sales-talk, irrelevant to what really happened. At best if provided him with analogies and dangerous analogies at that.

The danger was greater still when Wells shifted from man to society and treated even this in biological terms. He regarded society as a sort of animal, subject to the laws of evolution. This is a common trick of historians or, I would prefer to say, of writers who make sweeping generalisations about the past. They talk about old societies, mature societies, even about decaying societies – useful analogies perhaps, but no more. If a man has been around on the earth for a long time, he will really be 'old' – his bones will creak, his physical powers will be failing, within a fairly limited time he will die. But there is no reason whatever to suppose that any of this will apply to a society. It may amuse us, it certainly amuses me, to make out that Great Britain is a mature society, wise, experienced, sensible, while the United States are brash, new, blundering, just because our history starts with Boadicea and theirs with George Washington. But we know that it is nonsense, good for a laugh and no more. Wells took the claptrap seriously, as other pontificators about history do. All his thought, if it can be dignified with that word, revolves round the analogy with evolution. Animals adapted themselves to their surroundings, and those who adapted themselves best survived. Men will do the same in their social behaviour. Wells believed that he had only to point out what was wrong in society and evolution would step in to put it right. Things had been getting better up to now and therefore we were bound to arrive at Utopia.

Wells condemned the contemporary world in every novel and other sort of book that he wrote. The first words uttered by Mr Polly, as he sat on a stile, can serve as the theme for all Wells's writing: 'Hole! 'Ole! Oh! Beastly Silly Wheeze of a hole!' But why was the world a hole? It is easy to understand why Mr Polly felt so that afternoon. He owned a shop which did not pay and his wife produced meals which gave him indigestion. These are individual misfortunes which happen to many individuals. Wells insists on generalising them. He writes solemnly that Mr Polly was 'one of those ill-adjusted units that abound in a society that has failed to develop a collective intelligence and a collective will for order commensurate with its complexities'. There is an implication, you see, that in a well-ordered society there will be no inefficient shopkeepers and of course no indigestion.

Wells was not only generalising from Mr Polly. He was generalising from himself. He had been a shop-assistant. He had hated it.

He escaped to become a writer. Very considerately, he wanted this to happen to all other shop-assistants – a miracle, in fact; and, though considerate, like so much of Wells's or any other high-minded kindness, very wrong-headed. There are writers, potential or otherwise, who would hate to be shopkeepers. But there are far more shopkeepers who would hate to be writers. Wells had the snobbishness which nearly always goes with intellectual activities. He thought his way of life superior and he wanted to provide it for others.

This was the 'confusion' which he saw in society – too many shopkeepers, not enough devoted thinkers. There was another confusion which bulked large in Wells's novels and which indeed bulked large in his life – the relations between men and women. Somehow they rarely hit it off. Wells seems to have thought that, in a well ordered society, all would come right of itself, by which he really meant that women would fit in with men's moods. Sometimes they would be satisfied with casual relations; when required, they would settle for something more permanent. But they would never try to hold a man if he wanted to move off. The modern state, as he put it, 'must refuse absolutely to recognise or enforce any kind of sexual ownership'. This deserves a top prize for Utopia. I suspect Meredith was wiser when he said that woman would be the last thing to be civilised by man.

Wells started before the first world war by wanting to put society right. That war led him into wanting to put the world right as well. At once he jumped the whole way: there must be a world-state, and that without delay. The final illustration in his *Outline of History* is a map of the world, and scrawled across it in bold letters the words: The United States of the World. He often implied that this would come of itself, according to the supposed laws of evolution. For instince, he says in his *Experiment in Autobiography* :

> A planned world-state . . . is, we perceive, as much a part of the frame in which our lives are set as the roundness and rotation of the earth, as the pressure of the atmosphere or the force of gravitation at the sea level.

And again :

> The modern world-state which was a mere dream in 1900 is today a practicable objective; it towers high above the times. The

socialist world-state has now become a tomorrow as real as today. Thither we go.

But sometimes he had qualms that we were not going there at all. Wells always bounced easily from optimism to despair. In *Boon*, a book which he wrote in 1915, he discovered the Mind of the Race, which was working for salvation. But he concluded also that the Wild Asses of the Devil were loose – a more likely verdict on the twentieth century.

If the world-state was not coming of itself, what were we to do? Sometimes Wells implied that there was a superior moral force, pulling things the way in which he wanted them to go – in a phrase borrowed from Matthew Arnold 'that something not ourselves that makes for righteousness'. But he soon confessed that God, in his view, was merely another name for his own wishes. He wrote :

> My deity was far less like the Heavenly Father of a devout Catholic . . . than he was like a personification of, let us say, the Five Year Plan.

Wells admitted, indeed boasted, that he was very near the communist outlook. Just as the five-year plan was imposed on Russia by Stalin, the world-state was to be imposed by Wells and a few other enlightened intellectuals – what he called the Open Conspiracy. In his own words: 'If Russia has done nothing else for mankind, the experiment of the Communist Party is alone sufficient to justify her revolution'. He insisted however that there was one great difference. Communism was based on class-war and sought to set up the dictatorship of the proletariat. The Open Conspiracy would be composed of anyone intelligent enough to accept Wells's ideas, and principally by the men with real power. Wells thought that the captains of industry and finance would save the world. William Clissold, one of his fictional mouthpieces, announces : 'I shall travel on the Blue Train to the end of the chapter'. This seems to me another fantasy, more Utopian than the rest. All experience teaches that, if an élite run affairs, they do so in their own interests, and this is perhaps truer of businessmen than of any other so-called élite.

Wells became more and more convinced that knowledge would transform the world, if only there were enough of it. In *The Canford Visitation*, which he wrote in 1937, he imagines a supernatural voice, pointing the way of salvation:

There can be no escape for your world, for all mankind, from the ages of tragic conflict ahead of you, except so heroic an ordering of knowledge, so valiant a beating out of opinions, such a refreshment of teaching and such an organisation of brains as will constitute a real and living world university, head, eyes and purpose of Man. That is the primary need of your species now. It is your world's primary want. It must come now – if it ever is to come.

In *Babes in the Darkling Wood*, published in 1940, the hero says much the same :

> The Right Thing to Do will be to have a vast, ordered, encyclopedia of fact and thought for its Bible, and a gigantic organisation not only of research and record, but of devoted teachers and interpreters. A World Church, a World Brain, and a World Will. . . . We have to find out all that there is to be known and what is afoot in those various movements for documentation, for bibliography, for indexing, for all that micro-photographic recording one hears about distantly and dimly. Make understandings and more understandings. That is the reality of life for every human being.

This is the great contemporary delusion at its wildest : the belief that if only we accumulate enough facts, enough knowledge, the answer will emerge of itself. The facts will provide their own solution. Think of the pundits all over the world who are writing long solemn books about the problem of nuclear warfare and they are no nearer a solution. Yet any child could tell them what to do with nuclear weapons : 'Don't have them'.

Wells not only demanded ideas; he provided them. He had an unlimited faith in the power of education, and himself wrote books with an educational purpose – an outline of biology, an outline of economics, and, his most successful, an *Outline of History*. This at any rate is not only still read; it is the best general survey of man's history that there is. Wells wrote it to demonstrate that knowledge was superior to art and literature. He remarked slightingly : 'An industrious treatment of early nineteenth-century records would make Balzac's *Comédie Humaine* seem flighty stuff' – a view which Karl Marx would not have agreed with. The *Outline of History* was supposed to demonstrate that all recorded history had been moving fumblingly forward towards a planned world-state. It totally fails to demonstrate anything of the kind. It shows that men have always been in conflict and that the rich have always exploited the poor. Sometimes one state or one group in a civilisation has come to dominate all the others. This is done by superior force and nothing else. Most people, including Wells, sentimentalise their view of the past. They like to think that the Better Side wins. It doesn't. The Stronger Side wins. The Romans were not more civilised or more enlightened than the Greeks. They merely possessed a more efficient fighting machine. When Europeans established their authority throughout the world in the nineteenth century this was not because they were more civilised. It was because, in Hilaire Belloc's words: 'We have the Maxim gun, and they have not'. One conqueror, one potential uniter of Europe, perhaps represented a superior cause to the states he conquered. This was Napoleon. No one comes in for rougher treatment in Wells's *Outline of History*.

The *Outline* has a drawing of various national symbols, entitled Tribal Gods for which men would die. This is a true verdict on the history of the last 150 years. More men have died willingly for national loyalty than for any other cause. There is no heroism, and also practically no crime, which they will not perform in its name. If we draw any historical moral from this, it can only be that national states are not likely to vanish, though they may be conquered. Wells repudiated this moral: it did not accord with the world-state. He condemned men for their national loyalties. Though he wrote the *Outline* in order to show that history was going his way, in fact he demanded that men should abandon all their historical habits and behave in exactly the opposite fashion to that in which they had behaved throughout all recorded time. And of course they may. This is why it is so pointless to ask a historian to foretell the future. He can only say what will happen if men go on behaving as they have done in the past. For instance, if the past is any guide, the deterrent will one day fail to deter. There will be nuclear war, and all mankind will be destroyed. If you want the future to be different, the best thing is to forget history, not to try to extract morals from it.

Wells wanted a miracle, that men should change their nature. As he put it in the *Croquet Player*: 'Only giants can save the world from complete relapse and so we — we who care for civilisation — have to become giants'. He was far from becoming a giant himself. Though he condemned the tribal gods of nationalism in theory, no one was a more fervent patriot when it came to war against Germany. In the first world war he wanted to bomb Essen — 'a daily service of destruction to Germany'. In the second world war he declared that afterwards 'a few score thousand [German] criminals need to be shot', and then the world would be all right. Underneath he was too honest to imagine that his Utopia would really work. When he really imagined the future, in his scientific romances, he foresaw that a few clever men would still be exploiting all the rest. When the Sleeper awakes, for instance, 200 years hence, he discovers that the mass of mankind have become slaves, and the Sleeper raises an insurrection in the cause of old-fashioned freedom.

The contradiction was typical of Wells and rather endearing. He was by nature a radical, a rebel – one of the few Englishmen incidentally who still wrote diatribes against the monarchy. He knew instinctively that dictatorship, ordering people about, would not save them, and yet he could not think of any other way of doing it. In his ideal state, only one set of ideas would be allowed – his own:

> Only one body of philosophy and only one religion, only one statement of men's relation to the universe and the community, can exist in a unified world state.

This is a recipe for stagnation and disaster. Besides, if men turned to the writings of the master for instruction, what would they find? Instead of clear guidance, they would find chaos and confusion. Wells insisted, times without number, on the need for hard precise thinking. He was himself incapable of it. Every attempt at discussion in his books tails off with four dots in a row – a sort of 'to be continued in our next'. The great prophets of mankind are remembered by a single book, even if they wrote many. Rousseau is remembered by *The Social Contract*; Marx by *Capital*; Darwin by *The Origin of Species*. Wells put himself in their class. Indeed he claimed to be a better thinker than any of them. He wrote more than a hundred books. But when we ask: in which of them is the gospel according to Wells to be found? the answer is always: in the next book that Wells is going to write.

Actually his last book announced that there was no answer. Men had failed to listen to his teaching. Therefore they were doomed. He wanted his epitaph to be: 'God damn you all. I told you so'. He had imagined himself as God and was embittered when others did not acknowledge his divinity. But Wells was not God, was not even an inspired prophet. He was a spluttering imaginative little man in a hurry, bouncing from one contradiction to the next. His writings reflected the confusions and delusions of his age. There is not much wisdom in them, but there is a good deal of humanity. Maybe no one reads Wells any more for guidance – there are newer, equally muddled thinkers who provide that. We read Wells now for fun – the fun of the scientific romances, the fun of *Mr Polly*, even the fun to be found in *The Outline of History*. And fun is a great deal better than worshipping the golden calf of knowledge.

28. Stout Little Ghost.[1]

A review of *The Magic Years of Beatrix Potter* by Margaret Lane (Warne).

More than 30 years ago Margaret Lane wrote 'The Tale of Beatrix Potter,' which ranks high among the biographies of our century. Now the great archive of Beatrix Potter's drawings, letters and diaries (more than 200,000 words in code) has drawn her back to her favourite theme, which is also one of mine.

This is a biography with a difference. There is the same story of the solitary little girl and young woman who became for a few years a writer of genius and then settled down as a successful sheep farmer and happily married woman with her artistic genius exhausted. But the emphasis this time is on the evolution of Beatrix Potter's art and its translation into some of the greatest books for children.

Beatrix Potter was a gifted artist from her earliest years, always stronger on animals than on human beings. Millais said to her, 'Plenty of people can draw but you and my son John have observation,' on which Beatrix privately noted, 'John at that date couldn't draw at all, but I know exactly what he meant.' Beatrix was also a proficient naturalist, presenting – though not being allowed to read – a paper to the Linnaean Society on the spores of moulds. After seeing a meteor she commented, 'I do not often consider the stars . . . it is more than enough that there should be 40,000 named and classified funguses.'

Her principal characters lived with her long before they entered literature. Peter Rabbit was with her for nine years and she recorded after his death, 'Whatever the limitations of his intellect or outward shortcomings of his fur, and ears and toes, his disposition was uniformly amiable and his temper unfailingly sweet. An affectionate companion and a quiet friend.' Mrs Tiggy-winkle was 'a very stout short person': 'she enjoys going by train, she is always very hungry

[1]*Observer*, 1978.

when on a journey.' I doubt whether Beatrix had more than a cursory acquaintance with Mr Jeremy Fisher.

Beatrix once explained her secret: 'It is much more satisfactory to address a real live child. I often think that was the secret of the success of "Peter Rabbit"; it was written to a child – not made to order.' The censorship exercised by her publisher is very funny. He early cut out a scene from 'The Tailor of Gloucester,' showing rats carousing. He objected to *'all* the rest of Tom's clothes came off' and suggested *'nearly* all.' Beatrix replied, ' "Nearly all" won't do! because I have drawn Thomas already with *nothing*!' He changed wood-lice to creepy-crawly creatures and disliked the opening of Mr Tod as 'a story about two disagreeable people,' to which Beatrix replied, 'You are a great deal too much afraid of the public, for whom I have never cared about a tuppeny button.'

Beatrix Potter certainly did not care about critics or biographers. She described praise of her art as 'great rubbish, absolute bosh' and dismissed the critic with the tart postscript, 'When a person has been nearly 30 years married it is not ingratiating to get an envelope addressed to "Miss." ' Margaret Lane also received an abrupt rejection when she proposed to write Beatrix's life. 'My books have always sold without advertisement, and I do not propose to go in for that sort of thing now.' Margaret Lane persisted after Beatrix's death and, with the somewhat apprehensive assistance of William Heelis, Beatrix's husband, produced her marvellous biography. Now she has delighted us again. In conclusion she does not believe 'that the stout little ghost which haunts the place would still, after all this time, find it necessary to be angry.' In believing this, Margaret Lane is optimistic.

Margaret Lane is not altogether sound in her geography. At one point she places Sawrey in Cumberland which it never was. She refers to a non-existent Coniston Fell which should be Coniston Old Man. The Quaker Meeting House where Beatrix listened to a robin singing in the copper beech outside the porch, adding 'I doubt if his sentiments were religious,' is at Colthouse, which is some miles from Sawrey.

Margaret Lane has no special enthusiasm for 'The Tailor of Gloucester'. I rank it with the masterpieces of Balzac. On the other hand I do not regard 'The Tale of Samuel Whiskers' as indisputably 'her masterpiece'. May be they are all masterpieces. I am told that now only very middle-class children enjoys the works of Beatrix Potter. So much the worse for the rest of the juvenile population.

29. The Rogue Elephant.[1]

A review of *The Life of Hilaire Belloc* by Robert Speaight (Methuen).

Literature has its fashions like dress; and Hilaire Belloc is neglected at present along with his contemporaries. Will he survive at all? I find myself almost alone in the opinion that he and Wells are the writers of their generation safe for immortality. And this though I dislike most of his opinions – on history, on religion, sometimes on politics. I can feel nothing real in his serious verse, and even his prose style often irritates me. It is easier to catalogue his defects than his virtues. Yet there are no books that I look back to with more gratitude or read again with more pleasure.

Belloc exploded sham when it was more secure than it is now; but he resented the price he had to pay. He was a rogue elephant who enjoyed trampling down other people's fences and yet expected society to provide him with rewards. He was Lucky Jim born at a less suitable time. For nowadays Lucky Jim is happy enough at the devastation he causes and even achieves modest security as lecturer at a provincial university. Belloc missed election at All Souls and complained about it ever afterwards. When a young journalist asked his rule for happiness, Belloc replied: ' I have none. You can't be happy. Don't try. Cut it out. Make up your mind to be miserable.'

Belloc was always restless and always shouting – perhaps to silence his doubts and disappointments. He could not sit through a single act of a play; and, on arriving in a strange town, he immediately looked up the time of a train to take him away. His impatient assertiveness was a failure in the House of Commons and he wore his voice out on the hustings almost before the campaign began. One has the feeling that he could not drink a pint of beer without exclaim-

[1]*Observer*, 1957.

ing: 'Look, I am drinking beer.' His best book, *The Path to Rome,* takes place in the open air; all his books have to be read out of doors – you feel battered by them in a room. He had a rather tiresome trick of despising his readers, and not them only. When taking the chair at a debate between Shaw and Chesterton, he announced: 'They are about to debate. You are about to listen. I am about to sneer.'

His own dogmatism was ruthless. When asked how he could possibly believe that the Bread and Wine were really changed into the Body and Blood of Christ, he replied that he would believe that they were changed into an elephant, if the Church told him so. It is not surprising that he made few converts. Mr Speaight says rather that he restored the self-confidence of English Roman Catholics – and this may well be true.

Mr Speaight has written what is described as the official biography – that is, it was written at the request of Belloc's literary executors. The book is admirably full and surprisingly critical. Indeed it is rather odd that I should have to defend Belloc against his chosen biographer. Mr Speaight admires Belloc, but he is also rather embarrassed by him. He extols Belloc the sincere Roman Catholic and Belloc the romantic poet. He is less happy about Belloc the politician and social critic. His account of the Marconi Scandal, for instance, is as cautious and non-committal as any speculator could wish. The reader who wants to know what all the fuss was about must turn to the memoir of Belloc by his daughter and son-in-law, published last year. Suppose the affair had gone to a Special Tribunal, such as dealt with J H Thomas and Sidney Stanley, what would have been the verdict? My guess is that a future Prime Minister and a future Lord Chief Justice would have seen their careers sharply interrupted. The trouble with Mr Speaight is that he thinks there is nothing wrong with the English upper classes. Belloc slipped into this view later in life; and how relieved Mr Speaight is when Belloc strikes up in friendship with Lord Derby. But earlier on Belloc was savagely opposed to the system of influence and corruption by which our affairs are conducted.

Mr Speaight slides over Belloc's political novels. To my mind they are the best of their kind in English, as well as being very funny. You can see Mr Speaight, in his respectable, latter-day Roman Catholicism, puzzling what they are all about. They seem to him pure fantasy, and antiquated fantasy at that. Yet *Emmanuel Burden* throws a piercing light on the Imperialism which caused the Boer War; and, as to their being out of date, anyone who wants to know how our present Government was constructed will find a precise and detailed account of it in *A Change in the Cabinet,* which Belloc published in 1909. Of course, there is now a real difference between the Conservative and Labour parties, as Mr Speaight says. It is the difference between Eton and Winchester.

Mr Speaight is more effective in his appreciation of Belloc's historical writings, though their vision was more creative and the facts perhaps shakier than he makes out. He is warm, as other friends have been, in personal affection. Yet the full power of Belloc is somehow muted. One gets the impression that homecoming is the best part of a stormy voyage. No doubt Belloc felt this himself towards the end of his life; but he had done much navigating in rough weather before that. The Belloc of tumult and conflict is the one who is still alive.

IV SOCIALISTS and SOCIALISM

30.   Marx's Better Half.[1]

A review of *The Life of Friedrich Engels* by W O Henderson
(Frank Cass).

The original name of the firm was Marx and Engels: Socialism,
Wholesale, Retail and for Export. Later, when new partners joined
(Marxist-Leninism, Marxist-Leninist-Stalinism, Trotskyism) Engels
disappeared from the letter-heading. Now Yugoslavia is the only
Communist country I know where the portrait of Engels is displayed
alongside that of Marx in town halls and Government offices. Books
on Marxism, when they mention Engels at all, present him only as
Marx's loyal disciple, whose principal contribution was to provide
Marx with money.

Engels deserves more extended treatment. Though he had talent
where Marx had genius – Huxley to Marx's Darwin – he often for-
mulated Marxist concepts clearly before Marx did. His Communist
Catechism, for instance, with its 25 points is dull reading compared
to The Communist Manifesto, but all the ideas of the Manifesto are
already in it.

In some ways, too, Engels was the more interesting character.
Marx was a staid bourgeois apart from his ideas. Engels, despite being
a prosperous cotton merchant, tried to formulate a life style appropriate to a Socialist. He lived happily for many years with an Irish
factory-girl, Mary Burns, and, after her death, with her sister Lizzie
whom he married only the day before she died. Jenny Marx, Marx's
aristocratic wife, would not tolerate either of these women in her
presence and Marx conformed to the ban.

Dr Henderson has at last presented Engels as an independent
figure. His book is very much a DIY biography. The evidence, largely
from the Marx-Engels correspondence, is exhaustively marshalled.
Few conclusions are drawn and there is none of the psychological

[1] *Observer,* 1976.

153

penetration shown in the exciting book on Engels and Manchester by Steven Marcus. On the relations between Engels and his father, Henderson is content to quote the father's complaint, 'It is a heavy cross to bear that I have a son at home who is like a scabby sheep in the flock.' Marcus shows that the father helped the publication of *The Condition of the English Working Class in England in 1844* and later welcomed the son as a partner despite his revolutionary activities.

The Condition of the Working Class in England in 1844 was indeed the beginning of Marxism, far more so than Marx's cantankerous philosophising of the same period. Engels discovered the class war in industry between capitalists and proletarians and foretold that this could end only with the victory of socialism. Marx snatched at the idea and made it the foundation of his system. In 1845 Marx went to Manchester with Engels for four days, most of them spent in Chetham's Library. He went again for a single afternoon in 1865. These were the only occasions when Marx actually set eyes on the Lancashire cotton industry. Engels lived amongst it for 20 years.

The failure of the revolutions of 1848 pushed Engels back into a business career. An even stronger motive was Marx's constant need for money. Marx was a true Micawber who thought that the world owed him a living. Engels provided the answer. He kept Marx for over 30 years and on no mean scale. As Henderson points out, when Marx praised the Paris Commune for fixing the top salary of public officials at £240 a year, this was a great deal less than Engels paid Marx. He also bequeathed most of his fortune, some £30,000, to Marx's daughters or their descendants. Engels performed further services. He allowed Marx to father on him the illegitimate son of the Marx's housekeeper, Helene Demuth, and returned the boy to the true father, Karl Marx, only on his deathbed.

Engels's greatest service to Marx was in the realm of ideas. He turned Marx's brilliant insights into orderly exposition. Most of the precise statements of Marxism as a system derive from Engels. He often provided essential information. Marx, not surprisingly, had no idea how banking and finance worked in practice; Engels told him. Marx was a disorderly scholar, for ever turning aside from his central theme to run after attractive irrelevancies. The first volume of *Capital* was published only after many years of exhortation by Engels and then in an incomplete form. Marx did not complete the other two volumes at all. When Engels tried to make something of them, he found only a chaos of detached scraps, some in English, some in

French, some in German. Engels wrote most of the newspaper articles with which Marx supplemented his income, though Marx sometimes livened them up. When the first volume of *Capital* appeared, Engels wrote many reviews in German periodicals under different names and in different styles. His devotion never wearied.

Engels had also a remarkable life of his own. He kept two establishments in Manchester: bachelor's lodgings where he entertained his rich friends and a suburban house with Mary Burns where he entertained fellow socialists. He acquired considerable reputation as a writer on military affairs, not always getting things right. Though he was wrong in expecting an Austrian victory in 1866, he correctly divined Moltke's strategy in 1870.

Engels remained very much a German despite his 50 years in England. He was chairman of the Schiller Anstalt in Manchester and a founder of the Hallé Orchestra. During the Franco-Prussian war he raised money to provide relief for the German wounded and did not raise any money for the French. His views on the Slavs were indistinguishable from those of Hitler. He wrote in 1849:

> The universal war which is coming will crush the Slav alliance and will wipe out completely those obstinate peoples so that their very name will be forgotten ... The next world war will wipe out not only reactionary classes and dynasties but it will also destroy those utterly reactionary races. . . . And that will be a real step forward.

While in Manchester, Engels went out two days a week with the Cheshire Hunt, claiming that this was good training for the cavalry general of a future revolutionary war. In London he acquired a large house in Regent's Park Road and often ascended Primrose Hill, surveying London with a strategist's eye. After Lizzie Burns's death and Marx's, Helene Demuth kept house for him, a curious arrangement, and after her death Kautsky's divorced wife, which was also odd. Engels was now The General, acknowledged high priest of Marxism. He lived long enough to see the foundation of the Second International and addressed its Zürich conference of 1893, ending with the words, 'Long live the international proletariat.'

Marx and Engels in their deaths were characteristically divided. Marx had a conventional funeral and was buried beside his wife in Highgate Cemetery. Engels was cremated and his ashes were scattered in the sea off Beachy Head. The German Social Democrats claimed to be his ideological heirs. Henderson takes a different view. The biography of Engels ends with a sentence describing Lenin as 'the greatest of his disciples, the leader of the great revolution that Engels did not live to see.' So perhaps the firm should really be called Engels-Leninism after all.

31. Socialist Snobs.[1]

A review of *Fabian Essays*, introduced by Asa Briggs (Allen and Unwin).

Every movement has its sacred text, at first revered, later read for devotion, not for guidance. It would be difficult to deduce the splendours of the Papacy from the New Testament, and Rousseau would have been surprised at the uses to which Jacobins put the Social Contract. So too with the *Fabian Essays* – the seven lectures given to little groups of the faithful in the centenary year of the French Revolution. These lectures have survived when many thousand others have vanished into air. They became something like the foundation deeds of the British Labour Party on its intellectual side.

Now they appear again with a difference. Previous reprints, in 1908 and 1931, had prefaces by Bernard Shaw, the original editor. One, in 1920, had an introduction by Sidney Webb, estimating how far the essayists had been proved right and what they had left out. This edition has, for the first time, an introduction by an historian. The essays have become historical documents. They are no longer propaganda. As usual in such cases, it is difficult to recapture the effect of their first impact. Much of the essays seems commonplace; much seems wrong; most seems irrelevant. Every now and then, there is a phrase which has shaped the thinking of British socialists. If this is a dull book, no doubt that too has counted for virtue in the Labour movement.

The Fabians claimed to be rescuing socialism from Marx and they have been given credit for this ever since. This did not mean much more than that they rejected the idea of a sudden, violent revolution which many Marxists deduced from Marx's writings. Marx himself was less firm on this point, accepting at any rate the possibility of a

[1]*New Statesman,* 1962.

'Fabian' solution in England and the United States. Marxism was a system of evolutionary thought, despite its revolutionary asides, as Marx indicated by presenting a copy of *Capital* to Darwin. Nearly all these essays rest on crude Marxist assumptions. The last words of the book define the general spirit: 'It's coming yet for a' that'. Socialism was bound to come. Some of it was here already. More would soon arrive. There would never be a moment when the establishment of socialism could be finally and fully announced. Like the God imagined by Samuel Alexander, it would always be round the next corner. The Fabians demonstrated this truth, just as Marx had done, by an appeal to history, though in a more trivial, flimsier way. They recounted the horrors of the industrial revolution, showed how these had been restrained by legislation, and then projected the process into the future. This was the gradualism which Sidney Webb announced to the Labour party many years later. Events vindicated the Fabian outlook, or so Shaw claimed. The Bolsheviks, according to him, were completely converted to Fabianism by sheer force of experience, and Stalinism was Fabianism in action, a view with which the Webbs agreed.

The real difference between the Fabians and Marx was not over method, but over their failure to discover a driving force behind historical events. Their evolution was merely something which happened. The inevitability of gradualness sprang from the fact of democracy, by which they meant universal suffrage. Given that there were more poor people than rich, the poor would gradually vote the rich out of existence, and the rich would be so awed by the forces of evolution that they would acquiesce in their own extinction. The task of the Fabians was to be a bit more conscious about this progress and thus to help it on. To quote Shaw again, they must remain 'a minority of cultural snobs', graciously providing ideas for the 'illiterates and political novices' of the Labour movement. 'Cultural segregation is essential in research, and indiscriminate fraternization fatal'.

Shaw grew more intellectual and 'culturally snobbish' as he grew older. Some of the original essayists, though snobbish no doubt, were more passionate. The generous emotion even in Webb's essay is surprising. Only reference to the table of contents ascertains that the essay was not written by George Lansbury. Hubert Bland, an expert in many passions, was even more emotional. He was also the only essayist who clearly postulated the establishment of an independent Labour or Socialist party. The others still hankered after 'permeating' the Liberals. Webb, writing in 1920, pointed out that the essayists knew nothing about the trade unions or indeed about any aspect of the Labour movement. Their practical intention, so far as they had one, was to extend socialism unperceived, by means of local government; and the essays were appropriately published in the year when county councils, including the LCC, were established. It would need only a little ingenuity to reinterpret the essays as a sketch for Utopia by county council.

The Fabians were almost unaware of class. They were quite unaware of power. Marx was their superior on both counts. On one point they both fell down together. They assumed that the laws of capitalist economics would continue to operate under socialism, with the capitalists taken away. Their socialism was laissez faire without private property. Marx had no theory of international trade. The Fabians did not acknowledge that the rest of the world existed. Neither Marx nor the Fabians considered planning except for purposes of welfare. Unemployment would be automatically solved when the democratically-controlled local authorities put the unemployed to work. It is not surprising that Webb was, of all men, most at a loss when confronted with the great Depression in 1931.

Despite this, his essay, and his later introduction, are far better than any of the others. Shaw, of course, was a master of words, but he had little to say. His essay on Economics, which is supposed to refute Marx, is childish. It explains Ricardo's theory of rent in a primitive way and then deduces all the evils of society from this. His later prefaces grow increasingly frivolous, ending up with a plea for the abolition of democracy. Webb's essay, on the other hand, is creative. His introduction of 1920 is even more remarkable. This is a real exercise in self-criticism, writing about himself and his work as a matter of history. Webb, unlike the others, became a full-timer. He knew far more, read more widely, thought more deeply. Fabianism as the socialism of snobs will be always with us. Fabianism, as a system of ideas and policies, was really Sidney Webb and nothing much else.

32. Don't Forget the Literature.[1]

A review of *The Challenge of Socialism* Edited by Henry Pelling (Black).

Henry Pelling recently produced a striking book on the origins of the Labour party. He now adds to the subject by an anthology of Socialist writing in the series called The British Political Tradition. He has had a difficult task. The series is designed to show 'the richness of British political thought and discussion in the past two centuries' and previous volumes have traced radical or conservative ideas over this period. The ideas start rather simple and crude and they become more complicated as time marches on. Histories of art or philosophy used to be written in the same way, with each painter or thinker improving on his predecessor. This is the doctrine of evolution as applied to the world of ideas – not bearing much relation to the way things happen, but irresistible to the children of the Darwinian age. Pelling has done his best to make Socialism work in the same way. We begin with Spence and Godwin; go on to Owen and the Chartists; and bow politely to the anti-capitalist writers whom Max Beer rediscovered thirty years ago. Socialism gets gradually into its stride, becoming richer and deeper with the passing years. The SDF, the Socialist League, the ILP succeed one another; and we reach a triumphant conclusion, rather surprisingly, with a speech by Harry Pollitt. Human endeavour could go no further, at any rate so far as Socialism was concerned.

Pelling knows quite well that this method is not satisfactory. British Socialism did not 'evolve.' It appeared fully fledged in the eighteen eighties. The so-called forerunners appeal only to historical curiosity. No Socialist knew anything about them at the time; and, as Pelling remarks, we might just as well dig out the Levellers or

[1]*New Statesman*, 1954.

Thomas More. British Socialism had a certain international background, but no British background even unconsciously. Moreover it did not develop an existing traditional pattern. Socialism began as a challenge, not as a continuation; and Pelling admits this in his title. Even now the Labour party claims to threaten 'the British way of life,' though it does its best to preserve it. Pelling is not so clear on another point. British Socialism, unlike the Universe, had not only a beginning, but an end. It rested essentially on the prevailing outlook of late-Victorian England. It assumed, for instance, the perfectibility of man, as all radicals did; and it counted on the indefinite expansion of productivity, along with all the economists. Once admit that human wickedness and natural hardship are inevitable, and Socialism would have no sense. British Socialism was in fact the last flower of Victorian England and ended therefore when Victorian England ended, that is, with the abandonment of the gold standard and free trade in 1931.

This is made clear by Pelling's choice of extracts though not by his introduction. The passages chosen from writings between 1880 and 1930 are all devoted to advocacy of Socialism. Sometimes they argue; sometimes they preach; sometimes they merely describe the delights of Socialism or lay down that it is inevitable. But they all take it for granted that Socialism is a simple arrangement to make and that its results are bound to be infinitely beneficent. The passages from writings between 1931 and 1950 bring a change of tune. They are questioning, not dogmatic. The writers have difficulty in deciding what Socialism is; still more in how it can be attained; and are even doubtful whether its attainment will do much good. Some of their difficulties are due in appearance to the challenge of Communism in its turn. Much Socialist writing of the last twenty years has been more concerned to explain that Socialism is not Communism than to explain what it is. Putting the blame on Communism is exactly how the Americans behave at the present time to conceal the fact that they cannot discover a policy of their own, and British Socialists did much the same. They would not have argued about Communism so much if they had been clear what Socialism meant.

There is another and more profound difference between classical Socialist writing and that of the last twenty years. Recent Socialist writing is academic, written by dons for dons or at most for university students and WEA classes. The Left Book Club stocked the shelves of every undergraduate, and any economist who calls himself a Socialist is hard put to it to escape the House of Commons.

The works that were sold on the 'literature-stalls' of every Socialist meeting for half a century were of a very different character. The authors were usually not men with university degrees. They wrote clumsily. Even William Morris lapsed into polysyllabic sentences when he tried to explain the merits of Communism. Only Robert Blatchford was a writer of genius; and he, if alive today, would have found his home on the *Daily Mirror*, not in writing clever books. For classical Socialism was working-class Socialism – pamphlets written by working-men for working-men. Only Bernard Shaw belonged to traditional literary culture, and his contributions, with their brilliant remarks and polished sentences, seem detestably out of place, when set against the fumbling hard-headedness of Keir Hardie, 'Elihu,' and Bruce Glasier. It may be that a genuine working-class feeling and character has disappeared in this country and that middle-class values (whatever they may be) have spread their rot to the very bottom of society. Hence working-class boys like to dress as Edwardian dudes. They read the *Tatler*, not the *Clarion*. If the Labour movement ever wanted to escape from its present bewilderments, it might do worse than go back to the real Socialist writers, who at least knew what Socialism was and even how to get it. For a start it might adopt the panacea of every classical Socialist writer and ensure that no one lives by owning. That simple slogan would tear the smug fabric of present-day politics apart. Clever writing is all very well. But it will be a good thing for the Labour movement when we hear again the cry which followed the singing of the Red Flag and closed every Socialist meeting: 'don't forget the literature, comrades! don't forget the literature!'

33. A Socialist Saint.[1]

A review of *R H Tawney and His Times: Socialism as Fellowship* by Ross Terrill (Deutsch).

R H Tawney was the sort of socialist who could happen only in England. Other writers presented socialism in terms of economic change or administrative improvement. Tawney's concern was with morality. For him socialism was a religion, and he was bewildered when his close friend William Temple resigned from the Labour Party on becoming a bishop. Tawney was in his modest way a twentieth-century saint. Of all intellectuals he was the most acceptable to the inter-war Labour movement. He wrote one Labour programme – 'Labour and the Nation' – singlehanded. Crossman said of his most famous book : '*The Acquisitive Society* is my socialist bible,' and Gaitskell said at his memorial service : 'I think he was the best man I have ever known.'

Ross Terrill has written a book about Tawney's ideas rather than about his life. This was the right choice. To outward appearance Tawney's private life was much like that of any other professor of history. He wrote some outstanding works of history. He gave many lectures. He was assiduous in the Workers' Educational Association.

But Tawney was a professor with a difference. He lived up to his own principle of social equality. Despite the 'effortless superiority' (Asquith's phrase) that came from education at Rugby and Balliol, he was always on the side of the common man. In his own words: 'In the interminable case of *Dubb v Superior Persons and Co,* whether Christians, Capitalists or Communists, I am an unrepentant Dubbite.' When serving on the Somme during the First World War, his closest friend was a bricklayer – 'the man whom of all others I would choose to have beside me at a pinch.'

[1]*Observer,* 1974.

Thereafter he usually wore a tattered sergeant's jacket. At the London School of Economics, where he taught, he spoke scathingly of the snobbery which dominated Oxford. He never became an MA, because that degree was acquired merely by paying money. When Ramsay MacDonald offered him a peerage, he replied contemptuously: 'Thank you for your letter. What harm have I ever done to the Labour Party? Yours sincerely, R H Tawney.' The only practical lesson that can be drawn from his voluminous writings is that members of the Labour Party should refuse all political honours. Tawney's concern was with equality – not so much equality of reward as equality of esteem. He wrote:

> If men are to respect each other for what they are, they must cease to respect each other for what they own. They must abolish, in short, the reverence for riches, which is the *lues Anglicana,* the hereditary disease of the English nation. And human nature being what it is, in order to abolish the reverence for riches, they must make impossible the existence of a class which is important merely because it is rich.

The revolution Tawney wanted was a change of heart, exactly as did George Lansbury, who was also a saint in his way. Capitalism and the power of private wealth would simply disappear when men came to see that they were essentially immoral. This was the doctrine which he hammered out in book after book.

It was an admirable doctrine. Yet it is difficult not to feel that Tawney, despite his goodness and social simplicity, did not escape effortless superiority himself. It was all very well to be on the side of Henry Dubb – 'common, courageous, good-hearted, patient, proletarian fool.' Would the real Henry Dubb, if he had read any of Tawney's books (which he did not), have relished either the name or the description? For that matter would Tawney have liked to be addressed as Henry Dubb?

Though on Henry Dubb's side, Tawney was himself a Superior Person. His writings were addressed exclusively to the Superior Persons whom he claimed to despise. His books were sophisticated and allusive, the products of a classical education and beyond my comprehension, let alone that of Henry Dubb. Of the 354 articles by Tawney which Terrill lists, most appeared in the *Manchester Guardian* – a journal for Superior Persons – and not a single one in any newspaper read by Henry Dubb. It was no accident that Tawney's two admirers, Crossman and Gaitskell, were the products of that superior educational emporium, Winchester College. Tawney's socialism was essentially for public-school men. Tawney never contemplated the problem of power. No man saw more clearly the political monopoly possessed by the governing classes, yet all he could contribute to ending this was to reiterate that it was morally wrong. The revolution was to come simply by the rich and powerful reading Tawney's works and seeing the error of their ways. Events do not work out like this in real life. The rich and powerful are now trembling in their shoes not because their wickedness has been borne in on them, but because the trade unions are stronger than they used to be. At this terrible prospect the governing classes have forgotten the lessons of democracy they learnt at Balliol and are howling for a strong man or the rule of the Army.

The curious thing is that as an historian – a topic relatively neglected in Terrill's book – Tawney emphasised the triumph of power over morality. Tawney was a very distinguished economic historian. Of the three Labour academics in the inter-war years (Cole, Laski and Tawney) he was the only one to be elected a Fellow of the British Academy – a correct estimate of their respective merits. Many good judges rank Tawney's historical books among the greatest works on English history written this century. Their common theme is the social revolution of the sixteenth century when the village communities with their open fields were broken up and the land of England seized by a few rich men – the version of history that Cobbett had presented less professionally a century before. Cecils, Russells, Cavendishes and the other great families founded their fortunes on robbery and the ruthless use of power. If Tawney had gone on to study economic history in the nineteenth century, he would have concluded, as Marx did, that the great capitalist families made their fortunes in the same way.

What lessons did Tawney draw from this history as applied to the present day? Only that the heirs of these thieves and brigands would eagerly relinquish their spoils at the first breath of moral rebuke. I prefer the slogan I learnt in my socialist youth: 'The rich will do anything for the workers except get off their backs.'

Perhaps Tawney himself had doubts. Towards the end of his life he was trying to persuade a colleague to think well of the work of a young Marxist historian (presumably Christopher Hill). The colleague, an anti-communist, kept saying: 'But he's a communist, you know, he's a communist.' Tawney answered reflectively : 'Now is that a good thing or a bad thing?' R H Tawney was a great and good man, though I do not think that what he said was of much use to Henry Dubb.

34. Bolshevik Soul in a Fabian Muzzle.[1]

A review of The Life of G D H Cole by Margaret Cole (Macmillan).

Cole told his wife that *as a person* he was of no interest whatsoever: all that mattered was in his published writings which people could read if they chose. The remark was much in character. Cole had no interest in himself and very little in others. As Dame Margaret remarks in regard to his children: 'He accepted them as they came and was a kind father to them, but I doubt whether he would have felt any deprivation if he had had none.' Nevertheless Dame Margaret has done well to write his biography. Cole's books do not tell all about him. His very impersonality made him a most unusual person. Moreover he played a considerable part in Labour politics even if somewhat on the fringe. He was the outstanding Fabian of the post-Webb generation. He was, I think, the only Left figure never tinged with communism and yet equally free from anti-communism. He was the most successful socialist propagandist of his time in intellectual circles. No man was more worthy of remembrance.

Wives rarely make good biographers of their husbands. Dame Margaret Cole is the exception. She was associated with Cole's political activities almost from the first and presents them with some of his own clarity. Occasionally she slips too much from biography into general history and sometimes she exaggerates the importance of what were really coterie affairs. Broadly speaking she holds the balance right. She is equally admirable on the personal side of the story: frank as only a wife can be, devoted and yet without illusions. Cole was often prim, even priggish, and might easily have turned into a figure of fun. He was redeemed by an innocent sincerity which Dame Margaret has fully recaptured.

[1]*New Statesman*, 1971.

The extraordinary thing about Cole was that, though a left-wing socialist and an atheist, there was nothing of the rebel about him. His life, apart from the one point of his political beliefs, was one of complete orthodoxy. He had a traditionally classical education and bestowed the same education on his children. He liked the elegance of College life, particularly the table silver. His house at Hendon had large grounds, a tennis court and a badminton court. His interest in sex was minimal. He took Margaret Postgate out for country walks. One day, sitting beside her on a log, he put his arm round her and said: 'I suppose this has got to happen.' Thereafter he claimed that he had been forced into matrimony. When later he developed diabetes and was told that his enjoyment of sex would diminish, he replied: 'Thank goodness.' One of his secretaries reported: 'Womaniser was his last word in condemnation of any man.' Mostly he regarded women as a nuisance, fit only for domestic tasks. The young Margaret Cole used to boast she could not boil an egg. She had to learn this and other arts in order to care for her husband. He could not even make his own bed.

Cole was by no means a dull man despite his detachment. He was good company in an aloof intellectual way. He wrote detective stories and light verse, including an operetta on the general strike. He often developed affection for his favourite pupils and was at one time deeply 'in love' with Hugh Gaitskell – an attachment not without embarrassment for Gaitskell whose tastes were quite other. Cole got great pleasure from country walking – hence his admiration for William Cobbett, a man whose temperament was the reverse of his own. But it had to be tame country such as the Cotswolds with hills that were 'green to the top'. He never went to the industrial regions of England if he could avoid it and, though he sometimes went abroad to look at buildings, was always glad to be back in Hendon or Oxford. He spoke excellent French, but never bothered to learn German, let alone Russian, and tolerated foreigners only when they were socialists. Indeed, if written solely in personal terms, the life of Douglas Cole would present an impeccably donnish figure.

All this was changed by a single episode when Cole was young. He read *News from Nowhere*. He experienced a total conversion. From that moment he believed in the socialist Utopia which Morris had described and dedicated his life to it. He rejected utterly the society in which he had grown up and was as rigorous against Establishment as he had previously been rigorously for it. For Cole there was no halfway house. He insisted that he was an atheist, not an agnostic – *I know* that there is no god. He attended College chapel until he was 21. Then he informed the Master of Balliol that he had conformed out of respect for his parents' wishes and did not propose to attend chapel any longer. The Master forbade him ever to appear in chapel again. Cole was the only Fellow of an Oxford college who, when presiding at dinner, never mumbled the most innocuous words of grace. He stood tight-lipped for 15 seconds (not two minutes as John Sparrow alleges) and then sat down. On every other point of College procedure he was sternly orthodox. His attitude was shown in the education he sought in vain for his children : a traditional curriculum combined with positive atheism. Cole took the logical view that, since the upholders of existing society attached importance to religious ritual, he should be equally firm against it. What he disliked in God, apart from His non-existence, was that He was on the side of the capitalist system.

Cole's rejection of capitalism was total. Though comfortably off, he refused to invest his surplus money or even to take interest from his bank. When I remarked to him that he was making a present of the interest to the bank, he replied : 'Better that my banker should commit mortal sin than that I should.' Christopher Hill, as an undergraduate, was delighted to hear Cole say at a meeting : 'Of course, I should *prefer* the whole system smashed.' Cole did not merely detest capitalism. He also believed that a new and perfect society could be achieved and thought a good deal about this in practical terms. Economic reorganisation was not enough for him. He wanted a fundamental revolution in men's minds and in their behaviour to each other. Socialism without democracy was worthless in his eyes, and by democracy he did not mean a resort to the ballot box every five years, but working democracy every day. In the early part of his career he preached Guild Socialism, and many of his books were concerned with workers' control. In one of his last speeches he urged fellow-socialists not to think that 'socialists can afford to give up being *levellers*'. He regarded *News from Nowhere* as a concrete description of the future society.

There was a paradox, even a contradiction, in Cole's political life. Though revolutionary in outlook, he was practical and reformist when it came to action. Maurice Reckitt described Cole best as having 'a Bolshevik soul in a Fabian muzzle'. During the First World War he acted as expert adviser to the trade unions and esteemed Arthur Henderson above all other Labour leaders. He was assiduous on committees of investigation and research. He founded the Labour Research Department, the New Fabian Research Bureau, the Society for Socialist Inquiry and Propaganda and, at the end of his life, the International Society for Socialist Studies. He believed in the working-class movement. Translated into practical terms, this meant yet another group of two or three hundred middle-class intellectuals most of whom had never spoken to a working man in their lives. There was also a personal contradiction in his public behaviour. In private Cole was cool, rational and at worst slightly disdainful. Once on a committee he became ruthless and impatient. Beatrice Webb describes how, when defeated at a Fabian meeting, Cole said: 'I withdraw the words Fools. I substitute Bloody Fools,' and flounced out of the room. He often resigned in anger and then returned some months later without a word of apology. Despite his democratic principles, Cole never shook off the belief that there was in the world one Just Man.

This was not true when Cole moved from politics to education. Here he was infinitely modest and cooperative. The Cole Group which he ran in Oxford for many years was enormously influential and produced many leading figures in the present Labour Party. Cole did not tell the young men what to think. For most of the time he sat silent, encouraging them to think for themselves. He was an inspiration, not a director, a true educator, drawing his pupils out. Only Harold Laski rivalled Cole as a socialist educator, and Laski was incidentally the only human being whom Cole personally disliked. This was a curious lapse into jealousy, though the clash of personalities was also obvious enough. Cole thought that Laski was flamboyant and romantic. Certainly Cole was neither. He disliked the excitement of big public meetings, though he sometimes addressed them, and once teased me by saying: 'All you like in politics is fighting.' In a more affectionate way Cole also disapproved of Kingsley Martin and accepted Beatrice Webb's description of him as a flibberty-gibbet. Henceforth Martin signed his letters to Cole: 'Flibber T. Gibbet.' Kinsgley won that round.

Cole's books showed him at his best. There were over a hundred of them, all models of exposition and simplification. Cole was not, I think, an original scholar, and most of his books are now out of date except for his marvellous edition of *Rural Rides*. But this was what Cole intended. He served the cause of socialism with unquestion-

ing devotion, even though nearly half his life was harassed by diabetes. His last words, when his strength finally ebbed, were in
character: 'I'm sorry to be a nuisance.' Douglas Cole came as near to
complete integrity as any man of his time. I venerated him.

35.   Intellectual in Politics.[1]

A review of *Harold Laski* by Kingsley Martin (Gollancz).
Evidently when I wrote this review I still suffered like Harold
Laski from Hope.

There are few men of whom one can truthfully say that the world
would have been a different place without them. Harold Laski was
one of those few. His was the most important influence in remaking
English Social Democracy and giving it its present form. He deserved
a biography which should be more than a personal tribute; and he has
got it. Kingsley Martin has written a book which is a serious contribution to our political history and, what is more difficult still,
presents his dead friend without fear or favour. Anyone who sets
out to expose Laski's failings can save himself the trouble; Kingsley
Martin treats them fairly with a detachment which Laski himself
would have wished. There are some faults which may disturb the
historian. Events are occasionally run together. For instance, the fall
of Lloyd George and the creation of the first Labour Government
are both made to happen in 1921. More seriously, there is a lack of
proportion. After all, Kingsley Martin is a professional journalist,
despite his training as a historian; the present and future interest him
more than the dead past. Hence, the last ten years of Laski's life
occupy nearly half the book. Yet these were an epilogue and in many
ways an unsatisfactory one. The most interesting decade of Laski's
life was the Twenties, the years of his intellectual growth; and the
most important was the Thirties, the decade of the Left Book Club
and the Popular Front. This criticism does not alter the fact that
Kingsley Martin has written a very good biography, at once moving
and instructive.

Though Laski was to play an important part in the English Labour

[1]*New Statesman*, 1953.

movement, he came to it in an unusual way. He was a Jew, not a Nonconformist, by origin; in spirit, sometimes the nearest thing we have had to a Continental intellectual, sometimes an American liberal, but never a straight English radical. He learnt his Socialism from French writers of the eighteenth century and his politics from American lawyers; he learnt nothing from Cobbett or William Morris. He knew little at first-hand of the English working-class. He was born in a rich Manchester family; after Oxford, he spent his formative years in Canada and at Harvard; and he returned to the London School of Economics. Even at Oxford, as Kingsley Martin points out, it was Cole and G N Clark, not Laski, who were prominent in the famous tram strike; and when he came to write about trade unions, his interest in them was that of an academic lawyer. He wanted to show their similarity with the medieval Church and other 'corporate personalities,' not to present them as the fighting organisations of the English people. He thought it more important to manipulate politicians than to stir emotion. I remember how he once shocked me by his admiration for Disraeli and his dislike of Gladstone. Yet, by a strange twist of fate, his greatest success was to come when he emulated 'the People's William.'

This was certainly not Laski's intention. When he came to the London School of Economics, he had two ambitions. He wished to be a great political thinker; and he wished to exercise a decisive influence behind the scenes of political life. He did not achieve either ambition. Kingsley Martin says very fairly: 'academically Harold did not fulfil the promise of . . . his early books.' At first Laski tried to develop a theory of Pluralism, which he had learnt from Maitland and Gierke; it was a trail that led nowhere, and the *Grammar of Politics* now lies neglected on the shelves. Later he turned himself deliberately into a Marxist, and made more than one attempt to survey English and American history from a Marxist outlook. But though he knew a great deal of political philosophy, he lacked both detailed historical knowledge and the historian's temperament. I do not think that any professional historian could take Laski's writings on English history seriously; and though Norman MacKenzie (who has contributed the American chapters to this biography) does his best for *The American Democracy*, the verdict of scholars has not been in its favour. In private conversation Laski had the amiable weakness of inventing facts to support his argument; and in his writings, too, he inclined to believe that the facts would conform to the ideas, if only these were brilliant enough.

In much the same way, he thought that he could change the facts of the present by rational persuasion of a few individuals. He wrote constantly to Baldwin; he advised MacDonald on the composition of the first Labour Cabinet – or so he imagined; even during the second World War he tried to turn Winston Churchill into a Socialist by correspondence. Though he often talked in terms of class war, he really assumed that the English governing classes could be cajoled and argued into abdicating. He did not understand their skill, their tenacity or, above all, their ruthlessness; and he was hurt and surprised when they bit the hand that stroked them. It bewildered Laski when the Director of the London School of Economics, himself a 'liberal' pundit, objected to his writing for the *Daily Herald*; and the ban successfully imposed on Laski was certainly an odd demonstration of academic freedom, when one considers the political activities in which Heads of Colleges have subsequently engaged. But did Laski really suppose that Sir William Beveridge would weigh *The Times* and the *Daily Herald* in the same liberal scales? The failure of the libel action, in which he attempted to vindicate himself from the charge of preaching 'bloody revolution,' broke Laski's heart. Certainly the campaign against Laski by the Beaverbrook-Churchill combination showed few scruples. But was it reasonable for an advanced Socialist to expect sympathetic consideration of his views from a special jury and a High Court judge? The answer to mud-slinging is to sling better mud back. He who goes to equity must go with clean hands; he who challenges the ruling classes needs quite other equipment.

Laski got this unexpectedly. It was not his reasoning power, his assiduity, or his social contacts that made him an important figure; it was the following that he came to command. He built this first within the London School of Economics. Though his was not an original mind, he was an inspired and inspiring lecturer; even more, he was a devoted teacher. He gave himself to his pupils without reserve; and he gave himself to them all, brilliant and mediocre alike, as Norman McKenzie describes in his moving account of Laski as a teacher at Cambridge during the war years. The influential academic figures of the past – a Jowett or a Lowes Dickinson – worked through a few distinguished pupils; Laski created a heaven which went much wider. The Labour Government of 1945, for instance, had many of Cole's pupils among its members; none, I think, of Laski's. His influence operated in the junior ranks of the Labour movement and in India, Burma and West Africa. Kingsley Martin observes rightly that the most enthusiastic Education Officers in the Army during the war would often turn out to have been trained by Laski. High academics never took Laski seriously as a thinker but he had exactly the right form for the new audience of 'mass-intellectuals'.

It was this audience that gave Laski his unique position. The intellectuals of previous generations were a closed, limited body. Bentham changed English history by capturing a few dozen disciples. In the twentieth century the number of those who made Reason the master of their lives became much larger. The intellectuals ceased to be a small academic class; instead, their outlook was to be found indiscriminately in all walks of life. Here was the natural market for the Left Book Club; here was the wider audience waiting for Laski's guidance and inspiration. There was a decisive political consequence. Owing to the peculiar constitution of the Labour Party, the mass-intellectuals found their expression in the constituency parties, and there was a growing cleavage of outlook between these and the trade unions. The constituency parties needed their own representative and this need often sought strange outlets, from Oswald Mosley to Aneurin Bevan. Laski alone filled the role perfectly. He was not merely the spokesman of the mass-intellectuals, he was their personification. What use should he make of his power? This was a new problem, and Laski did not solve it. He might have remained a thinker and writer, inspiring others; he might have become a practical politician, fighting every detail. Laski tried to combine the two roles. Though he became chairman of the Labour Party, he would not contest a Parliamentary seat. Kingsley Martin passes a verdict that must be quoted in full:

No man, however disinterested or clever, can accomplish by letter, conversation and private memorandum, the feat of changing the policy of a great Party, since that is based not on the wishes or opinions of individuals, but on the interests of classes and groups. A man who wishes to lead a revolutionary movement, or even less ambitiously to redirect a Party's policy, must change the balance of power within the Party, must make it to the interest of its leaders to change their minds, or of their followers to change their leaders. That involves working with other men in a team, taking the knocks and rewards of party politics and inevitably to some extent losing the type of respect and influence which is paid to the scholar and teacher.

Laski realised this towards the end of his life, when he refused to stand again for the Labour Party Executive.

Yet perhaps his influence could not have been so great if he had shrunk from stark, practical responsibilities. Laski had something to contribute to the intellectual atmosphere of the time which only he could give. He strove with the problem which confronts every reasoning man – how to be both a liberal and a Marxist. No one who believes in liberty can ever work sincerely with Communists or trust them; yet no one who has Socialism in his bones can ever condemn Communism without reserve. This is the dilemma of our times; all Laski's later writings and all his political activity revolved round it. Sometimes he got the emphasis wrong, as in the days of the Popular Front. But essentially he was right. The answer to Communism is not anti-Communism; it is a democratic Socialism, equally convinced of its principles, but more tolerant in applying them. How much easier the situation in Europe would be today if the Labour Government had followed Laski's advice in 1945 and put itself at the head of European Social Democracy. How much more peaceful and secure the Middle East would be if this country had welcomed Jewish Social Democracy instead of following the barren anti-Semitism of Ernest Bevin and the Foreign Office. Laski knew, none better, the difficulties of his policy; he did not need any disillusioned Communist, returned from Utopia, to tell him the evils of Moscow rule. But he still believed that the world could be saved; and he tried to save it. In the last article he ever wrote, which was published after his death, he argued against Bertrand Russell's division of the world into two irreconcilable power blocs: 'Lord Russell builds his policy upon despair. I build my policy upon hope.' This was a noble legacy. If today in this country there is still no Communist movement of any size, if all Socialists can still be at home in the Labour Party, we owe it more to Harold Laski than to any other single man.

36.   The Road to Great Turnstile.[1]

A review of *Father Figures* by Kingsley Martin (Hutchinson),
the first and as it proved the only volume of his autobiography.

How to Succeed without Trying is a rare art. There is one still rarer,
a speciality of intellectuals : How to Succeed while Persistently Trying to Fail. Rousseau is the acknowledged master of this art. He was
perhaps the most influential writer of modern times, and his autobiography is a record of follies, mishaps and discomfitures. Kingsley
Martin is a latter-day Rousseau. He has had unique success as editor
of a weekly periodical. He increased the circulation of the *New
Statesman* fivefold, he actually made the paper pay; his influence and
importance were acknowledged all over the world. Yet, according
to his own account, he stumbled into greatness unawares. He shame-
lessly parades his failings and mistakes. Thus, at Cambridge, 'I spoke
at the Union, but was so nervous that I usually had to run to the
lavatory instead of speaking.' When in America, he wrote home :

> I am not really an able person in any important way. And yet I
> am not content to be second. I wish I could cease to be jealous and
> ambitious, and yet if I did I should cease to do any work at all.

He extracts comedy even from the hardships of the First World War,
when he served in the Friends' Ambulance Unit :

> I was told to empty a large bin of lime into small receptacles.
> Although warned, I rendered myself useless for several days by
> completely skinning my arms to the elbow. Then they sent me to
> clean out the gutters of the roof. I forgot that it was made of glass,
> and people washing many feet below were surprised when the roof
> fell in and I with it.

[1]*New Statesman,* 1966.

Fortunately Kingsley Martin, unlike Rousseau, has a sense of humour. Rousseau took his woes seriously. Martin laughs at them and even, I suspect, piles them on. He remarks when describing his friendship with Lowes Dickinson : 'Our talk was gloomy in the extreme – but we were very merry just the same.' He remained merry in a world where everything was going wrong and where he himself always expected the worst. He remained merry despite his own set-backs. Besides, his mysterious gift for success came into play, like a natural law. Though he stepped unerringly on every banana-skin in sight, he bounced up, after each fall, higher than before. When hoping for a fellowship at Cambridge, he was invited to dinner at Peterhouse and arrived home too late to change.

I just ate something in my rooms and thought no more about it. Next day I learnt that the whole high table had waited dinner for me until eight o'clock. My name was something worse than mud . . . I expect, looking back, I lost a good chance of staying in Cambridge and becoming a professor.

Perhaps a little exaggerated, but certainly a setback.

However, failure at Cambridge carried him to the LSE, which suited him much better; 'a wonderful home of free discussion, happily mixed race, and genuine learning. It seemed my natural home.' Then another fall. Martin wrote a little book about the General Strike and criticised the Samuel Commission. Beveridge, director of LSE, had served on the Commission and had largely written its report. 'A young member of his staff criticising his Royal Commission with such disrespect was really too much.' Martin was refused 'normal promotion'. Down again, and 'in the midst of this row', he was invited to succeed C E Montague as principal leader-writer on the *Manchester Guardian* at £1,000 a year – 'an extra-ordinary offer'. He wrote his own terms – £800 a year, but three months away from Manchester. Failure once more followed success. 'Within a month or two of my arrival I realised that things had gone wrong. The Scotts had decided that I was both incompetent and dangerously left-wing.'

In 1930 he was back in London, unemployed and prowling round for a job. Arnold Bennett summoned him to the Savoy and asked : 'What are your . . . p-p-politics?' Martin answered, 'rather too timid-ly', that he would call himself a socialist. 'I should hope so,' said Bennett, and with this Martin was in as editor of the *New Statesman*.

The paper was in poor shape after the erratic latter days of Clifford Sharp. It soon received a shot in the arm. Keynes, in his turn, summoned Martin and asked: 'Are you going to stand for the necessary interference with free trade and *laissez-faire*?' The answer proving satisfactory, Keynes handed over the *Nation*, of which he had grown tired. Not long after, events threw in *The Weekend Review* also. The amalgamated paper had a bit of everything: intellectual Fabianism from the *New Statesman*, emotional radicalism from the *Nation*, gaiety and satire from the *Weekend Review*. Martin himself was both serious and frivolous. 'I suppose my prime attitude was a dissenter's. A dissenter sees that the world is bad and expresses his moral indignation.' A few sentences later: 'Editing the paper was fun. We constantly laughed at ourselves.' He fought for the impossible without expecting to win. After a lifetime of gloom, however, he ends up cheerful: 'In 1965, I am not sure that the primitives will always conquer.'

Characteristically, in this last sentence, as often elsewhere, Martin has wondered beyond his brief. The present volume is intended as a first instalment, ending when Martin reached the editorial chair. Old students of Critic's Diary do not need to be told that the autobiographer provides a bit of everything, from anecdotes about personalities to dabblings in psychology. Schooldays, for instance, send Martin off on his old hobby-horse of flagellation. The deepest theme is indicated in the title. Martin was not only a dissenter. He was the son of a dissenter, with an equally fine record. Basil Martin was a Congregational minister who moved away from Christianity, became a Unitarian, and finally 'believed more and more in less and less'. His windows were broken during the Boer War, his furniture seized during passive resistance against the Education Act of 1902. Kingsley Martin loved his father. Not surprisingly, he managed to turn this into a grievance:

All boys in adolescence must break with their parents. My trouble was that my father gave me no chance at all to quarrel with him ... His causes became my causes, his revolt was mine ... I was much retarded because I did not work out these dissenting positions for myself, but freewheeled, as it were, with the momentum that I had gained from my father's lonely struggle against Calvinism.

This is the voice of Kingsley Martin, amateur psychologist, inventing explanations long afterwards. It is wrongheaded, like most psychology. I had much the same relationship with my father and have derived nothing but strength from his example. Father-son hostility is a great waste of time. It becomes an obsession, as it did with Samuel Butler, and it prevents a dissenter from getting on with his real job which is to kick against the world. Martin was lucky in his father, and he knew it. Perhaps he got a bit stuck in the relationship. As the title of his book indicates, he sought father substitutes, until he became a father figure himself in the editorial chair. He writes with deep affection of the older men whom he venerated: Lowes Dickinson in particular, but even – until disappointed – Beveridge and C P Scott. There are also plenty of contemporaries in the book, but they are written up from outside, adorned with anecdotes in a lively journalistic way. The young Martin seems to have had few friends of his own age. He gives the impression at Cambridge of being always on a bicycle – the machine of a solitary 'flibbertigibbet', Beatrice Webb's word for him. He remained a solitary flibbertigibbet throughout life.

There were other reasons for this detachment. Martin, despite his disclaimers, has always been a professional. He meant to be a professional historian – a fate he escaped fortunately for history and still more fortunately for himself. He became a professional journalist, he ended as a highly professional editor. He may boast that it was all done without hands. This only makes his professionalism the greater. The professional in any walk of life has no time for intimate social contacts. Moreover, in a typically intellectual way, Martin never knew much of what was going on around him. He was born in Hereford. He grew up in Finchley. What do they know of England who only Hereford and Finchley know? Instead, Martin knew a great deal about the rest of the world. The *Manchester Guardian* always set him to write leaders on Kenya. When the *New Statesman* made a profit, 'I forgot to get my salary doubled. Instead, I had a good conscience travelling round the world at the paper's expense.' He thinks he is unworldly. In fact, he has worldly-wisdom of a superior kind:

> The secret is never to spend as much as you earn and always to have something in hand. It's fatal to invest money . . . When the crash comes you lose the lot. You might have had fun with it.

Kingsley Martin has had fun. He provided fun for the readers of his paper. He now provides it for the readers of his autobiography. At the Day of Judgement, he will be asked, like Matthew Arnold: 'Why cannot you be wholly serious?' This will make him laugh more than ever.

37. Confusion on the Left.

This essay originally appeared in a volume entitled *The Baldwin Age*, edited with an introduction by John Raymond (Eyre and Spottiswoode, 1960).

The general election of November 1922 opened the Baldwin era, though Bonar Law was in nominal control for the first few months. 'Tranquillity and freedom from adventures and commitments' was the cry which put the second-class brains into power. On the Left there was a different spirit. Walton Newbold, returned as a Communist at Motherwell, wired to Lenin: 'Glasgow won for Communism.' It seemed a pardonable exaggeration. In Glasgow itself the Clydesiders of the ILP won 10 out of 15 seats and scented social revolution just round the corner. David Kirkwood shouted from his railway carriage to the crowd which sped the departure of the Clydesiders to Westminster: 'When we come back, this station, this railway, will belong to the people!' The promise was to be fulfilled, though only after a longer delay than Kirkwood or the crowd foresaw. Still less did they foresee Kirkwood as a member of the House of Lords; one of his associates Minister of Defence authorising the secret manufacture of atom bombs; and Maxton, supposed Robespierre of the group, the most loved and least effective member of the House of Commons. What did the Clydesiders achieve in practice? Only to make Ramsay MacDonald leader of the parliamentary Labour party by 61 votes to 56.

Ramsay MacDonald was to prove the left-wing counterpart of Baldwin, equally devoted to tranquillity and freedom from adventures and commitments. In 1922 he still seemed securely on the Left; still lunching every day at the 1917 Club; still frowned on by the respectable for his supposed pacifism during the Great War. In presence he was, in Shinwell's phrase, a prince among men. He had a ravishingly musical voice, every syllable ringing of Utopia. His ideas of social improvement were vague and undefined. In foreign affairs he saw clearly, wishing, in true left-wing fashion, to substitute conciliation and appeasement for alliances and the balance of power. He and Arthur Henderson were the principal targets for the abuse which flowed from Moscow. They were Social traitors, Social Fascists, and indeed the two men did more than any others to keep the British Labour movement free from Communism – a service for which they deserve to be remembered.

The British Labour party, now the official Opposition and soon to form the first Labour government, was a strange alliance of two distinct forces. On the one hand the trade union movement supplied the firm foundation and most of the money. Here the driving force was straight economic discontent. The post-war boom was over; large-scale unemployment had come to stay. The Red Flag flew on the Clyde, in Poplar, in South Wales. Here the King's writ did not run, and the Left supposed that they had only to capture central administration as they had already in these areas taken over local government. Policy and long-term planning seemed unnecessary. Capitalism would topple of its own defects, and the social revolution would come peacefully by a simple process of administrative change. The British Left believed as confidently as Lenin had done in 1917 that Socialism could be made in twenty-four hours. Socialism was preached in moral terms : men had to be persuaded that it was right and just. The only problem was to win a majority : then Socialism would follow of its own accord. The Labour movement had only to squeeze up wages and welfare until capitalism exploded and the trick would be turned. Hence while the Left preached and argued, it did not lead. Economic conditions, not leadership, would produce the desired result.

The other side of the Labour party was the section of the individual members, organised in the constituency parties. Henderson had created this new system in 1918 – a creation which changed the face of British politics. Previously individuals could join the Labour party only through the ILP or lesser bodies like the SDF and the Fabian Society. Now these bodies were doomed as mass organisations, though the ILP went on pontificating, with declining membership, until the end of the decade. Moreover, by this device the Labour party could offer a home to Radicals who had formerly been Liberal. Home Rule and sectarian disputes over education – the two issues which had sustained the Liberal party – were dead or dying. The great emotional question for the middle-class Left was foreign policy, and here the Labour party had a less spotted record. MacDonald had opposed the war from the first hour and the Labour party had denounced the Treaty of Versailles six weeks before it was signed. Also, though Labour would have nothing to do with the Communist party, it wished to end the boycott of Soviet Russia. The Councils of Action which had prevented war against Russia in 1920 were a proud memory; the mirage of Russian trade promised a solution for British economic difficulties and, though most men of the Left knew little of conditions in Russia, they rejoiced at the social revolution there and believed that the dictatorship would lose its force when other countries held out the hand of friendship. Left foreign policy had a simple prescription. Germany and Russia were justly aggrieved and the redress of their grievances would secure the peace and prosperity of the world.

The cleavage between the two sections of the Left was not absolute. Most trade union officials – and their more active followers – had started as Socialist intellectuals of a working-class sort; some indeed were Communists, though without understanding what this implied. Many of the 'politicians' had started in the trade union movement and the others recognised an obligation to promote economic improvement. Rather than a cleavage, there was a division of function. The trade unions expected that an enlightened foreign policy would give economic benefits, and the politicians preached welfare in order to have a free hand for their foreign policy. They were held together by a common morality: a passionate rejection of social evils and a conviction that these evils could be ended by the overthrow of the existing order. The Left was revolutionary in outlook, though not in method. The Baldwin era gradually forced the conclusion that it must become both or neither.

The promised land was not long delayed. Baldwin was no sooner in power than he went again to the polls on the question of Protection. The Labour party won 39 seats; the Conservatives lost nearly a hundred; and when Parliament met, Baldwin was defeated by the combined Liberal and Labour votes. Ramsay MacDonald became Prime Minister, first being sworn of the Privy Council – the only Prime Minister to need this preliminary. It was a revolutionary symbol, but the only one. Labour's success was not due to Socialism. It was the last victory of Free Trade – a respectable, and by now an antiquated, cause. In theory Labour stood for the community against private interests. In practice it defended balanced budgets, sound money and free trade. Planning and a directed economy were preached by Amery and a few enlightened Conservatives so far as they were preached at all. The first Labour government took office with minority support. Hence it could plead exemption from any startling act of legislation. It was supposed to show that Labour was fit to govern. Oddly, no one observed that this had already been demonstrated. Henderson had been a member of the War Cabinet and Clynes a successful Minister of Food. Nor was the Labour government remarkable as a showpiece. Most ministers became obstinate defenders of their departments, only Wheatley – Catholic business man from Glasgow – taking an initiative. A smug phrase cloaked this lack of thought of policy: Labour was 'in office but not in power'.

MacDonald was indifferent to the domestic record of his Government. Foreign affairs were what mattered to him. He began the appeasement of Germany and opened the road to Locarno, which the Conservatives followed later to general surprise. Indeed after 1924 there was no Right foreign policy: MacDonald's spirit prevailed in regard to Germany whether he was in office or not. Russia was a different matter. MacDonald had never shared the Left enthusiasm for the Bolshevik revolution and now recognised the Soviet government as grudgingly as he could. The Left wanted a union of hearts and also a trade treaty opening the Russian market to British goods. Negotiations lagged, then jammed. Ponsonby, MacDonald's under-secretary, actually announced breakdown early in August. A group of Left MPs took up the running and imposed agreement – the first of many Left revolts against the official leadership and for once successful. MacDonald and the Left were brought back to harmony by a series of unexpected twists. The Attorney-General – ill-briefed in the niceties of Left politics – started to prosecute a Communist editor for appealing to soldiers not to act as strike-breakers; then withdrew when Labour MPs protested. The Liberal and Conservative parties were indignant or claimed to be. The Government was defeated in the House of Commons, and MacDonald found himself fighting a general election as the patron of sedition.

The affair of the Zinoviev letter completed the reconciliation. It is a matter of little historical importance whether the letter was genuine or not. Labour men were unanimous that it was a fraud, manufactured by the anti-Bolshevik centre at Riga or perhaps by the Foreign Office itself. This was far from the 'fair play' which George V had desired for the Labour government. It was the gentlemen of

England playing dirty as only they knew how to. MacDonald had imagined himself as national leader, transcending party. Now he was back on the Left, again the ostracised idealist of the war years. The Zinoviev letter lost the general election for Labour or so it was said. But it also gave Labour a cover against accusations of failure. They had been tricked out of office, not defeated or discredited. Few bothered to analyse the Government's record, and the legend soon became established that everything had been going splendidly until Campbell and Zinoviev cropped up. There was little in the way of new thought or new policy. Ernest Bevin, with the constructive spirit which he was later to show as Foreign Secretary, proposed that Labour should not again take office with a minority. His proposal was rejected and from this decision to continuity of policy even with a majority was not a far step. The ILP, now at its last kick of life, proposed to arrive at Socialism by means of the Living Wage. This was none other than our old friend the belief that capitalism could be made to burst of itself if wage demands were pushed high enough.

Action, not thought, gave the Left its only outlet in these years. The General Strike was the most class-conscious act in British history (or rather the most working-class-conscious act – the upper classes never lose consciousness). Also, though no one cared about this, it was one of the few unselfish acts in anybody's history. But it did not fit into any pattern of Left development. There was no deliberate oscillation from political to industrial action, as some ingenious writers have suggested. The miners had been plodding steadily on with their struggle since Lloyd George swindled them over the Sankey commission in 1919. This struggle happened to reach climax in 1926. It had little to do with Left or Right, but was in truth a struggle for existence. Trade unionists did not need to be Communists, syndicalists, or even Socialists, to sympathise with the miners; they only needed to sympathise, and in trade union terms that could only take one form – the sympathetic strike. Certainly the avowed Left sympathised also and supported the strike as best they could. But what was there for a Left intellectual, or even for a trade union official, to do? Speeches appealing for solidarity were agreeable to deliver, but pointless when the audience was solid already. Nor was there anything to organise. The General Council met only four times during the ten days of the strike, and the *British Worker* was hard-pressed for news. 'Spirit splendid; all out', became monotonous. Some intellectuals who could drive motor-cars acted as couriers, carrying TUC secret instructions which contained no secrets. Many intellectuals could not drive. W H Auden, moving a car four miles during the ten days (from Old Marston to Oxford) was a symbol of Faith, not Works.

Things would have been different if the TUC had taken over the running of the country, but no one proposed this seriously. In fact, like most gestures of sympathy, once made it had served its purpose, and the only concern of those who had made it was to bring it to an end. The petering-out of the strike, and still more the defeat of the miners, certainly weakened the trade union movement. It had no effect on left-wing thought. The General Strike had been an instinctive reaction, not a policy. Once over, it was forgotten except for the resentment which Baldwin gratuitously provoked by legislating against the trade unions in 1927. This was always his way: soft words, harsh acts. Even so there was a short period of tranquillity and recovery – the true 'age of Baldwin' – which lasted until 1929. No great strikes; no riots by the unemployed; no alarms of war. The Labour party, securely established as the official Opposition, waited confidently for the swing of the pendulum. They would come into office on the great British principle of Buggins's turn. The Left became frivolous: gay young things of intellectualism. Enthusiastic tourists visited Soviet Russia, not to see new factories or the triumph of the social revolution, but to admire co-educational schools, divorce by consent and prisons allegedly without bars. Young writers found their spiritual home in Berlin and rejoiced at the moral emancipation shown by the homosexual prostitutes on the Kurfürstendamm. Hock became a left-wing drink; claret as shockingly Tory as it had been in the eighteenth century.

The general election of 1929 whispered the last enchantment of the Victorian age. Baldwin campaigned to the cry, 'Safety First'. The Labour party advocated a nebulous Socialism in moral terms coined by F D Maurice and Ruskin. The result was perverse. Labour got fewer votes, more seats, than the Conservatives; not enough, however, to escape another run of being 'in office, but not in power'. There was a victory celebration at the Albert Hall, Fenner Brockway registering triumph with outstretched arm in a salute not yet branded as 'fascist', and Ramsay MacDonald appearing in white tie and tails to announce that he was on his way to Buckingham Palace. Thereafter: nothing. The Labour party had no programme except to be indistinguishable from its predecessor. In MacDonald's words there was to be no monkeying. Unfortunately events disregarded his instruction. In October 1929 the great economic storm began to blow. Unemployment passed two million, soared to three. The gold standard rocked. The Labour party had no remedy for this situation. Planned economy was no part of classical Socialism. Marx, for instance, assumed that supply and demand, the law of the market, would continue to work under Socialism; only private profit would be eliminated. Soviet Russia had been operating a market economy and a gold currency since the end of the civil war. The first Five Year Plan, launched in 1928, had not yet made an impact on western minds. The New Deal had not appeared on the horizon. Keynesian economics were still in conception. Only Fascist Italy claimed, however falsely, to have a planned economy.

The Labour government could therefore offer only the classical remedy of balanced budgets and economy cuts. A few Socialists, Lansbury in particular, wished to shelter the poor from the storm and hang the expense. Mosley alone advocated this with unconscious Keynesianism. His policy was rejected, and he left the Labour party with some left-wing associates to form the 'New Party'. Later he took the full road to Fascism, and most of his associates drifted back to Labour, bringing economic direction with them in their baggage. But in August 1931, when the crisis reached its height, the Labour government was still unshakably orthodox in its economic thinking. Eleven members of the Cabinet agreed to reduce unemployment benefit by 10 per cent; nine refused. (Attlee, with his usual luck, was not in the Cabinet and so did not have to commit himself one way or the other.) The Labour government broke up. MacDonald went off happily with Snowden and Thomas to form a National government, which should save the pound – an ambition which fortunately it did not accomplish. Labour was massacred at the ensuing election and for an obvious reason. The National government claimed to have a remedy though it had in fact the wrong one. Labour did not even make the claim. Apart from the defence of unemployment benefit, its election campaign was fought solely on the ticket of Free Trade.

Yet, because of the way it had left office, Labour could again overlook its own faults and blame the manoeuvres or treachery of others. MacDonald, Baldwin or George V had tricked the simple, high-minded members of the Labour party. Arthur Greenwood, wearily fighting his election campaign in Lancashire, reiterated at every stop: 'It's not fair', as though the Socialist movement had a heaven-sent right to sunshine. After defeat the Left displayed old grievances, not new thought. The only conclusion which Laski, principal theorist of the party, drew from the affair was that the monarchy should be abolished. Yet Weimar Germany and the United States had the same economic difficulties and even dirtier politics. Still, some thought stirred as the dust subsided. John Strachey, breaking loose from Mosley, returned to Socialism with the only Marxist classic written in English, *The Coming Struggle for Power*. Yet he and other new thinkers of the Left squinted oddly. Mesmerised by Russia's Five Year Plans, they ignored the renewed terror and the massacre of the kulaks with which these were accompanied. Moreover, they knew nothing of America. They closed their eyes to the New Deal and described America right up to 1939 as a 'Fascist economy'. Soviet Russia was again the Utopia of the Left, now on grounds of economic efficiency, not of moral superiority. The Workers' State had become the model of planned economy.

The Left became more markedly intellectual as the decade proceeded – or perhaps intellectuals became more markedly Left. The Oxford Union had its only Communist president, Philip Toynbee. The October Club, avowedly pro-Communist, was for some years the largest political club in Oxford. Working men tried to find instructions for their trade union meetings in the poems of Auden and Spender. In this hubbub, the Left Book Club stood supreme. Each month it distributed two books as the 'Choice' – chosen, of course, not by the readers, but by a triumvirate of intellectual dictators, much as Lord Woolton decided later, though with more excuse, on the correct supply of calories and vitamins. Strachey, Laski and Gollancz provided a balanced intellectual diet, parcelling out near-Communism, proletarian 'literature', and sheer crankiness. Of the two first 'choices', for instance, one by a biologist (still turning the old hurdy-gurdy in 1958) looked forward to the time when artificial insemination would enable a Lenin (or a Stalin?) to father every child in the Soviet Union. The Left Book Club was often regarded as a subversive organisation. In reality it was a safety valve. Reading is a substitute for action, not a prelude to it, and the members of the Left Book Club worked off their rebelliousness by plodding through yet another orange-covered volume.

Economic problems predominated immediately after 1931: Free Trade, Imperial Preference, hunger marches by the unemployed. Within two years there was an unexpected change. Foreign affairs were thrust into the centre of the stage, and henceforth these were the great stamping-ground of the Left. Hitler caused much trouble, not of course for the British Left alone. Foreign affairs had been simple until he turned up. Appeasement of the aggrieved powers, Russia and Germany, would settle everything. Hence the Left had only to criticise the British government and oppose British armaments. But now? Most of the Left, though not all, agreed that appeasement of Hitler was hopeless and, besides, immoral. Resisting him was part of 'the struggle against Fascism'. How was this struggle to be waged? By co-operating with the National government? Or by continuing to attack it? The Left never solved the problem. Usually they avoided it. Collective security – operating sanctions through the League of Nations – was an evasion of this kind. Once allied to fifty-two other governments (the number that would supposedly work with the League), co-operation with the National government would pass unnoticed. The question caused great dispute. Labour party conferences were rent by it; leaders expelled and readmitted; bitter words spoken. Yet it was all quite pointless. The problem had no solution. For whatever the Left decided about co-operating with the National government to resist Hitler, the National government under MacDonald and Baldwin had no intention of resisting Hitler in co-operation with the Left or anyone else.

In 1935 resistance to aggression had a trial run against Mussolini – a sort of provincial preview before the real first night. The argument was the biggest family quarrel in the history of the Left. The Stalinist fellow-travellers, centred on the Left Book Club, clamoured for national unity and 'sanctions', a euphemism for war. The Socialist League – an intellectualist successor to the dying ILP – stuck to criticism of the British government and proclaimed: 'Our enemy is here.' This was a hard judgement on poor Baldwin, who had not an enemy in the world except perhaps Lloyd George. He was, however, a skilful political operator. Just when the Left had decided that its advocacy of collective security would enable it to defeat the 'imperialist' government at a general election, Baldwin announced that he, too, was enthusiastic for the League of Nations. The Left had failed to win earlier elections by claiming that it was indistinguishable from Baldwin. He however won the election of 1935 by claiming that he was indistinguishable from the Left. Once the election was over, he put the League of Nations back on the shelf and returned to his somewhat amateurish pig-farming.

The dress rehearsal had not been a success. Not surprisingly, therefore, the Left was as much at a loss as everyone else when Hitler reoccupied the Rhineland and the real problem presented itself.

Baldwin made an alliance with France, thus guaranteeing to lose a war where he had shrunk from winning one. The Left committed itself to rearmament, but not under the National government, one provision cancelling the other. What more could the Left do with Baldwin on their hands? They could not turn him out; the electorate had seen to that. It would have been equally futile to support him. Even the backing of a united House of Commons would not have convinced Baldwin that there was any better policy than twiddling his thumbs. It was, of course, this taste which endeared him to the electorate.

The Spanish Civil War brought the Left back to life, though not to effectiveness. Spain provided a concentrated meat-extract of all the emotions which the Left had experienced in previous years. Resistance to Fascism; class war; unity of the Left – difficult slogans at home, but easy to use in Spain. It was possible to admire the Spanish Communists without favouring Stalin, and the Spanish Republic became a Utopia as Soviet Russia had been in the 'twenties, with co-educational schools, enlightened prisons, and civil marriage. There was even a healthy anti-clericalism – a great improvement on Soviet Russia, for no one could feel anti-clerical about the Orthodox church. The one thing that went wrong was unfortunately the one thing that mattered. The Left failed to break the official refusal to supply the Spanish Republic with arms. Left meetings demanded 'arms for Spain'. Major C R Attlee gave the Communist salute to the International Brigade. No arms went to Spain.

Still, the agitation over Spain was a real struggle, as deeply felt as the General Strike ten years before. There was genuine and justified emotion. The Left were asserting the great principles of freedom and democracy, however unsuccessfully. They were seeking to resist the systems of dictatorship which plunged the world into war only three years later. What were Baldwin and the so-called governing classes doing during this great crisis? They were fussing over the question whether a middle-aged man should marry a woman who had two previous husbands, both living. Much can be said against the Left. They were romantic, idealistic, unworldly, often foolish. But one thing can be said in their favour. No one on the Left cared whom Edward VIII married, whether he married, when, or how often. The age of Baldwin was over so far as the Left were concerned. Totting up the account, I make one thumping debit and two credits. Ramsay MacDonald was the debit : the Left's present to the British people. The credits were the General Strike and support for the Spanish Republic – two honourable causes of which any political movement could be proud. It is true that the Left failed to decide what it meant by Socialism or how to get there. But these are problems to which no one has found a solution.

38.   Class War: 1926.[1]

A lapse into personal reminiscence on the occasion of the fiftieth anniversary of the General Strike.

The fiftieth anniversary of the General Strike is an excuse for some reminiscences by a member of the other ranks in the class war. In 1926 I was in my second year at Oxford. I had been a member of the ILP since 1921, when I was 15. I joined the Oxford University Labour Club as soon as I went up – not an easy process since my college, Oriel, had no college secretary and I had to seek out the club chairman, A L Rowse. I must have had an appetite for joining things. One evening an acquaintance at the Labour Club asked me: 'Why aren't you a member of the Communist Party?' Offhand I could not think of an answer, and on these inadequate grounds joined the Communist Party also.

The University Communist Party had at that time two members. Tom Driberg was one and I was the other. We held our meetings in Tom's elegant Christ Church rooms. The curtains were drawn; candles were burning and Tom shuffled round the room to the strains of a hot jazz record. We divided our duties. Tom sold the *Daily Worker* (or was it still the *Workers' Weekly*?) at the factory gates. I made Communist or at any rate left-wing speeches at the Labour Club. I did not take my political activities very seriously. I had a busy social life. I was in training with the college eight. Also I still had the foolish idea that lessons could be learnt from history. If another coal crisis came – and one was surely coming – either the union leaders would back down as they had done on Black Friday or the Government would back down as they had done on Red Friday. Maybe this time both would back down, as indeed they very nearly did at the last moment.

[1]*New Statesman*, 1976.

However, towards the end of April, it began to look as though there might really be a general strike. Perhaps the revolution was coming after all. Tom and I, who would presumably lead the revolution in Oxford, thought we should get instructions from headquarters. We went up to London in my car. At 16 King Street we found the shutters up and the door bolted. After much banging on our part there was a rattling of chains. An elderly Communist called Bob Stewart appeared. He eyed us sourly and said: 'There's no one here. I'm only the caretaker. Get along home with ye.' These were the only instructions I ever received from the Communist Party of Great Britain.

In Oxford undergraduates were being enrolled as strike-breakers and special constables. The Labour Club held a meeting to protest against the university's taking sides in the class war. A D Lindsay, the Master of Balliol, came and explained that the university was not involved: it had merely lent its premises to the government recruiting officers. The club did not accept this explanation and duly passed a motion of protest. The undergraduate volunteers were eager to be off. Many of them had fathers or elder brothers who had served in the war. Now, they felt, their own chance had come. Once more, 'God be thanked who has matched us with His Hour'. It was August 1914 all over again. The volunteers saw themselves gallantly at war against the revolution. One of them said to me: 'I wonder whether I shall ever come back.' The enrolment was Tom Brown's Last Stand. Nearly all the former public school boys enlisted. The grammar school boys stayed quietly in Oxford and went on with their work.

I, too, wanted to mount the barricades, though of course on the other side. There seemed little chance of doing this in Oxford, where all that was offered was missionary work in the surrounding villages. I decided to go home to industrial Lancashire. I sought permission from my college dean, Dr Wand, a muscular Christian, who was later Bishop of London. He puzzled over my request and then said: 'Other men have gone down to do their duty. I suppose you are entitled to go down to do what you think is yours.' At any rate I did better than some of my friends in Cambridge who got into trouble with their college authorities for refusing to enlist.

Norman Cameron was also anxious to join in the class war and came with me in my car to Preston. I found my father busy on the strike committee from morning to night, though I never discovered what he did – treasurer, deputy chairman, something like that. But what was there for me to do? There was no need to whip up support for a strike that was solid already. I put the problem to my father. He had a ready answer: 'You and I are the only two people in the Labour movement here who can drive a car. There will be plenty for you to do.' He exaggerated a little as he usually did: at least one union secretary had a car. But broadly what he said was true: driving a car was then a rare accomplishment.

There were union secretaries to take round the branches, strike pay to be distributed, returns of those on strike to be collected. Sometimes we went to encourage weaker strike committees in such Conservative strongholds as Blackpool. Norman Cameron also found useful activity. He joined a jobbing printer from the ILP and the two brought out a daily bulletin, most of which Norman wrote himself, though he did not contribute any poetry. I kept them supplied with newsprint which I collected from the *Daily Herald* in Manchester.

These longer journeys made a great impression on me. Nowadays a transport strike only means more cars on the roads. Then, in the words of the strike reports, 'everything stopped', at any rate in industrial Lancashire. The roads were empty. There were no trams, and mile after mile of deserted tram-lines has more impact than a mere absence of buses. I used to come back through a string of mining villages. In Preston and other towns the cotton mills and engineering shops were still open, and there were few strikers hanging around. In the mining villages there were strikers on every street corner. Only cars with a TUC sticker could pass. There were few local strike bulletins and the strikers distrusted the BBC news. They wanted to know how things were really going, and I had to address improvised open-air meetings, my first experience of public speaking.

Power seemed to be ours whenever we wanted to take it. I often asked my father when the strike committees would go over to positive action. He always gave me the same answer. This was not a general strike. It was a sympathetic strike in support of the miners, and it was the Government's job, not ours, to run the country. I am not sure whether my father was always so law-abiding. One evening a conspiratorial figure, with a hook instead of a right hand, called and talked privately to my father for a long time. Afterwards my father said 'I must go to London at once' and drove off. Perhaps he was merely reinforcing the TUC courier service that ran every day from London to Glasgow and back.

A day or two later my father came home radiant. He had just learnt from the one Labour member of the Watch Committee that the Government intended to arrest the leading members of strike committees and that his name was on the list. He said: 'They are losing their nerve. Now we shall see where the power really is.' He packed an overnight bag and waited hopefully for the knock on the door. It never came. Instead my father came home white-faced and with the duodenal pain that always racked him when he was upset. He said: 'The strike's over. We have been betrayed by our leaders.' That was all. My father never mentioned the strike again. When I next went home he was busy on the Board of Guardians. He claimed that his telephone was tapped for years afterwards but this may have been a product of his romantic imagination.

Norman and I went back to Oxford the same afternoon. The volunteers trickled back over the next few days. The special constables felt that they had performed a gallant service. The strike-breakers often resented that they had unloaded supplies far from essential. Many of them were distressed at the outcome: it had not occurred to them what the defeat of the strike would mean for the miners. Also they had developed a respect for what they called 'the other side'. They were not offended at what I had done. On the contrary, it created a bond between us; and we were far more friendly than we had been before. Their disapproval, so far as they had any, was directed against the 'shirkers' who had stayed in Oxford and not taken sides at all.

Soon afterwards those of us who had served on the right side had a dinner in New College. There were all the familiar faces from the Labour Club. One face was new to me; I asked who it was. The answer: 'He's a man called Gaitskell who turned up on the second day of the strike and said he wanted to help.' I have read somewhere that Gaitskell's rooms were wrecked because of his activities during the strike. You can expect anything from Wykehamists, but at any rate the wrecking did not take place the night I was there.

My experiences in the General Strike cured me of communism. In Preston the Communist Party had played no part in the strike, and the few Communists there were either useless or a nuisance. I decided that the Communist Party was not for me and quietly lapsed, thus escaping the soul torments that troubled so many intellectuals during the 1930s. The Communist Party was not the only ship that I abandoned. The college eight seemed to me unpromising and I used the excuse of my ten-day break in training to resign from it. I was right about that too: the Oriel first eight went down every night.

WAR

39.   Economic Appeasement

A review of *Economic Appeasement: Handel und Finanz in der britischen Deutschland-Politik 1933–1939* by Bernd Jürgen Wendt.[1]

British policy towards National Socialist Germany has been a heavily worked subject, at one time highly controversial and now settling down with more balanced perspectives. The emphasis has been on the political alternatives – whether to conciliate Germany by territorial concessions in Europe and elsewhere or to resist her by some system of alliances. Armaments have been discussed. Personalities have been canvassed. Public opinion has been assessed in a somewhat speculative way. Economic relations and policies have been relatively neglected. At the time they occupied the greatest attention. Hitler's rise to power was attributed, with much justice, to Germany's economic difficulties, and it was widely believed, though with less justification, that a return to prosperity would relax the harshness of Nazi dictatorship. At a more mundane level, the economic recovery of Germany – one of Great Britain's most important customers – was expected to contribute decisively to British recovery. Anti-Nazi writers accused the City of wishing to help Hitler as a bulwark against Communism. It would be probably truer to say that the City wished to help Hitler in order to help its own finances.

This is obviously a rewarding subject, and Bernd Wendt handles it well. With the opening of the British archives, he has been able to use the records of the Board of Trade and the Treasury as well as those of the Foreign Office. As he completed his research a year or two ago, it seems that the opening benefited him only until 1938. At any rate he has little from official sources about the last attempts at

[1]*English Historical Review*, 1972. Copyright © Longman Group and contributors.

economic appeasement in 1939. He has also relied greatly on articles in the principal economic journals and in *The Times*. Here his treatment is less satisfactory, perhaps unavoidably. He identifies Paul Einzig, the anti-Nazi writer in the *Financial News*. Otherwise most of the journalistic contributions are anonymous. As well Wendt has used the statements by the various economic associations – the cotton industry, the coal industry and creditors both trading and financial.

The story is one of great complexity. All economic interests wanted the recovery of Germany, but they wanted it for different reasons and in different ways. The coal and cotton industries wanted to increase their exports to Germany, which had brought them prosperity in the past; they did not want to achieve this by opening British and overseas markets wider to Germany in return. All industrialists wanted to be paid for the goods they had exported to Germany after the Reich had blocked foreign payments. Financial creditors also wanted to be paid with particular emphasis on restoring free exchanges. Here, too, there was a conflict of interest between the short-term creditors and the providers of long-term loans. Even the latter were split between the holders of German state bonds, raised under the Dawes and Young plans, and the holders of inferior securities. Finally there was a dispute as to whether the creditors from all countries should stand together or whether the British should make the best bargain they could for themselves. British industrialists and financiers favoured the latter course, much to the indignation of Americans and especially of the secretary of state, Cordell Hull.

All along there was equivocation. The British pursued agreement for its own sake as an immediate benefit. They also tended to believe that the Germans were as eager as they were for the restoration of a liberal international system. When this belief proved false, they fell back to the theory of Nazi extremists, led improbably by Himmler and Ribbentrop, and moderates, led by Goering. Schacht, the leading banker and for some time minister of finance, actively propounded this theory, though the only difference between him and the Nazis was that he wanted autarky with international approval and they did not care. There was much speculation as to where Hitler stood. As the only hope of success lay in his coming down on the moderate side, the British had to believe that this would happen. Despite the talk of Germany's retreating from autarky, the British were unconsciously moving towards it themselves. Though they would welcome a restoration of free exchanges, they did not intend to restore Free Trade or to abolish the system of Imperial Preference. In the last resort, the Germans were expected to surrender economic weapons of war which the British, thanks to their imperial legacy, could wield more respectably.

Political and economic judgements rarely went hand in hand. Wendt points the contrast between the house of commons debate on 13 April 1933, when speakers denounced the Nazi system, and that early in May, when they combined to praise the Anglo-German coal agreement. Soon after this things went the other way. Political appeasement hoped to bring Germany back to the disarmament conference. Economic leaders wanted to wield the big stick. It is curious to find Runciman, president of the board of trade, as the most ruthless of anti-Germans. The big stick was duly wielded on 14 June 1934 when the British government took powers to set up a clearing office. The German government gave way on this threat. On 1 November 1934 the two governments reached agreement on trade and exchange payments. British industrialists got a more secure access to German markets. British creditors got a gradual payment of some of their debts. This, though a British victory, was also a British concession. The agreement accepted the principle of bilateralism. British and Germans prepared to share out markets, and British creditors forgot about the claims of creditors in other countries. The City retreated from its international role.

The agreement of 1 November 1934 remained the basis of British economic policy until the outbreak of war. The Anglo-German naval agreement of 18 June 1935 was its political counterpart. Halifax followed its line when he visited Hitler in 1937. Throughout 1938 Neville Chamberlain hoped to get irrelevant political affairs such as Czechoslovakia out of the way so that the economic partnership should come into full effect. But there were always difficulties. The British regarded their retreat from liberal principles as a once-for-all concession. The Germans treated it as a first step towards complete autarky. Also the British held that there should be a sharing of the Balkans. The Germans wanted to monopolise the Balkans and yet to be admitted to the British empire as a tribute to their greater strength. The partnership was unequal. As Wendt puts it : how could a democratic system hold its own against a dictatorship without measures of compulsion which would infringe private enterprise and affect the living standard of the people? On top of this, there was the problem of America. The British wanted to preserve their independence and that of their Empire. They could not risk an open conflict with America for both economic and political reasons. Yet a trade war against the United States in South America was what the Germans wanted and, shortly before the outbreak of war, were on the point of getting.

Wendt insists rightly that economic appeasement did not end when British policy seemed to turn against Germany with the guarantee to Poland. Once more political differences were regarded as tiresome and irrelevant, troubles which must be got over by a mixture of firmness and conciliation. The renewed economic offers to Germany in July 1939 are well known, though much remains obscure and Wendt has little to add. He has to rely on the reports of Dirksen, the German ambassador, and these carried little weight. Wendt falls back on the idea that Hitler was now firmly resolved on war and so was uninterested in talk of economic concessions. This is speculation, though it may be right. Wendt is on stronger ground when he points to the confusion which prevailed throughout. The British always believed that, if they took one step towards autarky, the Germans would take two steps away from it. At the back of their minds, the British had a vision of a liberal economic order to which one day a prosperous Germany would return. They could not imagine a political authority which actually preferred autarky. How far Hitler did so consciously is a dark question, but German policy certainly worked out like this in practice.

Wendt tries to draw a moral. According to him, British policy towards Germany showed that the British were retreating from the world market and the British Empire. No longer an independent world power, the British turned to Europe for partnership. Hitler failed them. Now they have happily found their partner in the Common Market. It may be that Wendt's story is better read for its own sake, a fascinating historical episode which implies considerable revision of our views as to British policies before the Second World War.

40.　War in Our Time.[1]

A review of *Munich: The Price of Peace* by Telford Taylor (Doubleday, New York). I should add that, while I often indicate my agreement with Telford Taylor, he in his book often indicates that his disagreement with me. I may also add that we are not related.

The conference at Munich which led to the partition of Czechoslovakia was held over forty years ago on September 30, 1938. To judge from the books that still appear about it and the passionate feelings it evokes, the Munich conference was as significant as the congress of Vienna or the Paris peace conference of 1919. At first sight this is strange. As Telford Taylor rightly remarks, the conference settled nothing: its decisions had already been made in advance. 'Munich' was above all a symbol. A symbol of appeasement for some, a symbol of betrayal and weakness for others.

In a wider sense the Munich conference was the last time when Europe appeared as the centre of the world. The United States stood aside; Soviet Russia was excluded; and the four Great Powers – France, Germany, Great Britain, and Italy – imagined they were speaking for mankind. Munich marked the emergence of Greater Germany as the dominant power in Europe. Within seven years all was shattered. Germany was prostrate and partitioned; the other European Great Powers were diminished; Soviet Russia and the United States had become the masters of the world.

Telford Taylor's book is the most formidable and scholarly yet written about Munich. More than that, it surveys the entire course of European diplomacy from the peace conference of 1919 up to Munich and after. The sources used are unrivalled in extent. When I wrote my *Origins of the Second World War* nearly twenty years

[1]New York Review of Books, 1979. Reprinted with permission from *The New York Review of Books*. Copyright © *1979* Nyrev, Inc.

ago I had to rely largely on printed records such as selections of British and German documents. Telford Taylor, like other contemporary scholars, has had a free run of the British Cabinet papers, the Chiefs of Staff's reports, and comparable records from France, Germany, and, to some extent, Italy. The result is a book of 1,104 pages, hard going but none too long. No detail is neglected – for instance whether Hitler wore an armband on his left or his right arm. The most minor participants are meticulously catalogued. On a larger field the information about military affairs is particularly strong. We learn precisely what forces the Germans mobilized at the time of the Austrian and Czech crises and what the French could set against them. We can follow the arguments of the British Chiefs of Staff and the doubts some German generals expressed though to no great effect. This is more than a year-by-year, it is almost a day-by-day account.

Telford Taylor begins with the Munich conference itself. Since, as he says, the conference produced nothing new, this is an opportunity for a virtuoso 'I was there' performance such as some historians favour. There is nothing missing except the curious fact that, when the participants came to sign their agreement, there was no ink in the glittering inkstand. Then we go back to the beginning. First a quick run from the Paris peace conference to the German reoccupation of the Rhineland. Then a more detailed survey of the two years thereafter, which includes the Spanish civil war and the incorporation of Austria into Germany. Thus we arrive at the Czech affair, first with its background and the mounting tension during the summer of 1938, and then the actual crisis touched off by Chamberlain's visit to Hitler at Berchtesgaden. Finally a summary of events after Munich up to the outbreak of the Polish war and a brief assessment of what Munich meant and achieved.

There is little to criticise in this voluminous narrative except a few pedantic points. Telford Taylor is a little inclined to use 'Versailles' as a general name for the peace settlement, whereas the treaty of Versailles concerned only Germany and the peace conference was held in Paris. He attributes the succession states mainly to the initiative of the Great Powers and does not appreciate how much they made themselves. He inflates Italian grievances. Italy gathered all the fruits of the treaty of London except for North Dalmatia (not the whole of Dalmatia) and a vague promise of colonies. The alleged meeting of May 23, 1939 when Hitler foretold the certainty of war was probably a fabrication designed by some anti-Hitler sources to stir the British into action. These are not serious lapses.

On the greater issues Telford Taylor is emphatically right. In his view, which is also mine, Hitler was intent to make Germany the dominant power in Europe but had no clear idea how to do it. The reoccupation of the Rhineland was an improvisation. Only Schuschnigg's decision to hold a plebiscite surprised Hitler into action over Austria. After this Hitler intended the Czech problem to ripen gradually. Once more he was rushed into action by the Czech mobilization of May 21, 1938. Even then Hitler planned a surprise attack. This plan was upset by the prolongation of the diplomatic crisis. Hitler was rescued from the problem of how to launch a surprise attack that was not a surprise only by the dramatic appearance of Chamberlain from the air. As Telford Taylor rightly says, Chamberlain, not Hitler, gave the conclusion of the Czech crisis its final shape, though this is not to say that he caused it. Still Chamberlain was the midwife of the Munich conference. Telford Taylor is also right in dismissing the vaunted conspiracy of the German generals to overthrow Hitler as no more than late-night grumbling and hot air.

Diplomacy is well treated; as are military affairs, particularly the stress on the fact that the Luftwaffe was not equipped for strategic bombing. Some themes are in my opinion passed over or treated inadequately. The first is public opinion in the principal countries. I can write of this at first hand. I was an advocate of resistance to Hitler from the time he came to power and, though a member of the Labour Party, an advocate of intense rearmament after his reoccupation of the Rhineland. I was one of the few who addressed public meetings outside London during the fortnight before Munich, again advocating resistance. I must sorrowfully confess that these were the most difficult meetings I have ever experienced. There was not only fear of war, particularly fear of a repetition of the First World War. There was also a constant assertion that Hitler's claims were justified.

Telford Taylor quotes with disapproval a sentence of mine that the Munich settlement was 'a triumph for all that was best and most enlightened in British life.' I am sorry to disillusion him about my own attitude. The sentence was a bitter 'goak', to use a favourite word of Artemus Ward's, a writer now forgotten in England but not, I hope, in the United States. What I meant to convey was that all the most high-minded authorities in England had denounced the peace settlement of 1919 for many years. Hitler reaped where they had sown. I fear that I, too, had criticised the peace settlement during the 1920s. I was converted sooner than others. Certainly much of the British public had not been converted by September 1938.

I was in France during the first fortnight of September. On my return I told a friend on *The Manchester Guardian*: 'The French people will not fight. They may mobilise. They may man the Maginot line. But they will not fight.' No doubt this was only a personal impression but it was one derived from country towns and villages as well as from many talks with historians and journalists whom I knew in Paris. The French people and, I think, the French politicians felt secure behind the Maginot line and had ceased to care what happened beyond it. As to Germany, of course I never went there after Hitler came to power. But I think we can say of Hitler what Sorel said of Napoleon III, 'His origins condemned him to success.' Hitler, although a dictator, was acutely sensitive to public opinion. He never forgot the events of November 1918. Therefore he sought to provide a run of successes achieved by guile, not by actual war. What Mussolini and the Italian people thought is a matter of no great moment, though here, too, an easy triumph was the answer. Broadly speaking, the Munich conference secured what each of the participants thought their peoples wanted. It was easy for me at the time and is easy for Telford Taylor now to say that they, or at any rate Chamberlain and Daladier, were wrong, but wisdom and moral virtue are privileges accorded only to detached observers.

Another neglected theme is the effect of factors other than diplomatic and military on British policy. Telford Taylor does not seem to have read the book in German by Bernd Wendt on economic appeasement, a book based on papers in the Board of Trade, which British historians should have studied. From the onset of the Great Depression a main aim of British economic policy was the economic restoration of Germany. Coupled with this was the belief that National Socialism would lose its venom if Germany recovered her prosperity. Both the Board of Trade and the Bank of England strove to sustain the German currency. The Board of Trade tried to reach agreement with Germany over a partition of the Balkan market.

Walter Runciman was dismissed as an ignoramus when he was sent to Prague as mediator. But, as president of the Board of Trade, he knew a great deal about Eastern Europe. Like other British statesmen he was ready to recognise Germany as the economically dominant power there, but with some share still accorded to British interests. A British mission to negotiate in this sense was on the point of leaving for Berlin at the time of Hitler's occupation of Prague in March 1939, and these negotiations were renewed during the summer of 1939.

Neville Chamberlain fully endorsed these negotiations. Even Churchill, when hard pressed, spoke on May 27, 1940, of according Hitler 'the overlordship of central Europe.' British statesmen liked to think of themselves as realists. By 1938 they had ceased to hope that they could prevent Germany from becoming the dominant power in Europe east of the Rhine. They asked that this should be achieved by negotiation, not by force, that British interests should be not altogether excluded particularly in Romania, and they thought that Hitler would then be content. Alternatively, as we know from the negotiations in the autumn of 1939, they would be satisfied if Goering took the place of Hitler.

Telford Taylor never discusses what was the alternative. Sir Horace Wilson raised the issue in some notes he wrote for Chamberlain on September 10, 1938. Britain and Germany, he wrote, should be 'the two pillars that support orderly civilisation against the onslaught of disorderly Bolshevism.' Nothing should 'weaken the resistance that we can jointly offer to those who threaten our civilisation.' Alliance with Russia was the alternative to appeasement, as was recognised at the time by Lloyd George, Churchill and Sir Lewis Namier. Even they did not recognise the ultimate consequences.

A war between Nazi Germany and Soviet Russia would be disastrous from the British point of view at that time. If the Germans won, they would control all the resources of Russia as they nearly did in 1941. If the Russians won they would replace Germany as the dominant power in Eastern Europe. This was the actual outcome. Only those who believe, as I do, that Soviet overlordship, with all its faults, has been infinitely preferable to Nazi domination were entitled to advocate the Soviet alliance, and one can understand why British Conservatives of the 1930s hesitated.

Telford Taylor's outlook is very much concentrated on Europe, as is only natural. But the British international outlook of that time was not so concentrated. In the twenty years between the wars Great Britain was the only remaining world power. France and Italy had fallen out of that class if they were ever in it; the United States and Soviet Russia had not yet entered it. After the ending of the Anglo-Japanese alliance the British were trying to carry a world empire all on their own. They had little interest in European affairs except to be left alone. Their preoccupation, especially at the

Admiralty, was in the defence of the British Empire against Japan. Despite the alarms in Europe the underlying slogan of British policy, strongly urged by the imperialist Neville Chamberlain, was 'Main Fleet to Singapore'. Though the Second World War began in Europe, the British did most of their fighting outside Europe and from this aspect the war could be called the War of the British Succession. Of course these wider considerations were often obscured during a crisis such as the Czech affair. But I think a historian should not lose sight of them.

I have a final, larger reservation. Telford Taylor tells us not only what was done, but what should have been done. Thus, during the Abyssinian crisis, 'the wisest course, if bold, would have been to play the game of collective security to the hilt and bring Mussolini down, even if it meant war.' On the German reoccupation of the Rhineland, 'the French commanders should, if nothing better offered, have loaded their men into trucks and sent them across the border.' The British Air Staff should not have been frightened by the bombing capacity of the Luftwaffe. I thought at the time, and still believe, that Hitler was bluffing in the summer of 1938. In my opinion he meant what he said when he told his generals that he would attack Czechoslovakia only if he were certain that England and France would not intervene. I remain convinced that I was right. But this was the opinion of a contemporary observer, not of a historian.

In my view historians should not deal in this class of goods. The historian is like an onlooker at a game of poker. He sees the cards of all the players; he even knows what cards are in the deck and precisely how they are arranged. It is not surprising that he knows how the hands should have been played. This makes an amusing intellectual game, but it is no part of his business as a historian. The duty of the historian is to explain what happened, not to speculate on what might have happened. Even the greatest statesman makes mistakes. The historian can catalogue these mistakes; he cannot correct them and should leave the drawing of morals to the reader. The study of history enables us to understand the past better — no more and no less.

Telford Taylor however wishes to draw the moral himself. He takes issue with Keith Robbins, an English historian who has written a fine account of Munich.[1] Robbins concluded his study of Munich with these words: 'The only great lesson of Munich, the most diffi-

[1] *The New York Review*, March 22, 1979.

cult to learn, is that there are no great lessons. Historians, useless in predicting the future, achieve something if they prevent others doing so.' Telford Taylor however is determined to predict. He writes firmly : 'Munich has become a symbol of decisions to yield, wrongly reached because of fear and selfishness. . . . It is a potent and historically valid symbol of the dangers of not facing up to unpleasant realities. This is not a new lesson, but it is a great one, and it is the lesson of Munich.' This sounds very much like the policy defined by Harry Elmer Barnes as Perpetual War for the sake of Perpetual Peace.

In 1946 I visited President Beneš at the Hradschin Palace overlooking Prague. Taking me to the window, he said, 'Is it not beautiful? The only unspoilt city in central Europe, and all my doing.' When I raised my eyebrows, he added : 'By accepting the Munich settlement I saved Prague and my people from destruction.' I do not suggest that this was the lesson of Munich which a historian should necessarily accept.

41.   Catch-22 in the days of Munich.[1]

A Review of *'Appeasement' and the English Speaking World*
by Ritchie Ovendale (Cardiff: University of Wales Press).

Before the First World War the British Government took Dominions
aid and American sympathy for granted. Before the second both
were more essential and there was no certainty that they would be
forthcoming. In recent years this anxiety has been treated as the
key to Chamberlain's policy. Keith Robbins wrote of Munich, 'it
was taking an undue risk to make war without the certainty of
dominion support'. Chamberlain rarely put it so clearly. It seems
rather that doubts concerning the Dominions were called in aid of a
policy already determined. The documents also present difficulties.
At the Dominions Office, 'all significant papers on foreign affairs
have been destroyed under statute'; at the Foreign Office 'the
dominions intelligence files for 1938 have been destroyed'. Enough
remains to provide material for a book of considerable value.

The story starts with the Imperial Conference of 1937. At that
time all the Dominions except New Zealand were unwilling to be
involved in a European war. Smuts wrote: 'Our South African
representatives . . . will be extremely averse to South Africa or the
British Commonwealth being involved in any European conflict.'
Mackenzie King told the British ambassador in Washington: 'Canada
was resolved to maintain neutrality in any war at any price and on
no account would she be dragged into hostilities.' Chamberlain had
already embarked on appeasement and, as Ritchie Ovendale writes:
'The imperial conference convinced Chamberlain that his policy . . .
was the right one, but to say that it caused him to embark on it is
probably an exaggeration.'

At the Brussels conference in the autumn of 1937 the British

[1]*Times Literary Supplement,* 1976.

allowed others to shoulder the responsibility for inaction. Roosevelt gave this advice to the British Government:

1 It should not speak or think or act as though it were possible for me to be in any way an exponent of British Foreign Office policy.

2 It should never forget I cannot march ahead of our difficult and restive American public opinion; and

3 It must not try to push me in any way to the front or to thrust leadership upon me.

Jebb of the Foreign Office minuted: 'In my view sanctions [against Japan] would almost certainly mean war and the United States is not prepared to fight, even with the British Empire as an ally. Therefore there will be in fact no sanctions.' And a fortnight later: 'Generally speaking we seem to have put ourselves in the excellent tactical position of allowing the Dominions to torpedo a "sanctions" policy in advance before definitely committing ourselves one way or the other.' Once more the British Government was being pushed in the direction it wanted to go.

Dr Ovendale argues that the rift between Chamberlain and Eden that led to the latter's resignation was a clear-cut dispute over policy: Eden wishing to stake everything on close relations with the United States, and Chamberlain determined to approach the two Axis dictators directly. In reality the dispute was more blurred. Chamberlain held that it was useless to run after American aid. Eden on his side had no fundamental opposition to appeasement and objected only to the timing for it. Roosevelt's plan in any case did not amount to much. 'Certain minor powers would draw up an agenda for a conference to which all would be invited.' Would the minor powers have accepted this responsibility as mediators? If they had, would the major powers have allowed an agenda to be dictated to them? Both seem unlikely. Roosevelt wanted to act as peacemaker without committing himself in any way. No doubt this was all that American opinion would allow him to do.

The Czech crisis was a showpiece for support of appeasement by the Dominions. Smuts again expressed their general opinion:

As regards the Dominions they will fight for Great Britain if attacked, they will not fight in the battles of Central or South

Eastern Europe. I have even doubts whether they will fight again for France and Belgium.

However, as the crisis moved from talk to possible action, the Dominions began to abandon their reserves. On September 25 the High Commissioners were still saying that 'the German proposals *can't* be allowed to be a *casus belli*'. But on September 26 they agreed that if it came to war 'the Dominions would, however reluctantly, be in sooner or later, on the side of the United Kingdom'. On September 26 also the British Government reminded the Dominions that 'with the constitutional position of the king no dominion could remain neutral in international law'. Clearly the British Government assumed that when Father says 'turn' we all turn. This was surely a misreading of the Statute of Westminster but no Dominion government disputed it.

Roosevelt's contribution to the Czech crisis is memorable. He hoped that if the Western powers went to war they would rely solely on blockade :

Blockade must be based on loftiest humanitarian grounds and on the desire to wage hostilities with minimum of suffering and the least possible loss of life and property, and yet bring the enemy to his knees.

Roosevelt was anxious that others should act though he would do nothing himself. In March 1939, he told the British ambassador :

If the British wanted cooperation what they ought to make America believe was that they had enough backbone to retain their position by their own efforts and lick the other going on their own as they had done before. 'What the British need is a good stiff grog.'

This was a Catch-22 situation. The British must show they merited American support by taking independent action. If they took independent action this would prove that they did not need American support. British relations with the Dominions were another version of the same catch. If appeasement were successful, the Dominions would be pleased but their aid would not be needed. If appeasement failed, Dominions aid would be needed but they would be reluctant to give it.

The British knew that they were cheating the two Pacific Dominions when they talked of sending a fleet to the Far East. Chamberlain suggested that the Dominions should be warned that it might not be possible to send an adequate force. Chatfield replied:

> It appeared quite out of the question to put forward a satisfactory argument to the Dominions for weakening the assurance which we had given them. In fact, in his opinion, it would be dangerous to do so and would have an extremely bad effect on Dominion opinion. Even if we only sent a force of seven or eight capital ships to the Far East, we could trust to our superior efficiency to hold the position and to contain the Japanese fleet.

Stanhope went further: 'If one or two capital ships were sent to Singapore they would be a deterrent to Japan, especially if the United States fleet moved to Honolulu'. No plans were made for moving any ships to the Far East. The Dominions concerned were not warned.

Lord Halifax claimed later that the Dominions were disillusioned by Hitler's occupation of Prague. This is not confirmed by the records. Smuts wrote on April 6, 1939:

> Chamberlain's Polish guarantee has simply made us gasp – from the Commonwealth point of view. I cannot see the Dominions following Great Britain in the sort of Imperial policy the dangers of which to the Commonwealth are obvious. We still remember Lloyd George's Chanak escapade.

Dr Ovendale sums up firmly: 'The Commonwealth was not united after Prague, nor was support from the United States any more likely than it had been during the Munich crisis'. When war was actually on the horizon Roosevelt's only suggestion was that 'there be no declaration of war so that he could possibly avoid implementing the neutrality acts'. Mackenzie King was 'horror-struck by the talk of bringing Churchill and Eden into the cabinet' and told Chamberlain that Hitler's offer to Poland seemed 'significant and sincere'.

Dr Ovendale writes at the end of *'Appeasement' and the English Speaking World*:

> It seems strange that Canada did fight, particularly in the light of views frequently expressed about the dangers of becoming involved

in British quarrels in Europe. There was no strategic reason for Canada's fighting; Roosevelt had guaranteed Canada's security in his Kingston speech in September 1938.

The Dominions continued to favour appeasement until the last moment and, as we now know, even beyond it : they urged negotiations with Hitler in October 1939 and again in the summer of 1940. But, as Dr Ovendale writes : 'When it came to the choice what counted most were ties of sentiment and kin. The Dominions were not directly threatened by Hitler : they fought for Britain.'

British policy was not determined by either the Dominions or the United States. Appeasement was promoted for purely British considerations though it was no doubt desirable to keep the Dominions and the United States in a good temper. The British Government simply assumed, like an amateur theatrical company, that 'it would be all right on the night' and with the Dominions it was.

42. The War of the British Succession.[1]

A review of *Allies of a Kind: the United States, Britain, and the War against Japan, 1941–1945* by Christopher Thorne (Hamish Hamilton) and *Imperialism at Bay: the United States and the Decolonisation of the British Empire 1941–1945* by William Roger Louis (Oxford).

I am inclined to patent my new name for the Second World War in Asia.

During the Second World War and for a generation after it Germany occupied the centre of the stage; Japan seemed remote and almost irrelevant except of course to those engaged in the war against her.

With the passage of time perspectives have changed. The war against Germany now appears as, let us hope, the last episode in the long struggle for the mastery of Europe which had occupied most of modern history. The Far Eastern war had deeper consequences: within a short time it ended the white domination of Asia which had characterised the previous 200 years.

This was totally unexpected. The British fought to restore the Empire they had lost at the end of 1941; the Americans, though by no means anxious to restore the British Empire, assumed that it would be replaced by their own predominance, suitably cloaked in idealistic phrases. Both were disappointed. Japan, though defeated in battle, won a moral victory. Asia for the Asians ended the age of Imperialism.

This is a tremendous theme and here at last are two magnificent books devoted to it. Christopher Thorne's is a staggering achievement. Its 700 pages survey not only Anglo-American relations and the war

[1]*Observer,* 1978.

against Japan. They also illuminate the problems of China, India, South East Asia and Australasia. Thorne's research ranges over the continents. He is a master of diplomacy as well as of war and also, what is perhaps even more important for an historian, a master of personalities. All the participants from Roosevelt and Churchill downwards come alive. Churchill's outlook is summarised in a single phrase: 'Why be apologetic about Anglo-Saxon superiority? We are superior.'

Roosevelt was at his most devious in his patronage of both Britain and China. He could have said with Pearl Buck, 'If the American way of life is to prevail in the world, it must prevail in Asia.' Revealing, too, was the remark of the American Chiefs of Staff that, if Puerto Rico were ever to be given its freedom, its inhabitants would first have to 'voluntarily and under no duress acknowledge the facts' and grant the United States unshakable defence rights there.

The British had comparatively little military strength to spare for the Far East: only 10 per cent of the British servicemen who died in the war died there. But their ambitions were none the less limitless. As Churchill said, 'All, all shall be restored.' The Americans regarded the British as tiresome and somewhat ineffective allies. If the British were to act at all, it should be with the aim of reopening land communications with China, on whom the Americans set exaggerated hopes in both the military and political spheres. The British, judging China more realistically, strove for an offensive towards Burma and South-East Asia, which they did not achieve until the war was almost over.

The Far Eastern war was a racial war by implication and often in practice. Thus Roosevelt, though anxious to end British rule in India – perhaps even by 'reform on the Soviet line' – also thought that the Indians needed an infusion of Nordic blood. As Thorne remarks, 'The saviour of the East, it seems, was to be neither a Gandhi nor a Curzon, but Siegfried with a sitar.'

Both the British and the Americans thought that they alone understood the Asiatics and that their partners did not. Their partnership was often strained. The British broke one of the main American diplomatic codes, though they ended their eavesdropping once America was in the war. Roosevelt remarked, 'I do not mean to be unkind or rude to the British, but in 1841, when you acquired Hong Kong, you did not acquire it by purchase.' To which Oliver Stanley, the British Colonial Secretary, replied, 'Let me see, Mr President, that was about the time of the Mexican War, wasn't it?'

Often the records quoted by Thorne give the impression that the British and Americans were more concerned to thwart each other than to get on with the war against Japan. Or rather they ran both struggles at the same time. In the last resort they were forced together and became 'allies of a kind.' There were ties of common interest and common ideals, but there was also much misunderstanding and some hostility.

Roger Louis presents the same relationship, as limited to the Anglo-American debate on the future of colonial possessions after the war. As this debate was conducted between diplomats or academics it had fewer of the open brawls that marked the arguments between the respective chiefs of staff or the somewhat irresponsible pronouncements of President Roosevelt. The British prided themselves on their record of colonial administration and insisted that they could maintain it, even in the mandated territories, without international supervision. The Americans preached trusteeship which would replace imperialism by international control.

There followed a curious twist. The Americans, though anxious to eliminate all other empires, wished to acquire one for themselves. Their eyes were set on the Pacific Islands which they proposed to transform into a ring of strategic bases directed against Japan.

The arguments went on throughout the war. In the end they proved irrelevant. At the San Francisco conference the British, faced with Australian as well as American pressure, succumbed to the principle of trusteeship for their mandated territories and later dismembered their entire Empire for reasons quite unconnected with American promptings. As for the Americans, they duly secured strategic control of the Pacific Islands but, as Japan ceased to be a danger, the islands proved to be so many white sea-elephants, nor did the islands help the Americans much when they tried to assert their supremacy on the mainland of Asia and in Vietnam.

As often happens in war the British and Americans were trying to provide against past dangers and did not foresee the future problems with which they would be faced. In the eyes of both British and Americans the Far Eastern war was the war of the British Succession. As things worked out there was no successor except the peoples of Asia themselves.

43. Alarm in High Places.[1]

A review of *Ministry of Morale* by Ian McLaine (Allen & Unwin).

The Ministry of Information was not accorded a volume in the official civil history of the Second World War. It died unhonoured and unsung. Presumably it was felt to be beneath the dignity of an official history. This is not surprising. The comedy extracted from the MOI files by Ian McLaine surpasses even the fantasies provided by Evelyn Waugh in 'Put Out More Flags.' Indeed this is the funniest book I have read for a long time.

The key to the story was provided by a member of MOI when he wrote, 'The whiter the collar, the less the assurance.' The mandarins of MOI, surveying the world from the heights of the Senate House in Bloomsbury, knew nothing of this. A colleague wrote of Harold Nicolson, one of the highest mandarins: 'He was quite ignorant of the habits and attitudes even of the middle classes. As for the working classes he seemed to regard them as barbarians to be feared, admired and placated.' Their alarms were derived from what 'they had heard in the club the previous evening or on the train in the morning.'

Starting from this outlook, the directors of MOI expected panic even during the Phoney War and even more during the Blitz. They exhorted others to show the courage that they did not possess themselves. Their ideas of successful propaganda were curious. One of them suggested as iconography 'A long-bowman from the Hundred Years' War, standing with his feet outspread (to represent steadiness) and drawing his bow (to represent vigour).' He added this explanation: 'The archers, who provided the mainstay of the English Army, were drawn from the lower classes.'

[1]*Observer,* 1979.

In fact the despised working classes were unshaken by the Blitz, though they took such sensible precautions as they could. As McLaine writes, 'They were not to know that those servants of the Government employed, among other things, to extol their heroism were at the same time breathing hearty sighs of relief that their task had not been to stem a tide of panic and defeatism.'

The pundits of MOI took Goebbels as their model. They recorded sadly that the public harboured 'little sense of real personal animus against the average German man or woman' and urged that this must be replaced by 'personal anger . . . against the German people and Germany.' Harold Nicolson remarked, 'It is so strange that in this moment of anxiety there is no hatred of Hitler or the Germans.'

Hence there followed the Anger Campaign which ran stories of German atrocities which, though true, were not believed. When this campaign miscarried, the MOI resorted to the opposite tack of promising a better world after the war with copious doses of a more egalitarian social system. After penning one such string of promises Nicolson descended to the Senate House refectory of which he recorded, 'It is absolutely foul. . . . We have got to queue up with trays with the messenger boys.'

The Religious Department provided its quota of Christianity, together with an appeal that 'we should refrain from condemning the Pétain *internal* programme in France.' Not surprisingly the public were reported 'to suspect that certain of their leaders would betray them as Pétain and Laval had betrayed the French people.'

British bombing of Germany supplied its element of embarrassment. Sir Arthur Harris, chief of Bomber Command, made no secret of the fact that his aim was to destroy German morale by indiscriminate bombing of German cities. The Air Ministry did not like this, MOI still less so and maintained a rigid denial of what Bomber Command was doing. To the surprise of MOI the mass of people were indignant that German cities were not being bombed more heavily.

Soviet Russia's appearance as an ally furnished the richest comedy of all. MOI faced the insoluble question : how were they to welcome the new ally and rejoice at its victories without suggesting that the Soviet economic system worked with great success? No answer was ever found. When Communists organised pro-Soviet meetings, the local Mayor was instructed to take over the meeting himself. Alexander Werth, supposedly a left-winger, recommended from Moscow 'that people like Pollitt should be shut up – preferably by

Moscow, which might perhaps also be asked to instruct the British CP to go all Union Jacky.' The Communist shop-stewards needed no such instruction : for the duration of the war they were the most effective strike-breakers in British history.

Lord Clark, himself a member of MOI, wrote of it recently, 'It was a perfectly useless body, and the war would have been in no way affected if it had been dissolved and only the censorship retained.' This applies only to its unnecessary attempts to boost morale. The British people did not fight for some high ideal or a better social system. Simply, as people often said, 'We're not having those Nazis here.' They were determined on victory. In the summer of 1940 people often stopped me in the street and said, 'Poor old Hitler, he's done for now he has taken us on,' and so it proved.

In other ways MOI performed useful services. Its regional offices explained the mountain of regulations to the public. After an air raid people did not want to be exhorted to steadfastness. They wanted to know where to find accommodation and new ration books, and this is what the MOI regional office told them. Once Brendan Bracken took over, MOI became an effective body, pressing the service departments and the Cabinet for the earlier release of news and exercising 'a very high degree of common sense.'

I add a word of warning to future researchers. McLaine relies heavily on the reports of Home Intelligence. These were supplied by amateurs such as myself who allegedly recorded their impressions from meetings or private conversations. I took little notice of these impressions and merely put down what I myself thought at the time or wanted to advocate. I suspect that most contributors to Home Intelligence did much the same. Home Intelligence was in fact propaganda in reverse. We were trying to instil some common sense into the mandarins of the Senate House. We did not have much success.

44. Boom and Bombs.[1]

A review of *Trenchard* by Andrew Boyle (Collins).

Trenchard was the first Chief of the Air Staff and held the post
longer than any of his successors. He is rightly named 'father of the
Royal Air Force', though he disliked the phrase. He was also a
remarkable character on his own account. Mr Harold Macmillan,
generously coining a blurb for a rival publisher, has called him 'a
great man: great in stature, great in courage and great in achievement'. He was big rather than great. In physique he was outsize
and made himself bigger by his powerful voice. His generation
knew him as 'Boom'. He was a man of few words, but these few
were penetrating. His brief speeches should be printed in capital
letters. On paper, he was crisp, clear and effective. He was the man
to send when disorder threatened. He quelled a mutiny at Southampton in 1919 among the troops returning from France. He restored
duty and disclipline in the Metropolitan Police after a bad period in
the Thirties. He deserves the excellent biography which Andrew
Boyle has written. It is a bit long and a bit too laudatory. But it is
easy to read, clear on the issues and brings a good deal of new
information – some from Trenchard's papers, more from his vivid
conversation in old age.

The important thing in Trenchard's life was his creation of the
Royal Air Force. Thanks to him, it became an independent force,
instead of being divided between the two existing services, the army
and the navy. This was a remarkable achievement, particularly
against such a formidable opponent as Beatty, the First Sea Lord.
What inspired Trenchard was more important still. He believed
that the principal function of the RAF was to drop bombs. Of course
he recognised that it had other functions also: patrol work for the

[1]*New Statesman*, 1962.

navy, and direct combat in cooperation with the army at the front – a task which he himself directed for much of the First World War as commander of the Royal Flying Corps. Independent bombing was the new and most important task. The next war, he believed, would be won by dropping bombs, not by land fighting. He applied this doctrine in practice and made the RAF predominantly a bomber force. The doctrine had vital consequences. It shaped British policy before the Second World War and British strategy during much of the war itself. In Trenchard's view there was no defence against bombing; there was only the 'deterrent' of a superior bomber force. Baldwin was repeating Trenchard's doctrine when he said: 'the bomber will always get through'. Hence British policy had to be cautious, or even craven, so long as the German bombers were thought to be more formidable than the RAF. On the other hand, the excessive confidence of Bomber Command also sprang from Trenchard's doctrine. He was responsible, in the last resort, for the strategical air offensive which has recently been scrupulously examined in an official history.

Trenchard's biography shows how this doctrine originated. It sprang from dogma, not from experience. During the First World War the RFC, forerunner of the RAF, worked with the army, observing enemy movements, fighting German aeroplanes. Trenchard was in command, not as a particularly skilled pilot, still less as a technician, but simply because he knew how to command. He was a competent regimental officer of high character, devoted to Haig, whom he resembled. Late in 1917 Rothermere was made first Secretary for Air – perhaps as a manoeuvre by Lloyd George to keep Rothermere's brother Northcliffe quiet. Trenchard was recalled from France to become Chief of the Air Staff; and, according to him, for an odd reason. Rothermere said that he and Northcliffe were about to launch a press campaign against Haig, and needed Trenchard as cover. Trenchard, being loyal to Haig, at first refused the job; then, most strangely, accepted. He soon quarrelled with Rothermere, though over another question. He insisted on sending all available aeroplanes to France. Rothermere was playing up to public opinion which had been frightened by German air raids and wanted to keep most of the aeroplanes in England. Trenchard was dismissed, and Lloyd George, regarding him as an ally of Haig's, approved. Meanwhile Trenchard's old post, commanding the RFC, had been filled. He was hastily put in charge of a new independent bombing force at Nancy. This again was a gesture to satisfy British public opinion, which was clamouring for 'retaliation'. Few bombs were dropped on Germany, and to little effect. Trenchard talked big rather than acted; and his talk convinced him, if not others. He, previously the advocate and practitioner of air power as a wing of the army, now became the champion of the independent bomb.

This new faith grew stronger when he returned as Chief of the Air Staff after the war. He fought for his own independent position and that of the RAF. He needed a decisive argument. He found it in Iraq. In 1922 warning pamphlets and a few incendiary bombs subdued a tribal rising at a cost of £10,000, where a military expedition would have cost £500,000. This trivial affair made a decisive mark on British history. The RAF won its independence. It became the cornerstone of British power in the Middle East. The lesson of the Iraqi villages was applied to the cities of Europe. They, too, could be bombed into subjection, much as Trenchard cowed the mutinous troops at Southampton with his booming voice. The bomber aeroplane was the strategical equivalent of a fist banged on the table. Boom and Bomb became one. In the middle twenties Trenchard was planning to bomb France – an unlikely enemy, but a possible rival. When Germany appeared as a real danger, bombing was again offered as the only answer.

Mr Boyle praises Trenchard as the man who prepared victory in the Battle of Britain. This is not so. The Battle of Britain was won by Fighter Command and radar. Trenchard had despised the one and knew nothing of the other. What Trenchard prepared was the strategical air offensive of 1940-41, which was a total failure, and, more remotely, the air offensive of 1942-44, which, though more successful, did more damage to this country than to the Germans. Like Haig, his hero, Trenchard was an extremely resolute and dogged commander, whose weapons did not come up to expectations and whose plans did not correspond to the facts. He was a strategical player who called above his paper. It is all dead stuff now, at any rate in Trenchard's terms. The conventional bomb and the conventional aeroplane have had their day as weapons of war. Still, it makes an odd story. Trenchard would not have hit on independent bombing if he had not become involved in an obscure intrigue of Northcliffe and Lloyd George, and if the tribes of Iraq had not been troublesome. Coventry, Hamburg and Dresden all paid for it. Maybe our strategy now is based entirely on cool, rational calculation. But it is just possible that there are still some in high places who think that Boom and Bomb are the same thing.

45.   Bombing Germany.[1]

A review of *History of the Second World War. The Strategic Air Offensive against Germany 1939–1945* (H.M.S.O. 4 Vols) by Sir Charles Webster and Noble Frankland. This volume has a special interest. It is one of the few works of official history in which the authors held their own against objections by the service Chiefs.

The bombing of Germany by British aeroplanes began on 15 May 1940. It continued, though not without interruption, until the end of April 1945. No part of war policy stirred more argument then and since. Some held that the war could be won by bombing alone. Sir Arthur Harris, Commander-in-Chief of Bomber Command, wrote in 1942: 'Victory, speedy and complete, awaits the side which first employs air power as it should be employed.' Others, equally extreme, believed that the bomber offensive was an immoral waste of effort. The full account in the official history, now published, will start the argument afresh. The volumes are a model of scholarly accuracy and impartiality, a bit cumbersome and long-winded, but never failing to tell the truth as far as it can be ascertained. They are a great achievement, and it is sad that Sir Charles Webster has not lived to receive the praise which is his due.

Many will use these volumes as an opportunity to denounce those in charge of British policy from Sir Winston Churchill to Sir Arthur Harris. Others will extol British courage and achievement. In my view, the historian is not concerned to fight past battles over again, still less to fight them differently. His duty is to explain. We can safely assume that all leaders in wartime make mistakes; we can also assume that the mistakes were honest mistakes and that there were good reasons for making them. Criticism after the event places one

[1]*New Statesman,* 1961.

piece on the board differently without appreciating that this affects every other piece. For instance, the bomber offensive did not knock Germany out in 1943. Nevertheless, it prevented the Germans from putting a far greater air strength on the Eastern front and so helped the Soviet victories. What indeed would have happened to Soviet determination without it? The present authors conclude cautiously and wisely :

> Strategic bombing . . . made a contribution to the war which was decisive. Those who claim that Bomber Command contribution to the war was less are factually in error. Those who claim that its contribution under different circumstances might have been yet more effective disagree with one another and often overlook basic facts.

The basic fact is that Bomber Command operated in the unknown and that it had to proceed by trial and error. It started the war with the wrong strategy and inadequately prepared for that. Its pre-war plan was for precise bombing by daylight of selected targets. This proved impossible, as the *Luftwaffe* was also to discover. Sir Charles Portal, Chief of the Air Staff, refused to believe that a long-range fighter could be invented. He was wrong, as the Americans showed in 1944; and this was one of the great mistakes of the war. But it was supported in this country by all informed opinion. Night bombing seemed to be the only alternative. This, too, was supported by informed opinion for mistaken reasons. It was held that the morale of the German people was weaker than that of the British. This turned out to be quite untrue. The Germans sustained much greater blows than the British had done without any shaking of morale until the very end. It was also held that German industry was already fully stretched and that relatively small losses would bring Germany to her knees. This was a catastrophic error. Germany's economic mobilisation was on a small scale and had made few inroads on civilian production, which declined much less than in Great Britain. Air attack actually stimulated her war production, which reached its peak in July 1944 when independent strategic bombing was already over. One can argue that the production would have been still greater without the air attacks; one can equally well argue that the increase would not have taken place without the stimulus from air attacks.

What seems broadly true is that strategic bombing demanded more economic effort from Great Britain than it inflicted economic damage on Germany. But even this is not a decisive argument. Strategic bombing, when it started, sprang from the motive that there was nothing to which British resources could be more usefully devoted. This was unanswerable. Churchill endorsed it. He never believed, as is sometimes alleged, that bombing could win the war; he believed rightly that it was the best contribution which Great Britain could make towards winning the war in the circumstances of the time. The claim of Sir Arthur Harris that bombing alone could win the war was never tested by events for he was never given either the free hand or the resources which he laid down as necessary.

There was a narrower issue in dispute – that between area bombing which Harris favoured and the bombing of precise targets, which Harris dismissed as 'panaceas'. We can see in retrospect that Harris was right, though not always for the right reasons. Area bombing was the only operation of which the hastily trained crews of Bomber Command were capable. Precision bombing would have demanded a long period of training, during which no bombing would have taken place and supplies to Bomber Command would have been cut down in favour of competing needs. Bomber Command, in fact, had to bomb in order to justify itself; and area bombing was its only possibility. Moreover some of the 'panaceas' were inaccessible; others were not the 'panaceas' which they were alleged to be. For instance, Bomber Command was repeatedly urged to attack the ball-bearing factory at Schweinfurt, a difficult operation. It ultimately did so with disappointing results. The Germans discovered to their surprise, and still more to that of the Ministry of Economic Warfare, that they had enough ball-bearings in stock to keep them going until new production was started.

Still, the strongest argument for area bombing was that Sir Arthur Harris believed in it. He had brought new inspiration to Bomber Command after the failures of 1941. He alone understood the operational needs and difficulties of his Command. Nor was it irrelevant that he had personal access to Churchill and strong support from Cherwell. A commander who claims to know how to win the war when others are doubting will always do much to carry the day.

The situation changed once the allied armies landed in France. The German night fighters lost the guidance of their advanced radar stations. Bomber Command could undertake precision bombing against German oil supplies and did so with tremendous effect. This, of course, does not prove that it could have been done successfully while Western Europe was under German occupation. Strategic bombing had been intended to make an allied invasion unnecessary; instead it helped to make it successful. As with most past controversies, careful study of the record does not enable us to decide for one side or the other. It only enables us to understand what they were arguing about and why they argued as they did.

Can we draw any moral or guidance for the future? Fortunately not about strategic bombing in the strict sense. Strategic bombing, as practised in the last war, is now as obsolete as bows and arrows. A new war, if it comes, will undoubtedly be much more devastating, probably much faster, at any rate quite different. But, though weapons change, men remain the same. The lasting interest of this story is in the human sphere – how decisions were shaped, not how they were carried out. As technical power increased, confusion of counsels increased also. There was never a single strategic direction of Bomber Command. Sir Arthur Harris often determined strategy. Sir Charles Portal gave instructions for operations. Lord Cherwell influenced strategy as well as providing scientific assistance – or sometimes, as in the case of *Window* (the device of dropping tinfoil to interfere with German radar), retarding it. The Ministry of Economic Warfare tried to determine bombing policy. The Admiralty wanted Bomber Command diverted to the war against the U-boats and often got its way. For a short period in 1944, Sir Arthur Tedder was put in supreme charge in order to prepare for the invasion. Things were done to impress public opinion or were sometimes prevented by it. Other things were done to impress the Americans or to prove them wrong. The Prime Minister intervened with ideas of his own.

In all this turmoil one almost forgets the crews of Bomber Command who ultimately had to carry out the conclusions of these conflicting authorities: 59,000 lost their lives. If the past be any guide, all the expectations of all the experts who are now preparing for war will turn out to be wrong and the experts will go on being wrong while the war is being fought. In the end, no doubt, someone will win. Clemenceau said that war was too serious a business to be left to soldiers. Nowadays it is too serious a business to be left to anybody.

46.   More Luck Than Judgement?[1]

A review of *Science and Government* by C P Snow (Oxford).

In the summer of 1940 the Royal Air Force startled the world by winning the Battle of Britain. Many contributed to this victory, from the pilots to the Prime Minister, Winston Churchill. Their courage and sacrifice might have been in vain if it had not been for the British possession of that unique instrument, radar. The credit for its possession, and for the fact that it was in full operation by 1940, is mainly due to one man – a relatively unknown scientist, Sir Henry Tizard.

Tizard was not an originator; he was not a practical worker in the laboratory; least of all was he a parliamentary politician. He was the first and greatest of the 'back-room boys', the more or less acknowledged scientific adviser to pre-war Governments. Tizard hit on radar as the decisive weapon for British defence before its practical effectiveness had been demonstrated; he set the best scientific minds at work on its development; and he then personally supervised the preparations for its operation.

The Battle of Britain was his victory. Yet when the German aeroplanes tumbled from the skies and Hitler abandoned his invasion plans in frustration, Tizard was not acclaimed. He was not rewarded or given other great tasks. Instead he sat disregarded, never again to exercise influence on the conduct of the war or even be invited to do so.

He went into obscurity as President of Magdalen College, Oxford, and re-emerged only when the Labour Government took office after the war. Sir Charles Snow is perhaps a little hard when he writes of Tizard's election at Magdalen : 'The Establishment in England has a knack of looking after its own.' This is not how it appeared to the

[1]*Observer*, 1961.

Fellows of Magdalen, most of whom were remote from 'the Establishment' I know. I was one. But no doubt things look different from outside.

Tizard's fall had a crude personal explanation. On 10 May Churchill became Prime Minister. He had long had a scientific adviser of his own, F. A. Lindemann (later Lord Cherwell), Professor of Experimental Philosophy – in other words Physics – in the University of Oxford. Lindemann would tolerate no rival near the throne. Within three weeks of Churchill's taking office, Lindemann forced Tizard's resignation and deprived him of all future say in the conduct of the war. Lindemann became scientific dictator for the duration, and gave the Government advice which was as disastrously wrong as Tizard's had been proved triumphantly right. He asserted that the war could be won by bombing attacks on German working-class housing. Tizard claimed that Lindemann's estimate of destruction was five times too high; P M S Blackett, an associate of Tizard's, decided independently that it was six times too high; survey after the war showed that it had been ten times too high. Tizard summarised correctly: 'The actual effort in manpower and resources that was expended on bombing Germany was greater than the value in manpower of the damage caused.' After examining the evidence, it is hard to dispute this verdict.

This is the story Sir Charles Snow tells in the Godkin Lectures which he delivered at Harvard. He tells it with the gifts – rarely combined – of a scientist, an experienced Civil Servant and an accomplished literary artist. The result is as fascinating as one of his best novels, with the added advantage of being a true story, or at any rate of dealing with real persons. The two men concerned are enough to make it tingle in itself. Both were remarkable men of great ability, though neither had the creative genius of a Rutherford. Both sought to put science – and their own talents – at the service of the State. They went about it in different ways.

Tizard was the ideal scientist for Civil Servants – or, as Sir Charles Snow writes, for 'the Establishment'. He was the perfect chairman of a committee, choosing the right men for it and getting the best out of them. His favourite field of influence was the Athenaeum, where he would catch the ear of Hankey or Bridges – themselves the backroom boys of Government – and leave them to carry the politicians.

Lindemann, though an extreme Tory, cared nothing for 'the Establishment', and despised Civil Servants as he despised nearly everyone else. A man of considerable wealth, he moved in Society. There he met Birkenhead and Churchill. He made Churchill his hero, and Churchill repaid his admiration to the full. It was this personal connection alone, and not any detached examination of his qualifications, which made Lindemann scientific dictator during the war.

In this position, Lindemann was a lone wolf. He did not consult other scientists. He ran his private statistical office, to produce figures which suited his arguments. So long as Churchill ruled, he reigned supreme; and when Churchill fell, he fell with him – to return after the Conservative victory of 1951.

Sir Charles Snow draws a number of morals from his cautionary tale. The conflict between Lindemann and Tizard was fought, from first to last, behind the scenes. This, Sir Charles insists, was inevitable. Decisions over great scientific questions – radar, bombing or (one may add) nuclear war – must be taken in 'closed politics'. This, again to follow Sir Charles, has three forms: committee politics, hierarchical politics, and court politics. Tizard was a master of the first and second; Lindemann won by using the third. One can call it, more crudely, 'personal intrigue.'

Sir Charles Snow condemns the outcome emphatically. 'It is dangerous to have a solitary scientific overlord ... We have seen too much of that, and we should not like it to happen again.' He also condemns Lindemann's qualities as a scientist. Lindemann, he says, was a believer in gadgets, and 'anyone who is drunk with gadgets is a menace.' 'It isn't wise to be advised by anyone slightly mad.'

Yet Sir Charles insists that we must have scientists active in all the levels of Government. This is not merely so as to explain their technical achievements or to carry them through. 'Scientists have something to give which our kind of existential society is desperately short of ... That is foresight.' 'Scientists have it within them to know what a future-directed society feels like.'

He ends with this warning: 'We [and he now apparently means Western society as a whole] are immensely competent; we know our own pattern of operations like the palms of our hands. It is not enough. That is why I want some scientists mixed up in our affairs.' This is an odd conclusion to a story which has shown one particular scientist mixed up in our affairs only too well.

The literary magic of Sir Charles Snow at first carries all before it. Then doubts begin. First on the personal side of the story. Here the novelist seems to have taken control almost to the point of caricature.

I knew Lindemann slightly, and have never met anyone more dislike-able. I knew Tizard intimately when he was President of Magdalen – perhaps better than any non-scientist did. I served him devotedly, and remained friendly with him after he left Oxford. Yet I cannot swallow either of Sir Charles Snow's pictures. No one would guess from this account that Lindemann, almost single-handed, transformed the Clarendon laboratory at Oxford from a mid-nineteenth-century shed into an institution of international reputation, rivalling the Cavendish at Cambridge, nor that he assembled round him some of the most distinguished scientists in the world.

Though he could perhaps claim no great discoveries himself, he made it possible for others to make them. He was primarily respon-sible for bringing refugee German scientists to England when Hitler came to power, and for setting their great talents to work. His was the decision which authorised the continuation of nuclear research during the war up to the point where practical execution could be handed over to the Americans. They were given the secrets, inciden-tally, by Tizard – his last public work during the war.

Tizard, in contrast, seems too favourably drawn. He was all that Sir Charles says. But he had his weaknesses. He liked to settle things behind the scenes: a quiet committee meeting ending in a recom-mendation, drafted – I must say incomparably – by himself, and then formally carried at some larger body. Open debate shook him; oppo-sition unnerved him. I suspect that, like Sir Charles Snow, he saw in all such debates a struggle for power, and therefore regarded argu-ment as an attack on his position. I did not share this view, though it is now widely held. In my opinion and experience, most men are more concerned to defend their interests and to prove themselves right than to grasp power. Strong intellectual convictions (often of course wrong-headed) are the great motive force, and men quarrel over power only when no real issue divides them. Tizard was as much a dictator as Lindemann, but he disliked publicity. He wanted to be an anonymous dictator, a dictator off-stage. Perhaps he had lost confi-dence when I knew him, but I wonder whether his tidy complacency was not in itself enough to provoke Lindemann. I doubt whether Lindemann opposed radar, as Snow makes out, but he wanted it (and other things) done in emergency and haste. Tizard insisted on work-ing 'through the usual channels.'

I have further doubts, if we lift the conflict off the personal plane. How simple Sir Charles makes it look: radar, the cool scientific solution; bombing, the wild impulsive guess. Was it really so? Did not both express the different personalities of the two men? Tizard was meticulous, cautious, worrying about the inventory of college furniture or about his pension. Lindemann was blustering and aggressive: he looked as though he banged his head against a stone wall for half an hour each day to keep it in trim. Without knowing any of the scientific arguments, it was easy to guess that one would back radar, and the other indiscriminate bombing.

Radar was not adopted after a careful array of the evidence in its favour. The argument was simply: 'It is this or nothing.' Tizard backed a 'hunch' and it worked. Lindemann similarly backed a 'hunch' over bombing and it failed to work. But in the situation where Russia seemed to be losing and the Americans had hardly begun to come into the war, the argument was the same: 'this or nothing.' Either Great Britain could win the war by destroying German housing or she could not win the war.

Sir Charles seems to imply that Lindemann was alone in advocating indiscriminate bombing. This is not so. Churchill always inclined to believe that bombing could win the war. Bomber Command held this belief fanatically from first to last, as Sir Arthur Harris, I think, still does. Was Lindemann all that wrong in endorsing it?

Assuming that Germany could not be defeated on land – and that was a reasonable assumption early in 1942 – the war would still be going on in 1945. The Allies then might have the nuclear bomb, thanks to Lindemann. Is it not possible that they would have then won by bombing? In any case, Tizard, as Sir Charles Snow remarks, had no rival solution. He did not think the war could be won. In May, 1944, he anticipated that, if the Allies landed in northern France, they would be thrown out. In the end, therefore, Lindemann turned out to be right, though for the wrong reasons.

All this seems to me a warning against Sir Charles Snow's faith in the foresight of scientists. Neither Tizard nor Lindemann showed much foresight. Sometimes they guessed right; sometimes they guessed wrong; and the only way the guesses could be tested was by trying them out. The scientist can rarely be sure that his guess will work. He can only back a 'hunch' and be acclaimed as a genius if it comes off. He is a gambler, not an actuary. Darwin's guess about Natural Selection, for instance, remained a brilliant hypothesis until the development of Mendelian genetics provided a solid basis for it after his death. Rutherford guessed rightly that the atom could be split; he guessed wrongly that the result would be of no practical importance. Had he foresight or not?

The story of nuclear physics is throughout a poor tribute to the foresight of scientists. They guessed at random according to their personal or political inclination, from Teller's obsessive anti-Bolshevism at one end of the scale to Max Born's near-pacifism at the other.

As nuclear weapons developed, scientists have shown much casualness and irresponsibility, but, with a few honourable exceptions (including Sir Charles Snow), little foresight. They have shown less, in my opinion, than the politicians, and infinitely less than those who marched from Aldermaston to London. Both Lindemann and Tizard are good examples. Neither believed beforehand that the nuclear bomb would work, though both helped it forward in different ways. Both of them apparently thought that 'nature' or science itself would somehow look after any problems which might arise. It is reported of Lindemann: 'The idea of such destructive power being available in human hands seemed to repel him so much that he could scarcely believe that the universe was constructed in this way.' When the Bomb was proved to work, Lindemann derived sardonic pleasure from the thought that mankind would now certainly be blown to pieces, and some pride from the thought that British hands would help to press the button.

Tizard, a good Civil Servant as ever, passed the responsibility to others. He said in a lecture after the war: 'Science [i.e., Sir Henry Tizard and those who worked with him] is grandly impartial, aiding and arming the oppressed as well as the oppressor. It leaves man where it finds him, sinking down to the primeval brute or rising grandly to God from whom he truly comes.'

I read this, to me, blasphemous sentence one day in the Athenaeum. Seeing Tizard, I said to him: 'I suppose you mean that you scientists make a mess of things, and then we poor chaps, whom you condemn as scientifically illiterate, have to clear it up.' He replied: 'Well, you can try.' I suppose I should be grateful for this permission. Scientists of the younger generation hold that anyone who shows foresight should be locked up.

47. Scientists at War.[1]

A review of *Most Secret War* by R V Jones (Hamish Hamilton) and *The Secret War* by Brian Johnson (BBC).

The Second World War was a combat between scientists as well as between fighting men. It was a combat that Great Britain won and much of the credit for this goes to R V Jones, Professor of Natural Philosophy since 1946 at the University of Aberdeen.

His book is a record of great achievements in such things as radar, breaking the secrets of German Beam navigation and detecting the German preparations for flying bombs and rockets. It is also a personal story of one man's war. This puts it in the first rank among war books. Indeed I am inclined to say that in its combination of science and human character it is the most fascinating book on the Second World War that I have read.

Jones's ostensible position was modest : Assistant Director of Intelligence (Science). In fact most of the advances in Air Intelligence during the war derived largely from him. Jones's great strength was that he did all his own work. When he went to a meeting he spoke from a brief he had written himself. Also he had no pre-conceptions. Others had and this caused him great difficulty.

This is illustrated by his troubles over Window, the device that made German radar unworkable. Watson-Watt, who had pioneered radar, was passionately against Window. As Jones says : 'It hurt him emotionally to think of radar being neutralised, even German radar.' Then there were the two great seniors, Tizard and Lindemann (Lord Cherwell). Though they fought each other, they resisted the ideas of anyone else even more strenuously. Over Window Lindemann said : 'You will find Tizard and me united against you.' To which Jones replied : 'If I've achieved that, by God, I've achieved something.'

[1]*Observer*, 1978.

Cherwell was also persistently sceptical about rockets, and both Tizard and Cherwell did not really believe that nuclear energy would ever be released. Jones adds the explanation: 'They clung to the hope that God had not so constructed the universe that he had put such power in the hands of men.' As to rockets, precautions against them were finally resolved by a non-scientist, Smuts, who said simply: 'Well the evidence may not be conclusive, but I think a jury would convict!'

The book is not confined to scientific arguments. There is high adventure, as in the raid on Bruneval which revealed more secrets of German radar. Very often Jones's task was not so much to solve a scientific problem as to guess what was in the mind of his German opponent. It was a great strength for Jones that he had always been something of a practical joker and some of his best strokes were by way of being practical jokes. He also knew how to win over superior officers who were at the start somewhat suspicious. Jones discovered that one such officer was an enthusiast for model trains and so played trains with him. Another was an enthusiastic maker of jam and Jones won his heart by providing a supply of quinces.

The Germans were defeated not only by superior wits. The European Resistance also made great contributions. Jones writes with particular warmth of the French, the Poles and the Belgians. Foreign labourers provided much of the information about the German rocket base at Peenemünde. When Bomber Command was given the task of attacking Peenemünde it insisted on making the housing estate nearby, and not the installations, its target: 600 foreign labourers were killed as against 130 German scientists, engineers and other staff.

Churchill steadfastly supported Jones as 'the man who broke the bloody Beam.' After the war this support was not enough. Jones had hoped to remain in intelligence. He was confronted by a plan which Blackett imposed, dividing Intelligence between the services. No doubt Blackett, being originally a naval officer, wished to preserve the autonomy of the Admiralty. Jones found that, having been in charge of Scientific Intelligence throughout the war, he was now consigned to be a single member of a committee of 13, only one of whom had any experience of Scientific Intelligence at all. He wisely decided to become a Professor at Aberdeen. Blackett's arrangement has continued to prove inefficient and clumsy.

Brian Johnson's book with a similar name grew out of the BBC television programmes on the war of the scientists. It is of course less personal than Professor Jones's book and also more technical. Indeed its accounts of the great discoveries and how they were made go just beyond the technical point where a non-scientist such as I am can understand them.

The earlier chapters cover much the same ground as that treated by Jones, often with more technical details and illustrations. They are liveliest when Jones himself contributes. These chapters narrate the Battle of the Beams, the development of radar and the battles against the terror-weapons, V-1 and V-2, terminating with an appearance by Werner von Braun.

The later chapters describe subjects in which Jones was less involved. There is first the Battle of the Atlantic with all the devices, successful and otherwise, for the protection of convoys. An entertaining chapter presents the miscarriages of many ingenious projects, including The Great Panjandrum. I am sorry to hear nothing of the iceberg that was to serve as an unsinkable aircraft carrier. Finally there is some elucidation of Enigma and their deciphering instruments. Here again a great debt was owed to the Polish Resistance.

My impression is that the glamour of Enigma is now a little overdone. Certainly it was a great stroke to be able to read the German messages. But they were not always read correctly and sometimes they could not be read at all. The Germans achieved some surprises right until the end of the war, as witness their Christmas offensive in the Ardennes. But somehow decoding retains its glamour as other exercises in Intelligence do not.

48. Shameful Record.[1]

A review of *Britain and the Jews of Europe, 1939–1945* by Bernard Wasserstein (Oxford).

During the Second World War there was perpetrated what Churchill justly described as 'probably the greatest and most horrible crime ever committed in the whole history of the world': the mass murder of the Jews by the Germans, done, to quote Churchill again, 'by scientific machinery by nominally civilised men in the name of a great State and one of the leading races of Europe'. Confronted with this crime the countries that claimed to be truly civilised offered little beyond expressions of ineffective sympathy and perhaps, though Dr Wasserstein contests this, could have done nothing except to strive for the unconditional surrender of Germany.

Under the shadow of the gas chambers it is often almost forgotten that in the earlier stages of the war the so-called Jewish 'problem' was the exact reverse of what it became later. Rather than the Germans refusing to let the Jews out of Europe and the Allied countries being unable to secure their release, the Germans until some time in 1941 wished to expel the Jews from Europe and the allied countries refused to take them in. This earlier aspect was the particular concern of Great Britain. She was the undisputed leader of the Allied coalition until the end of 1941; indeed to all intents and purposes she was the allied coalition. Moreover she exercised the mandate for Palestine, which as the Jewish National Home seemed their obvious place of refuge. But in 1939 the British government committed themselves to the White Paper which imposed severe restrictions on the entry of Jews into Palestine. They failed to foresee that penning the Jews into Europe was ultimately to pass sentence of death on millions of

[1]*English Historical Review*, 1980. Copyright © Longman Group Ltd. and contributors, 1980.

innocent people. Instead they clung to the White Paper with bureaucratic insistence. Wasserstein opens his book with a chapter on this
early theme – 'sealing the escape routes'. This covers much the same
grounds as Nicholas Bethell's recent *The Palestine Triangle*. Both
books use the same sources from the British records. Both are essential
reading for all who care for the honour or rather the dishonour of
this country. Later the two writers part company. Bethell remains in
Palestine; Wasserstein becomes concerned with the fate of the Jews
in Europe. Both writers are inclined to write of British 'policy' as
though it followed a coherent course. In fact it was shaped, as often
happens, by a host of conflicting authorities. The High Commissioner
in Palestine and his staff were rigidly determined to enforce the
White Paper. They were seconded by the Colonial Office, the body
immediately responsible for the affairs of Palestine. The Middle East
command was obsessively concerned to secure its strategical position
by appeasing the Arabs. The Foreign Office was troubled only when
American opinion proved restive. At a later stage the Air Ministry
also became involved. The War Cabinet had little time to spare for
Palestine and when it spared any spoke with muffled voices. Some of
its members – Herbert Morrison out-spokenly, Anthony Eden more
circumspectly – were anti-semitic. Only Churchill continued to show
sympathy with the Jews until the murder of Lord Moyne, and there
is nothing more striking in the story than the total failure of the
supposedly all-powerful prime minister to enforce his will on numer-
ous occasions. In the background was British public opinion, sometimes anti-semitic, more often impatient for some undefined action.
The Jewish Agency, once the partner of British governments and
still effectively represented by Weizmann, was a potent factor.

The White Paper was sustained by arguments similar to those used
by Sir Charles Trevelyan during the Irish Famine when he opposed
any large-scale relief for the starving Irish : it was against the rules
and therefore could not take place. In Palestine this was supported
by the cry of alarm, urged also against Jewish entry into Great
Britain, that the Nazis would include secret agents among the refugees. This was a pretext : not a single Nazi agent was ever discovered.
More fundamental was the hostility towards the Jews shown by
members of the Colonial Office, whether from anti-semitism or from
exasperation provoked by the pertinacious arguments of the Jewish
spokesmen. H F Downie, Colonial Office, commented on an article
by an American Zionist : 'This sort of thing makes one regret that the
Jews are not on the other side in this war'. J S Bennett, Colonial

Office: 'The Jews have done nothing but add to our difficulties by propaganda and deeds since the war began'. Sir John Shuckburgh, Colonial Office: 'I am convinced that in their hearts they [the Jews] hate us and have always hated us; they hate all Gentiles'. A R Dew, Foreign Office: 'In my opinion a disproportionate amount of time in this office is wasted in dealing with these wailing Jews'. Wasserstein tells the whole lamentable story. Refugees were arrested on arrival in Palestine. Some were interned in Cyprus, some in Mauritius. It has been suggested that the Jewish authorities in their zeal for Zionism were determined that the refugees should come to Palestine and nowhere else. In fact they offered to send refugees elsewhere only to learn that there was nowhere else for them to go. When it proved impossible for the British to stem the flow of refugees, they acted to prevent the movement of refugee ships. When one such ship, the *Salvador*, was wrecked in the Sea of Marmora with the loss of two hundred lives, T M Snow, Foreign Office, commented: 'There could have been no more opportune disaster from the point of view of stopping the traffic'. This policy culminated in the affair of the *Struma*, a ship carrying 769 Jewish refugees. Her engine broke down off Istanbul. The Turks would not allow the refugees to land. The British government insisted that the ship should be sent back into the Black Sea. Some British officials protested. Oliver Harvey, Foreign Office: 'Must HMG take such an inhuman decision? If they go back they will all be killed'. A Walker, Foreign Office: 'I do not at all like the idea that we may be acting as accessories in bringing about the death of these miserable people'. The *Struma* was ordered back into the Black Sea. On 25 February 1942 she sank. There was one survivor.

Thereafter Hitler rescued the British from their difficulties by refusing to allow Jews to leave any part of his inflated Reich. However, this was not the end of trouble for the British. In 1944 it was suggested that the Hungarian government might allow some 5,000 Jews to leave Hungary if the British would issue 'bogus' immigration certificates for Palestine. The British acquiesced. The device came too late: no holders of these certificates reached Palestine before the liberation of Hungary. The British authorities could pride themselves that they had upheld the White Paper to the end. Indeed they had more than maintained it. The war ended with the quotas for Jewish entry laid down in the White Paper not filled. The record of admissions to the United Kingdom itself was less deplorable. There had been a fairly generous admission of Jews before the war and most 'enemy aliens' were left undisturbed when the war began. At the height of the alleged panic after Dunkirk, there was a wholesale internment of these refugees on the Isle of Man. This alarm followed on the stories that the German conquest of Holland had been assisted by thousands of fifth columnists. De Jong has shown that these stories had no foundation. Even Churchill believed them and wrote after the war: 'There were known to be twenty thousand organised Nazis in England at this time'. The *Manchester Guardian* applauded the policy of 'intern the lot' and so, I am afraid, did I. The alarm was a fiction invented by MI5. However, it can be pleaded that the internment was conducted in a civilised way, with university courses flourishing on the Isle of Man, and that most of the internees were released in the autumn. Wasserstein suggests that there was an underlying current of anti-semitism in England until quite late in the war. A Mass Observation survey of April 1940 reported that anti-alien sentiment was pronounced among 'the middle and upper classes ... It is becoming the socially done thing to be anti-refugee'. Later, anti-semitism was undoubtedly stoked by right-wing Poles, who had been admitted to Great Britain on a much larger scale than Jews had been. My own impression is that anti-semitism was negligible among ordinary people. Wasserstein should not attach much credence to the Ministry of Information reports on public opinion: these reports had to sound the alarm in order to justify MOI's existence. At any rate the refugees, so grudgingly received, more than paid for their welcome: most of the advances in nuclear physics during the war were made by them.

From the beginning of the war the Jews were not only anxious to be rescued: they wished to take an active part in the war against the Nazis. There were ambitious proposals to raise a Jewish army or at any rate a Jewish contingent in Palestine. Churchill welcomed the proposals enthusiastically and ordered that they should be carried out. His orders were resisted at every stage. The arguments were of the usual kind: there were not enough arms for British soldiers, let alone Jews; the creation of a Jewish army would enable Hitler to claim that the Allies were fighting to establish a Jewish domination of Europe; the Jews had no state of their own and there was therefore no one to authorise their army; if the Jews fought, it would be only for Zion. The decisive argument was that British officers other than Orde Wingate did not want Jews. They were too argumentative, they knew the rules and thought themselves as intelligent as their officers. No Jewish army was raised.

The latter part of Wasserstein's book is dominated by the horrors of 'The final solution', the policy of mass murder initiated by the Germans in 1942. There were many expressions of condemnation and interminable negotiations with the United States, a Power more generous in words than in deeds. No protests or resolutions were likely to shake the determination of Hitler and the Nazis. There were some curious episodes when questionable intermediaries suggested that the Germans were prepared to exchange some Jews for Allied supplies of raw materials or equipment. Probably these suggestions were the product of busybodies. However a cabinet committee warned against 'the danger that the proposal may be genuine'. Any idea of aiding the enemy by helping to supply his needs was rejected out of hand. There was also the risk that the Soviet government might see in any such bargain the preliminaries of a separate peace. In April 1945 Himmler, presumably hoping to save his skin, released some thousands of Jews and allowed them to proceed to neutral territory. Churchill ruled: 'no truck with Himmler'. This order of Churchill's was obeyed. Another was not. Jewish spokesmen asked that the murder camps at Auschwitz and Treblinka should be bombed. Churchill and Eden agreed. Sir Archibald Sinclair, secretary for air and himself a former Zionist, was instructed to act. Instead the Air Council replied with objections that would have been equally valid against the attempts to aid Warsaw in September 1944. Churchill repeated his order. The Air Council then pleaded that it had no detailed maps of the area. The Jewish authorities in London duly provided such maps for the Foreign Office, which decided not to forward them to the Air Ministry and the latter made no further enquiry.

When Richard Crossman saw the first direct reports from Buchenwald, he noted: 'Though we had heard and reported many stories of Nazi massacres of Jews and Slavs, we had never believed in the possibility of "genocide" ... Now we were to realise that our propaganda had fallen far behind the truth'. This may be part of the explanation. Men were reluctant to believe the stories of atrocities when they had accepted too implicitly similar stories from the First World War. Moreover, as Wasserstein writes, 'the average British official lived in a different mental world from that of the Jewish refugee. The Pall Mall club and the Palestine internment camp were not merely different places: they were different psychological universes, conditioning attitudes and reflexes which rarely found points of contact'. For whatever reason, British civil servants, mostly no doubt of impeccable

243

character, promoted or at best condoned policies which exacerbated the sufferings heaped by Hitler on the Jewish people. Wasserstein concludes : 'And so they came and looked and passed by on the other side'.

49. Christ Stopped at Potsdam.[1]

A review of *Shattered Peace: The Origins of the Cold War and the National Security State* by Daniel Yergin (Houghton Mifflin).

In September 1945 Senator Claude Pepper called at the Kremlin. Stalin remarked to him that the 'Grand Alliance' had been created by the single circumstance of a common enemy. Stalin went on :

> That tie no longer exists and we shall have to find a new basis for our close relations in the future. That will not be easy but Christ said, 'Seek and ye shall find'.

Stalin's biblical injunction came too late. It had been followed at Yalta with outstanding success. At Potsdam the Americans began to abandon it and from Potsdam the path ran with occasional interruptions to the Berlin blockade, which marked the confirmation and also the limitations of the cold war.

This interpretation is not new, but Daniel Yergin draws on more sources than any previous writer. In his view US policy was shaped by two rival axioms concerning the USSR. The Riga axioms were held by nearly all US diplomats before the second world war. These axioms were simple : Soviet Russia was dedicated to world revolution and would promote it by military force. The Yalta axioms were held by Roosevelt and a few associates : the USSR was a world power concerned with security and the US could do business with it. Roosevelt's death took the drive out of the Yalta axioms and the end of the war seemed to make them less necessary. Moreover Truman, unlike Roosevelt, liked quick, clear-cut solutions. Henry Wallace remarked, 'Truman's decisiveness is admirable. The only question

[1]*New Statesman*, 1978.

is as to whether he has information behind his decisiveness to enable his decisions to stand up.' `

Truman certainly received plenty of information. It ran all one way: a revival of the Riga axioms. It was expressed by George Kennan in his 'Long Dispatch', the longest document in the records of the State Department. It culminated in document NSC-68, drafted in 1950.

> The Kremlin is inescapably militant. It is inescapably militant because it possesses and is possessed by a world-wide revolutionary movement, because it is the inheritor of Russian imperialism and because it is a totalitarian dictatorship.

The USSR's 'fundamental design' necessitated the destruction of the US and thus the US was 'mortally challenged' by the USSR. These axioms were dogma and rested on no evidence. Indeed all the evidence runs the other way. In the immediate post-war years Stalin deliberately thwarted the advance of the communist parties in France and Italy. His concern in the USSR's border states was security, not the advance of communism. His supposedly aggressive designs, as in Iran or at the Straits, also sprang from security and he abandoned them when they were resisted. Throughout these years, the USSR was a frightened power desperately on the defensive. Apart from security, Stalin's other main aim was to gather reparations from Germany, an aim which curiously led him to champion German unity when the Western allies had already abandoned it.

These objections are irrelevant. US policy was pursuing a dogma rather than responding to events. Byrnes remarked at Potsdam:

> Someone made an awful mistake in bringing about a situation where Russia was permitted to come out of a war with the power she will have ... The German people under a democracy would have been a far superior ally than Russia.

Truman was not yet convinced: 'I like Stalin. Stalin is as near Tom Pendergast [the Missouri political boss] as any man I know. He is very fond of classical music.'

But when Byrnes, as secretary of state, switched round and actually negotiated with the Russians, Truman lost patience. 'Unless Russia is faced with an iron fist and strong language another war is in the making ... I'm tired of babying the Soviets.' By 1946 the Americans had lost interest in bargaining and conducted negotiations publicly in order to appeal to 'world opinion', or in more practical terms to whip up US anti-communism. Yergin rather neglects this aspect and writes as though US policy was made only by diplomats. Surely there was a wider pressure from those who disliked the USSR's socialism. The concrete needs of US imperialism should be added. The conflict over Iran, for instance, had nothing to do with stemming communism or even with checking Soviet power. The Americans were after Iran's oil and were more concerned to exclude the British, now their humble client, than to thwart their Soviet enemy.

At this stage the Riga axioms took on a more positive form. Originally they had merely followed the negative line of disregarding the USSR. Now they demanded positive action in the name of national security. Any step taken by Russia beyond its borders in the name of Soviet 'security' would by definition clash with what became known as American 'national security'. As Kennan postulated, 'We must make the Russians understand that they must confine their security demands to our concept of security demands.' Another 'expert' pronounced : 'The basic objective of the USSR appears to be a limitless expansion of Soviet Communism accompanied by a considerable territorial expansion of Russian imperialism.' Yet throughout the period, and indeed to the present day, there has been no expansion of Soviet Communism and no territorial expansion of Russian imperialism. As against this, American expansion has not been far from limitless, as witness Greece and Turkey, or where it has been limited this came from military defeat, as in Vietnam, and not from modesty.

Nuclear power was a complicating factor. At first it gave the Americans an illusion of complete superiority. Then they discovered that it could not be used as a bargaining weapon. And in the end it has restrained the Americans more than it has restrained the USSR or any lesser power. As Yergin points out, the Americans were frightened by their own success. Moreover the armed forces justified their ever-increasing demands by inflated and often deliberately false estimates of Soviet strength and then were terrified by their own estimates. Here is another factor that Yergin hardly considers. Expenditure on armaments stimulated the US economy and continues to do so. If peace broke out, the US would be in desperate straits. Fortunately for American capitalism, imaginary fears once started can rarely be dispelled : they are absorbed into the system and run on happily of themselves.

The immediate post-war period moved gradually to a climax in

1947 and 1948. The first catalysis was the economic crisis in western Europe. The Marshall Plan aimed both to stabilise Western capitalism and to draw a clear line against any communist advance. For the first time the iron curtain became official US policy. Capitalism was duly saved; communism was duly checked in the West. But there was a corollary. The Soviets also consolidated their security in Eastern Europe. Non-communist Hungary and a little later non-communist Czechoslovakia were victims of the Marshall Plan. When the State Department considered censuring the USSR at the Security Council, one official objected, 'The Soviets might level counter charges against us as concerning MacArthur's actions in Japan'. No appeal was made to the Security Council.

The decisive step came in 1948 when the US and Britain set up a separate state in western Germany. Most of the troubles in the four-power control commission had come from France. But France had to be swept into the new policy and Soviet Russia got all the blame for obstruction. In fact the USSR needed German unity in order to exact reparations from the western zones – no doubt one reason why the US and Britain abandoned unity. The Russians inaugurated the blockade of Berlin in defence of German unity, believing that it would force the western powers to the conference table. Instead the Anglo-Americans successfully ran the air lift. War seemed near but faced with nuclear war or nothing the US chose no war. Yergin reveals a curious fact in a footnote – the B-29s, sent to England and pointedly known at 'atomic bombers', had not been modified to carry atomic bombs. Probably the Russians knew this all along. The Berlin blockade duly ended at the conference table, though German unity fortunately was not preserved.

There has been no serious danger of war in Europe since 1948. The Americans have fought what would once have been called colonial wars. There was a false alarm in 1962 over Cuba when the Americans got the appearance of victory and the Soviets got what they wanted – the independence of Cuba. Now both Eastern and Western blocs are losing their rigidity. Nuclear weapons are no longer the monopoly of the two superpowers. The rise of communist China has upset the calculations of both the US and the USSR. The phrases of the cold war are used now more by academic pundits than by diplomats. Détente is talked about and even occasionally practised. The two superpowers have not changed their characters. But maybe they are coming to recognise that bargaining is a better way of advancing their own security. As Yergin concludes,

This means a return to the Yalta axioms as the basic mode of dealing with the Soviet world, and perhaps a vindication for Franklin Roosevelt and his aims and methods.

Yergin may err on the optimistic side, but there seems just a chance that Christ did not stop at Potsdam after all.

50.   Delusions of Grandeur.[1]

A review of *Independence and Deterrence: Britain and atomic energy 1945–1952* by Margaret Gowing (Macmillan).

On 3 October, 1952, British scientists, led by William Penney, exploded an atomic bomb at Monte Bello, Australia. Penney was knighted, receiving a telegram from Churchill, then prime minister: 'Well done, Sir William.' Penney had written a little earlier: 'The discriminative test for a first-class power is whether it has made an atomic bomb and we have either to pass the test or suffer a serious loss in prestige both in this country and internationally.' Now Great Britain seemed to have passed the test. The decision was shortlived. A month later the Americans exploded their first thermonuclear device; in August 1953 the Russians tested their first thermonuclear bomb. British scientists had invented the bow and arrow just when America and Russia were perfecting the quick-firing rifle.

Margaret Gowing tells the Why of this extraordinary story in her first volume and the How in the second. Although her book is 'official history' – the first on a peacetime theme – it is impeccably honest and ruthlessly frank. Mrs Gowing has every gift, presenting political decisions, scientific technicalities and bureaucratic entanglements with equal grace. If the reader is at the end still bewildered, that is not Mrs Gowing's fault. What she says of the secrecy involved applies more generally: 'The policy ... went beyond rational explanation.'

At the end of the war the Americans had developed the atomic bomb, but the British assumed that the wartime American partnership with themselves and the Canadians still applied. Instead the Americans repudiated President Roosevelt's obligations and cut off all information. When later Attlee achieved a promise of cooperation from Truman, Dean Acheson remarked: 'We had to unachieve

[1]*New Statesman*, 1974.

that.' One motive for the British bomb was therefore to impress the Americans so that they would return to cooperation after all. The impression was not made. A Congressman said after the explosion at Monte Bello: 'We would be trading a horse for a rabbit.' There was also the idea that the British would have some say in America's use of the bomb if they had one of their own. Conversely the British would be free to use their own bomb without asking America's permission. The delusion of British independence was exposed by the Suez affair.

British policy was, however, 'largely the instinctive response of a country which had been a great world power and believed itself to be one still.' In March 1948 Bevin sounded the alarm against Russia: 'Unless positive and vigorous steps are taken it may well be that within the next few months, or even weeks, the Soviet Union will gain political and strategic advantages which will set the great Communist machine in motion, leading to the establishment of World Dictatorship.' This seems irrelevant when the British bomb could not be ready for five years. The Chiefs of Staff, however, cheerfully reported that Soviet Russia would not have a bomb for ten years and by then Great Britain would be far ahead. The Chiefs of Staff wanted the bomb for its own sake. At last they would have the 'deterrent' which they had advocated before the war and which the Battle of Britain had shown to be not the only defence. In their enthusiasm for this 'deterrent' the Chiefs of Staff altogether neglected the means of delivery. It was enough to have the bomb without providing any way in which it could be used.

The British people were never told what they were being committed to. The Cabinet learnt vaguely of the bomb in 1947; the House of Commons had an innocuous question and answer slipped past it in 1948. A Ministry of Supply official remarked complacently: 'If you want to know how much we are spending on guided projectiles, you will not find it on the face of the Estimates', and this applied even more to the atomic bomb. The Labour government spent £100 million on it without the knowledge of parliament.

Nearly all scientists welcomed the bomb without reserve. Even J D Bernal was a member of the first committee which blessed it. Only two scientists took a more rational line. One was Patrick Blackett, later President of the Royal Society, who had shown during the war that he understood practical questions of strategy better than most military men. When Blackett submitted a memorandum against manufacturing atomic bombs, Attlee commented: 'The author, a

251

distinguished scientist, speaks on political and military problems on which he is a layman.' The memorandum was ignored. The other sceptical scientist was Sir Henry Tizard, theoretically the government's chief adviser on defence. He wrote: 'We are not a Great Power and never will be again. We are a great nation, but if we continue to behave like a Great Power we shall soon cease to be a great nation.' He asked: how do we add to the deterrent effect of the American atomic bombs by letting it be known that we have none but hope to make a few later – when moreover the few would be obsolete? Tizard's reward was to be excluded from all dealings with the atomic bomb. What Mrs Gowing says of the engineers involved can be said also of the scientists: 'They were neither attracted nor repelled by a realisation that their immediate aim was to produce the material for bombs.' For them the bomb was just another job. This is what German scientists and engineers had felt about the gas chambers. Even the three defectors (Nunn May, Fuchs and Pontecorvo) had no general revulsion against making bombs: 'Indeed Fuchs seems to have positively revelled in the business.'

Politicians, Chiefs of Staff and scientists all rejoiced that by making atomic bombs Great Britain would assert herself as a Great Power. I must confess that when we launched the Campaign for Nuclear Disarmament in 1958 we had the same delusion. We thought that, if Great Britain renounced atomic weapons, this moral gesture would have tremendous impact throughout the world. The Cuban crisis showed that it did not matter what we did one way or the other. Of course it was more sensible not to make nuclear weapons than to make them, but we had ceased to count in the world. In Mrs Gowing's words, 'for Great Britain it was a race of the Red Queen's variety'. The Red Queen at least stood still. Great Britain slipped steadily backwards. Nuclear weapons are presumably still made, but no one except the Chiefs of Staff and the scientists attaches any importance to them. They ensure that we shall be blown up on the first day of the next war, but that will probably happen in any case.

Index